First World War
and Army of Occupation
War Diary
France, Belgium and Germany

52 DIVISION
157 Infantry Brigade
Headquarters
17 July 1917 - 25 June 1919

WO95/2898/1

The Naval & Military Press Ltd
www.nmarchive.com
Published in association with The National Archives

Published by

The Naval & Military Press Ltd

Unit 10 Ridgewood Industrial Park,

Uckfield, East Sussex,

TN22 5QE England

Tel: +44 (0) 1825 749494

www.naval-military-press.com

www.nmarchive.com

This diary has been reprinted in facsimile from the original. Any imperfections are inevitably reproduced and the quality may fall short of modern type and cartographic standards.

Contents

Document type	Place/Title	Date From	Date To
Heading	WO95/2898-1		
Heading	52nd Division 157th Infy Bde Bde Headquarters Apr 1918-Jun 1919		
Heading	52nd Division Disembarked Marseilles From Egypt 17.4.18 B.H.Q. 157th Infantry Brigade April 1918		
War Diary	East Of E. Jelil	01/04/1918	02/04/1918
War Diary	Sarona	03/04/1918	03/04/1918
War Diary	Surafend Camp Ludd	04/04/1918	07/04/1918
War Diary	Kantara	07/04/1918	07/04/1918
War Diary	Alexandria	08/04/1918	11/04/1918
War Diary	At Sea	12/04/1918	16/04/1918
War Diary	Marsailles	17/04/1918	22/04/1918
War Diary	St Vallery	23/04/1918	30/04/1918
Operation(al) Order(s)	Brigade Order No. 95 by Brig General C.D. Hamilton Moore D.S.O. Commanding 157th Inf Bde	01/04/1918	01/04/1918
Miscellaneous	157th Infantry Brigade Administrative Instructions No.5.Issued With Brigade Order No. 95.	03/04/1918	03/04/1918
Miscellaneous	157th Infantry Brigade Administrative Instructions No.6		
Miscellaneous	On His Majesty's Service.		
Miscellaneous	War Diary H.Q. 157 Inf Brigade From 1st-31st May 1918 Volume III		
War Diary	Aire	01/05/1918	06/05/1918
War Diary	Neuville St Vaast	06/05/1918	09/05/1918
War Diary	Vimy Ridge Maroevil St Nazaire 1/20000	13/05/1918	15/05/1918
War Diary	La Fulie Farm Vimy Ridge	10/05/1918	12/05/1918
War Diary	Vimy Ridge S23c 1/20000	12/05/1918	17/05/1918
War Diary	Vimy Ridge	18/05/1918	22/05/1918
War Diary	Vimy Ridge S23c 3.4	23/05/1918	24/05/1918
War Diary	Mt. St. Eloy	25/05/1918	31/05/1918
Operation(al) Order(s)	157th Infantry Brigade Order No. 97	05/05/1918	05/05/1918
Miscellaneous	Appendix II O.C. 6th B.L.I.	18/05/1918	18/05/1918
Miscellaneous	Appendix III O.C. 459 6th N. Battn	18/05/1918	18/05/1918
Miscellaneous	Addendum No. 1 to 157th Bde No. 7/696	18/05/1918	18/05/1918
Miscellaneous	Appendix IV O.C., Units	18/05/1918	18/05/1918
Miscellaneous	Appendix Va O.C.,	18/05/1918	18/05/1918
Miscellaneous	Defence Scheme Mericourt Sector 157th Infantry Brigade		
Miscellaneous	Index		
Miscellaneous	157th Infantry Brigade Defence Scheme Mericourt Sector		
Miscellaneous	Boundaries Of Areas.		
Miscellaneous	Appendix II Communications		
Miscellaneous	Appendix III Medical Arrangements.		
Miscellaneous	Appendix IV List of Co-ordinates.		
Miscellaneous	Reserve Brigade Provisional Defence Scheme	29/05/1918	29/05/1918
Operation(al) Order(s)	157th Infantry Brigade Order No. 101	26/05/1918	26/05/1918
Miscellaneous	On His Majesty's Service.		
Heading	War Diary H.Q 157th Inf Bde From Feb-30th June 1918 Volume III		
War Diary	Mt St Eloy	01/06/1918	01/06/1918

War Diary	Vimy Ridge (Willerval Section)	02/06/1918	20/06/1918
War Diary	Mt St Eloy	21/06/1918	30/06/1918
Operation(al) Order(s)	157th Infantry Brigade Order No. 103	06/06/1918	06/06/1918
Operation(al) Order(s)	157th Infantry Brigade Order No. 104	08/06/1918	08/06/1918
Operation(al) Order(s)	157th Infantry Brigade Order No. 105	12/06/1918	12/06/1918
Operation(al) Order(s)	157th Infantry Brigade Order No. 106	12/06/1918	12/06/1918
Operation(al) Order(s)	157th Infantry Brigade Order No. 107		
Miscellaneous	Amendment To Brigade Administrative Instructions No.103	18/06/1918	18/06/1918
Miscellaneous	157th Infantry Brigade Administrative Instructions No.103	17/06/1918	17/06/1918
Miscellaneous	Action Of Reserve Brigade	19/06/1918	19/06/1918
Miscellaneous	Operation Orders By Major R. Blair Comdg 1/7th Bn The Cameronians (Sco Rifles)	18/06/1918	18/06/1918
Miscellaneous	Operation Orders By Major R. Blair Comdg Bn The Cameronians (Scottish Rifles)	27/06/1918	27/06/1918
Operation(al) Order(s)	157th Infantry Brigade Order No. 108	27/06/1918	27/06/1918
Miscellaneous	157th Infantry Brigade Administrative Instructions No.105	27/06/1918	27/06/1918
Miscellaneous	Appendix VIII War Diary	28/06/1918	28/06/1918
Miscellaneous	Provisional Defence Scheme	28/06/1918	28/06/1918
Heading	H.Q. 157 Infy Bde Vol 4		
Miscellaneous	D.A.G. 3rd Echelon Base		
Heading	War Diary H.Q. 157th Inf. Bde From 1st-31st July 1918 Vol III		
War Diary	Vimy Ridge (Chaudiere Section)	01/07/1918	15/07/1918
War Diary	Mericourt Sector	16/07/1918	16/07/1918
War Diary	Vimy Ridge	17/07/1917	17/07/1917
War Diary	Mont St Eloi	18/07/1918	19/07/1918
War Diary	Auchel Area	20/07/1918	30/07/1918
War Diary	Barlin	31/07/1918	31/07/1918
Miscellaneous	Appendix I O.C.,	01/07/1918	01/07/1918
Miscellaneous	Newton Mortars		
Miscellaneous	Appendix Instructions Re.Field Artillery Barrage.	30/06/1918	30/06/1918
Operation(al) Order(s)	157th Infantry Brigade Order No. 106	02/07/1918	02/07/1918
Operation(al) Order(s)	157th Infantry Brigade Order No. 110	03/07/1918	03/07/1918
Miscellaneous	157th Infantry Brigade Administrative Instructions No.106.	03/07/1918	03/07/1918
Operation(al) Order(s)	Brigade Order No. 111	10/07/1918	10/07/1918
Miscellaneous	Defence Scheme Left Section 52nd Division Mericourt Sector 157th Infantry Brigade		
Miscellaneous	Index		
Miscellaneous	157th Infantry Brigade Defence Scheme Left Section 52nd Divisional Sector		
Miscellaneous	Appendix I Boundaries Of Areas		
Miscellaneous	Action Of Artillery		
Miscellaneous	Communications		
Miscellaneous	Appendix IV Medical		
Miscellaneous	Appendix V List of Co-Ordinates		
Map	La Targette		
Operation(al) Order(s)	Brigade Order No. 112	14/07/1918	14/07/1918
Miscellaneous	157th Infantry Brigade Administrative Instructions No.107.	14/07/1918	14/07/1918
Operation(al) Order(s)	157th Infantry Brigade Order No. 113	15/07/1918	15/07/1918
Miscellaneous	Table "A"	17/07/1918	17/07/1918

Miscellaneous	157th Infantry Brigade Administrative Instructions No.108	15/07/1918	15/07/1918
Operation(al) Order(s)	157th Infantry Brigade Order No. 114	19/07/1918	19/07/1918
Miscellaneous	Table "A"		
Miscellaneous	Reference Brigade Order No. 114	19/07/1918	19/07/1918
Operation(al) Order(s)	157th Infantry Brigade Order No. 115	23/07/1918	23/07/1918
Operation(al) Order(s)	157th Infantry Brigade Order No. 116	29/07/1918	29/07/1918
Miscellaneous	Table "A"		
Miscellaneous	O.C. 6th H.L.I.	29/07/1918	29/07/1918
Miscellaneous	157th Infantry Brigade Order No. 117	30/07/1918	30/07/1918
Miscellaneous	157th Infantry Brigade Administrative Instructions No.111	30/07/1918	30/07/1918
Operation(al) Order(s)	157th Infantry Brigade Order No. 118	30/07/1918	30/07/1918
Miscellaneous	Ref.Trench Map 51	31/07/1918	31/07/1918
Miscellaneous	H.Q.157 Infy Bde Vol 5 Agst 18		
Heading	D.A.G. 3rd Echelon B.E Force		
War Diary	Roclincourt	01/08/1918	05/08/1918
War Diary	Roclincourt (A.28.b.7.3)	06/08/1918	17/08/1918
War Diary	Mont St Eloi	17/08/1918	17/08/1918
War Diary	Bois De La Haie X.13a.9.9	18/08/1918	18/08/1918
War Diary	Chateau de-la Haie	19/08/1918	21/08/1918
War Diary	Agnez-Les Duisans	22/08/1918	23/08/1918
War Diary	Echeux (Ref. Map Sheet 51c SW)	24/08/1918	24/08/1918
War Diary	Echeux	24/08/1918	24/08/1918
War Diary	Henin	25/08/1918	31/08/1918
Operation(al) Order(s)	52nd Division Order No. 127	24/08/1918	24/08/1918
Operation(al) Order(s)	157th Infantry Brigade Order No. 120	05/08/1918	05/08/1918
Miscellaneous	O.C. 5th Bn. H.L.I.	04/08/1918	04/08/1918
Operation(al) Order(s)	157th Infantry Brigade Order No. 119	04/08/1918	04/08/1918
Miscellaneous	Appendix II 4th 5th /8/18	05/08/1918	05/08/1918
Operation(al) Order(s)	157th Infantry Brigade Order No. 121	11/08/1918	11/08/1918
Miscellaneous	Appendix III	11/08/1918	11/08/1918
Miscellaneous	Warning Order	13/08/1918	13/08/1918
Miscellaneous	Appendix VI	13/08/1918	13/08/1918
Operation(al) Order(s)	157th Infantry Brigade Order No. 122	15/08/1918	15/08/1918
Miscellaneous	Table "A"	17/08/1918	17/08/1918
Miscellaneous	157th Infantry Brigade Administrative Instructions No.113.	15/08/1918	15/08/1918
Miscellaneous	Appendix VII	15/08/1918	15/08/1918
Operation(al) Order(s)	157th Infantry Brigade Order No. 123	16/08/1918	16/08/1918
Miscellaneous	Table "A"		
Miscellaneous	O.C. 5th Bn. H.L.I.	17/08/1918	17/08/1918
Miscellaneous	Warning Order	16/08/1918	16/08/1918
Operation(al) Order(s)	157th Infantry Brigade Order No. 124	20/08/1918	20/08/1918
Operation(al) Order(s)	157th Infantry Brigade Order No. 125	22/08/1918	22/08/1918
Miscellaneous	O.C. 5th Bn. H.L.I.	22/08/1918	22/08/1918
Miscellaneous	Appendix X	22/08/1918	22/08/1918
Miscellaneous	157th Infantry Brigade Administrative Instructions	23/08/1918	23/08/1918
Operation(al) Order(s)	157th Infantry Brigade Order No. 130	24/08/1918	24/08/1918
Miscellaneous	Appendix XI	24/08/1918	24/08/1918
Miscellaneous	H.Q. 157th Infantry Brigade	04/09/1918	04/09/1918
Map	British Trenches In Red		
Map	France		
Miscellaneous	H.Q. 157th Infantry Brigade	04/09/1918	04/09/1918
Operation(al) Order(s)	157th Infantry Brigade Order No. 131	24/08/1918	24/08/1918
Miscellaneous	Appendix XII	24/08/1918	24/08/1918

Operation(al) Order(s)	157th Infantry Brigade Order No. 132	25/08/1918	25/08/1918
Miscellaneous	Appendix XIII	25/08/1918	25/08/1918
Miscellaneous	5th, 6th & 7th HL 9c (157th L.I M.B For Information)	26/08/1918	26/08/1918
Miscellaneous	Appendix XIV	26/08/1918	26/08/1918
Miscellaneous	Addendum To 157th Infantry Brigade Order No. 134	26/08/1918	26/08/1918
Operation(al) Order(s)	157th Infantry Brigade Order No. 134	26/08/1918	26/08/1918
Miscellaneous	Appendix XV	26/08/1918	26/08/1918
Operation(al) Order(s)	157th Infantry Brigade Order No. 135	27/08/1918	27/08/1918
Miscellaneous	Appendix XVI	27/08/1918	27/08/1918
Operation(al) Order(s)	157th Infantry Brigade Order No. 136	31/08/1918	31/08/1918
Miscellaneous	Appendix XVII		
Miscellaneous	Appendix XIX	31/08/1918	31/08/1918
Operation(al) Order(s)	H.Qrs. 157th Inf Bde. War Diary Volume III September 1918		
War Diary	S4a 2.4 (Near Boisleux Au Mont)	01/09/1918	01/09/1918
War Diary	T.4.a & B Henin Hill	02/09/1918	02/09/1918
War Diary	H.21 (W. Of Bulleucourt)	03/09/1918	03/09/1918
War Diary	Near Queant German Hutments C.12.b.95.85 57c 1/20000 M.E.	04/09/1918	06/09/1918
War Diary	Corps Reserve Near Croisilles Sr, T30 (Sheet 57c.S.W.)	07/09/1918	16/09/1918
War Diary	V.28.d.0.0. (57c Se) (Inchy En Artois Sector)	16/09/1918	16/09/1918
War Diary	V.28.d.0.0. (Inchy En Artois Sector)	17/09/1918	25/09/1918
War Diary	Near Moeuvres	26/09/1918	30/09/1918
Miscellaneous	Summary Of Operations 157th Infantry Brigade From August 20th, 1918, To September 7th, 1918		
Miscellaneous		20/08/1918	20/08/1918
Miscellaneous	Captured Personnel And Material		
Miscellaneous	157 Inf Brigade Order No. 137	01/09/1918	01/09/1918
Operation(al) Order(s)	157th Infantry Order No. 138	02/09/1918	02/09/1918
Operation(al) Order(s)	157th Infantry Brigade Order No. 139	05/09/1918	05/09/1918
Operation(al) Order(s)	157th Infantry Brigade Order No. 140	06/09/1918	06/09/1918
Miscellaneous	157th Infantry Brigade Administrative Instructions Issued With 157th Infantry Brigade Order No. 140	06/09/1918	06/09/1918
Miscellaneous	157th Inf Bde Administrative Instructions 1	07/09/1918	07/09/1918
Operation(al) Order(s)	157th Infantry Brigade Order No. 141	15/09/1918	15/09/1918
Miscellaneous	Table "A"	16/08/1918	16/08/1918
Operation(al) Order(s)	157th Infantry Brigade Order No. 142.	13/09/1918	13/09/1918
Miscellaneous	157th Infantry Brigade Administrative Instructions No.2	19/09/1918	19/09/1918
Miscellaneous	Warning Order Appendix IX	18/09/1918	18/09/1918
Miscellaneous	O.C. 5th Bn. H.L.I.	19/09/1918	19/09/1918
Miscellaneous	O.C. 5th H.L.I.	19/09/1918	19/09/1918
Operation(al) Order(s)	157th Infantry Brigade Order No. 143	21/09/1918	21/09/1918
Operation(al) Order(s)	157th Infantry Brigade Order No. 144	24/09/1918	24/09/1918
Operation(al) Order(s)	157th Infantry Brigade Order No. 145		
Miscellaneous	157th Infantry Brigade Administrative Instructions Issued With Reference To 157th Infantry Brigade Order No. 145	25/09/1918	25/09/1918
Heading	War Diary 157th Infantry Brigade Headquarters October 1918 Volume III		
War Diary	Near Moeuvres	01/10/1918	01/10/1918
War Diary	F.30.a (57c N.E)	01/10/1918	07/10/1918
War Diary	Grand Rullecourt	08/10/1918	19/10/1918
War Diary	Mont St Eloy	19/10/1918	19/10/1918
War Diary	Menin Lietard	20/10/1918	20/10/1918
War Diary	Wagnonville	21/10/1918	23/10/1918
War Diary	Flines	24/10/1918	26/10/1918

War Diary	Landas Area	27/10/1918	27/10/1918
War Diary	Lecelles Area	28/10/1918	30/10/1918
War Diary	Rumegies	31/10/1918	31/10/1918
Miscellaneous	Casualties For Month Of October, 1918		
Miscellaneous	Strengths At End Of Month Of October 1918		
Operation(al) Order(s)	157th Infantry Brigade Order No. 146	04/10/1918	04/10/1918
Miscellaneous	Table "A"	04/10/1918	04/10/1918
Operation(al) Order(s)	157th Infantry Brigade Order No. 149	05/10/1918	05/10/1918
Operation(al) Order(s)	157th Infantry Brigade Order No. 150	06/10/1918	06/10/1918
Operation(al) Order(s)	157th Infantry Brigade Order No. 151	12/10/1918	12/10/1918
Operation(al) Order(s)	157th Infantry Brigade Order No. 152	19/10/1918	19/10/1918
Miscellaneous	After Order		
Operation(al) Order(s)	157th Infantry Brigade Order No. 153	20/10/1918	20/10/1918
Operation(al) Order(s)	157th Infantry Brigade Order No. 154	23/10/1918	23/10/1918
Operation(al) Order(s)	157th Infantry Brigade Order No. 156	27/10/1918	27/10/1918
Operation(al) Order(s)	157th Infantry Brigade Order No. 157	27/10/1918	27/10/1918
Heading	Summary Of Operations 157th Infantry Brigade From Midnight 7th/8th September 1918 To Midnight 7th/8th October 1918.		
Miscellaneous		07/09/1918	07/09/1918
Miscellaneous	Lessons Learnt Suggested Improvements In Training. Tactics And Equipment		
Miscellaneous	Prisoners And War Material Captured		
Miscellaneous	Statement Of Casualties For Period.		
War Diary	Rumegies	01/11/1918	03/11/1918
War Diary	Fontaine Bouillon (P.17.b.6.7) Sheet 44.S.E.	04/11/1918	30/11/1918
Heading	Report On Operations From 1st November 1918 To 14th November 1918 157th Infantry Brigade		
Miscellaneous			
Operation(al) Order(s)	157th Infantry Brigade Order No. 158	03/11/1918	03/11/1918
Miscellaneous	Table "A"	04/11/1918	04/11/1918
Operation(al) Order(s)	157th Infantry Brigade Order No. 159	06/11/1918	06/11/1918
Operation(al) Order(s)	52nd Division Order No. 145	07/11/1918	07/11/1918
Operation(al) Order(s)	157th Infantry Brigade Order No. 160	07/11/1918	07/11/1918
Miscellaneous	To All Recipients Of 157th Infantry Brigade Order No. 160	07/11/1918	07/11/1918
Operation(al) Order(s)	157th Infantry Brigade Order No. 161	10/11/1918	10/11/1918
Operation(al) Order(s)	157th Infantry Brigade Order No. 162	10/11/1918	10/11/1918
Operation(al) Order(s)	157th Infantry Brigade Order No. 163	14/11/1918	14/11/1918
Miscellaneous	157th Bde GA.140		
War Diary	Maisiere Erbisoeul Glin Area	01/12/1918	28/02/1919
War Diary	Maisieres-Erbisoeul Area	01/03/1919	20/03/1919
War Diary	Soignies	21/03/1919	14/06/1919
War Diary	Antwerp	21/06/1919	24/06/1919
War Diary	Boulogne	25/06/1919	25/06/1919

52ND DIVISION

157TH INFY BDE

BDE HEADQUARTERS

APR 1918-JUN 1919

52nd Division.

@@@@@@@@@@@@@

Disembarked MARSEILLES from EGYPT 17.4.18.

B. H. Q.

157th INFANTRY BRIGADE

APRIL 1918.

Instructions regarding War Diaries and Intelligence Summaries are contained in F. S. Regs., Part II. and the Staff Manual respectively. Title pages will be prepared in manuscript.

WAR DIARY

~~or~~

~~INTELLIGENCE SUMMARY.~~

(Erase heading not required.)

Army Form C. 2118.

VOL III

157 Infy Bde April 1918. A.I.

Place	Date	Hour	Summary of Events and Information	Remarks and references to Appendices
EAST OF E. JELIL.	1/4		Cold windy day with heavy rain showers. Arrangements for relief of Brigade being made. All baggage which is not required is being sent to SARONA. Received Divl Order No 101 which states that the 52nd Divn (less Artillery) will shortly embark for France. The Command of the Left Sector of 21st Corps front passed from 52nd Divn to the 7th Divn at 12.00.	
	2/4		The relief of the Brigade by the 21st Indian Brigade commenced at dusk.	
			2nd Batn The Black Watch relieved 7th HLI in the Right Sub Section	
			1st " Guides Infy " 6th HLI in the Left " "	
			1/8 Gurkhas " 5th HLI " Right Sub Section Reserve	
			20 Punjabis " 5th A&SH " Left " " "	
			The relief was completed by 01.00 on 3rd. The Battns marched independently to Sarona. The last Battn arrived there at 05.30.	H M Hewison Capt 157 Bde.

D. D. & L., London, E.C. (A8004) Wt. W1771/M2031 750,000 5/17 Sch. 52 Forms/C2118/14

Instructions regarding War Diaries and Intelligence Summaries are contained in F. S. Regs., Part II. and the Staff Manual respectively. Title pages will be prepared in manuscript.

Vol III

WAR DIARY
or
INTELLIGENCE SUMMARY.
(Erase heading not required.)

157 Infy Bde.
APRIL 1918

A2.

Army Form C. 2118.

Place	Date	Hour	Summary of Events and Information	Remarks and references to Appendices
SARONA	3/4		Battalions prepare to move to SURAFEND CAMP LUDD. MG Coy and L T M Battery are relieved and proceed to Sarona. The Brigade group marches to Ludd. The head of the column passes the starting point, light railway crossing at ARGYLL ST SARONA, at 18.30. and arrives at Surafend Camp at 23.00.	
SURAFEND CAMP LUDD.	4/4		All ordnance stores belonging to the E.E.F. are handed in and S.B. Respirators and Waterproof sheets drawn	
	5/4		All S.B.R. tested. All field kitchens, watercarts, limbers &c returned to ordnance and all horses returned to remounts.	
	6/4		The Brigade entrained at Ludd. The marching out state was	[illegible] Capt 157 Bde

	Officers	O.R.
Bde Hqrs	4	69
5th HLI	30	850
6 HLI	24	452
7 HLI	30	864
5th A&SH	38	976

	Officers	O.R.
MG Coy	9	214
L T M Batty	4	81
2nd L F A	5	251

D. D. & L., London, E.C.
(A8001) Wt. W1771/M2031 750,000 5/17 Sch. 52 Forms/C2118/14

Instructions regarding War Diaries and Intelligence Summaries are contained in F. S. Regs., Part II. and the Staff Manual respectively. Title pages will be prepared in manuscript.

VOL III

WAR DIARY
or
INTELLIGENCE SUMMARY.
(Erase heading not required.)

154 Infy Bde
APRIL 1918

A3

Army Form C. 2118.

Place	Date	Hour	Summary of Events and Information	Remarks and references to Appendices
SURAFEND CAMP	6/4.		The train timings for the Brigade Group was	
LUDD.			1st Train — Depart LUDD — Arrive KANTARA	
CONTD.			5th H.L.I — 6/4/18 — 08 51 — 7/4/18 — 00 39	
			2nd Train	
			4th H.L.I — " — 11 51 — " — 03 44	
			3rd Train	
			Bde. Hqrs. 6th H.L.I — " — 14 51 — " — 06 56	
			4th Train	
			5th A & S Hdrs — " — 17 51 — " — 10 01	
			5th Train — 20 51 — " — 13 23	
			Hqrs RE 157 MG Coy DIV SIG Coy DIV Hqrs. Hqrs Div Train APM & DADOS	

D. D. & L., London, E.C.
(A8004) Wt. W1771/M2031 750,000 5/17 Sch. 52 Forms/C2118/14

Instructions regarding War Diaries and Intelligence Summaries are contained in F. S. Regs., Part II. and the Staff Manual respectively. Title pages will be prepared in manuscript.

Army Form C. 2118.

WAR DIARY
or
INTELLIGENCE SUMMARY.
(*Erase heading not required.*)

Vol III — 157 Infy Bde — APRIL 1918 — A4

Place	Date	Hour	Summary of Events and Information	Remarks and references to Appendices
SURAFEND CAMP	6/4		6th Train. Depart Ludd. Arrive Kantara	
			410th Field Coy R E — 6/4/18 - 23.51 — 7/4/18 16.26	
LUDD	Contd.		157. L.T.M. Batty	
			1/2 L F Ambulance	
			217 Coy A. S. C	
			219 Coy A. S. C	
			The trains left up to time and arrived at Kantara before the scheduled time.	
	7/4		The Brigade remained at Kantara during the day and	
KANTARA.			entrained at Kantara West at the following times	Henderson Capt 157 Bde
			The trains being made up in the same order as they were on way down from Ludd to Kantara.	

D. D. & L., London, E.C. (A8001) Wt. W1771/M2031 750,000 5/17 Sch. 52 Forms/C2118/14

Instructions regarding War Diaries and Intelligence Summaries are contained in F. S. Regs., Part II. and the Staff Manual respectively. Title pages will be prepared in manuscript.

Vol III

WAR DIARY
or
INTELLIGENCE SUMMARY.
(Erase heading not required.)

157 Infy Bde
APRIL 1918

A5

Army Form C. 2118.

Place	Date	Hour	Summary of Events and Information	Remarks and references to Appendices
			Train times from KANTARA to ALEXANDRIA.	
KANTARA	7/4		Depart Kantara / Arrive Alexandria	
			1st TRAIN — 5th HLI — 7th 20.50 — 05.40	
			2nd " — 7th HLI — 22.30 — 06.45	
			3rd " — BDE HQRS & 6th HLI — 24.00 — 08.45	
			4th " — 5th A & S. H — 8th 01.50 — 10.45	
			5th " — M G Coy, 410 Field Coy, Divisional Signal Coy, Hqrs R E, Div Hqrs, Divnl Train, A. P. M, D A D O S — " 03.45 — 13.10	

W.M. Henderson Capt.
157 Bde

D. D. & L., London, E.C.
(A8003) Wt. W1771/M2031 750,000 5/17 Sch. 52 Forms/C2118/14

Instructions regarding War Diaries and Intelligence Summaries are contained in F. S. Regs., Part II. and the Staff Manual respectively. Title pages will be prepared in manuscript.

Army Form C. 2118.

WAR DIARY
or
INTELLIGENCE SUMMARY.
(*Erase heading not required.*)

VOL III — 157 Inf Bde — APRIL 1918 — A6

Place	Date	Hour	Summary of Events and Information	Remarks and references to Appendices
ALEXANDRIA	8/4		Brigade Headquarters, 5th, 6th & 7th H.L.I. detrained at SIDI GABER and went in to Camp at SIDI BISHR. The 5th A.&S. Hdrs embarked on the KAISER-I-HIND. Leave to Alexandria was granted to 25% of the men.	
	9/4		Brigade Hqrs and 7th H.L.I. embarked on INDARRA.	
	10/4		5th and 6th HLI embarked. 5th on the OMRAH and 6th on CALEDONIA.	
	11/4		The convoy consisting of seven ships and escorted by six Japanese destroyers sailed from Alexandria at 14.30.	
At Sea.	12/4 13/4 14/4 15/4 16/4		During the voyage the weather was fine & the sea smooth. The usual ship routine was carried out & there is nothing to report.	

D. D. & L., London, E.C. (A8001) Wt. W1771/M2031 750,000 5/17 Sch. 52 Forms/C2118/14

Instructions regarding War Diaries and Intelligence Summaries are contained in F. S. Regs., Part II. and the Staff Manual respectively. Title pages will be prepared in manuscript.

WAR DIARY
or
INTELLIGENCE SUMMARY.
(Erase heading not required.)

Army Form C. 2118.

Vol III — 157 Infy Bde — APRIL 1918 — A7

Place	Date	Hour	Summary of Events and Information	Remarks and references to Appendices
MARSAILLES.	17/4		We arrived at Marsailles early in the morning and got alongside about 08.30. The Brigade disembarked at 13.30 in a downpour of rain and marched to MONTFURON CAMP.	
	18/4		Remained at Marsailles. 10% of the men were given leave to visit the town.	
	19/4		The Brigade entrained for Noyelle.	
	20/21/4		En route for Noyelle.	
	22/4		Bde Hqrs arrived at Noyelle at 10.00 & went in to Billets at St Vallery. The 5th HLI & the 6th HLI were also billeted in St Vallery. The 5th A.S.H. and 7th HLI arrived at Noyelle & stayed overnight at rest camp there. Gen. Hamilton Moore left for five days leave to England.	H M Hewson Capt 157 Bde

D. D. & L., London, E.C. (A5004) Wt. W1771/M2031 750,000 5/17 Sch. 52 Forms/C2118/14

Army Form C. 2118.

Instructions regarding War Diaries and Intelligence Summaries are contained in F. S. Regs., Part II. and the Staff Manual respectively. Title pages will be prepared in manuscript.

WAR DIARY
or
INTELLIGENCE SUMMARY.
(Erase heading not required.)

VOL III — 157 Inf Bde. APRIL 1918. A 8

Place	Date	Hour	Summary of Events and Information	Remarks and references to Appendices
St VALLERY	23/4		The 7th HLI marched to CAYEAUX & went in to billets there. The 5th A&SH marched to PENDÉE and had one company billeted in LANCHERES and one in SALLONELLE.	
"	24/4		Bde Hqrs and Battalion drew transport and bicycles from ABBEVILLE.	
"	25/4		Major Braid Gas officer to VII Corps lectured in the St Vallery town hall to 100 officers & men of 5th HLI from 09.00 to 11.00 and to a similar number of 6th HLI from 14.00 to 16.00.	
"	26/4		Major Braid lectured to 5th A&SH at PENDÉE and to the 7th HLI at CAYAUX	

H. [illegible] Capt
157 Bde

D. D. & L., London, E.C. (A8004) Wt. W1771/M2031 750,000 5/17 Sch. 52 Forms/C2118/14

Instructions regarding War Diaries and Intelligence Summaries are contained in F. S. Regs., Part II. and the Staff Manual respectively. Title pages will be prepared in manuscript.

WAR DIARY
or
INTELLIGENCE SUMMARY.
(*Erase heading not required.*)

Army Form C. 2118.

A9

Place	Date	Hour	Summary of Events and Information	Remarks and references to Appendices
St. VALLERY	27/4		Billeting parties from the Brigade proceeded to AIRES by motor lorries.	
"	28/4		Brigade entrained for BERGUETTE. The first train with one Company of 5th 6th & 7th HLI and Bde Hqrs left at 18.30	
"	29/4		5th 6th & 7th HLI with Brigade Hqrs went in to camp at La Lacque the 5th A & S H to quarters in the Artillery Barracks at AIRES.	
"	30/4		BGC and Commanding Officers make a reconnaissance of the line which the Brigade is to hold when ordered to man battle stations.	

H. M. Henderson Capt
a/Bde Major 157 Bde

D. D. & L., London, E.C.
(A8001) Wt. W1771/M2031 750,000 5/17 Sch. 52 Forms/C2118/14

Instructions regarding War Diaries and Intelligence Summaries are contained in F. S. Regs., Part II. and the Staff Manual respectively. Title pages will be prepared in manuscript.

WAR DIARY
or
INTELLIGENCE SUMMARY.
(*Erase heading not required.*)

Army Form C. 2118.

A.10

Place	Date	Hour	Summary of Events and Information	Remarks and references to Appendices
			Strength of Brigade on date of Embarkation.	

	Officers.	O. Ranks
Bde Hdqrs	8	93
5 H.L.I.	40	1010
6 H.L.I.	38	857
7 H.L.I.	45	937
5 A&SH	41x	1030x
157 M.G. Coy	11	225
	183	4132.

x Includes 1 off & 127 OR of Town Major's party. SARONA.

D. D. & L., London, E.C.
(A8001) Wt. W1771/M2031 750,000 5/17 Sch. 52 Forms/C2118/14

Instructions regarding War Diaries and Intelligence Summaries are contained in F. S. Regs., Part II. and the Staff Manual respectively. Title pages will be prepared in manuscript.

WAR DIARY
or
INTELLIGENCE SUMMARY.
(Erase heading not required.)

Army Form C. 2118.

A. 11

Place	Date	Hour	Summary of Events and Information	Remarks and references to Appendices
			Strength of Brigade 26-4-18.	

	Officers	O Ranks.
Bde. Hdqrs.	6	64
5th H.L.I.	43	1027
6th H.L.I.	37	893
7th H.L.I.	45	945
5th A&SH	38	1011
	169	3940

D. D. & L., London, E.C.
(A5001) Wt. W1771/M2031 750,000 5/17 Sch. 52 Forms/C2118/14

Appendix 1

SECRET. Copy No. 13

BRIGADE ORDER NO.95
BY
BRIG. GENERAL C.D.HAMILTON MOORE.D.S.O. COMMANDING 157th INF. BDE.
1st April 1918.

Reference PALESTINE Sheet XIII.

1. MOVE. The 157th Infantry Brigade Group as detailed below will march to SURAFEND Camp (S.30.b.) on 3rd April 1918.

The head of the column (5th H.L.I.) will pass the Starting Point at 1930 and Units in order named will follow at 30 yards distance.

2. STARTING POINT. Light Railway Line at SARONA.

3. ROUTE. Track running along left bank of the NAHR EL BARIDEH,
SHEIKH AMRAD (J.25),
MAIN ROAD H.36.d.9.3.
Thence along RAMLEH - JAFFA Main Road.

4. ORDER OF MARCH.
Brigade Headquarters,
5th H.L.I.
6th H.L.I.
7th H.L.I.
5th A.&.S.H.
~~157th M.G.Coy.~~
~~157th L.T.M.Bty.~~
410th Field Coy. R.E.
2nd L.F.A.
Company A.S.C. Divisional Train.

5. TRANSPORT. Each Unit's Transport will march behind the Unit to which it belongs.
The strictest march discipline will be maintained.
Transport Officers will ensure that any breakdown which may occur will be pulled clear so as not to delay the column.

6. ACKNOWLEDGE.

H.M. Harrison
Captain,
a/Brigade Major, 157th Infantry Brigade.

Issued at 1700 on 1st April 1918.

Copy No.1 to Brigade Commander.
2 5th H.L.I.
3 6th H.L.I.
4 7th H.L.I.
5 5th A.&.S.H.
6 157th M.G.Coy.
7 157th L.T.M.Bty.
8 Bde. Transport Officer.
9 Bde. Reserve S.A.A.
10 410th Fd. Coy. R.E.
11 A.D.S. 2nd L.F.A.
12 O.C. Divisional Train.
13 War Diary.
14 do.
15 File.

Copy No. 16

Appendix 2.

S E C R E T.

157th Infantry Brigade Administrative Instructions No.5.
Issued with Brigade Order No. 95.

Ref. map PALESTINE Sheet XIII. NIGHT 3rd/4th APRIL 1918.

1. SUPPLIES. Supplies for consumption 3/4th April will be drawn from SARONA Dump at 0830 on 3rd instant.
Instructions regarding drawing of supplies at SURAFEND will be issued when received.

2. WATER. Drinking. } SURAFEND Water Area, EAST of Camp.
Watering. }

3. TRANSPORT. The Transport will be available to all Units on their Mobile Scale, with following amendments:-

1 G.S. limbered wagon will be required for Bde. Reserve.
Baggage and supply wagons of Divisional Train will be available, i.e., 4 wagons per Battn. They will report to Units for loading at 1400 on 3rd prox. The Train wagons will march under the orders of O.C. Divisional Train behind the Brigade.

Field Cookers and Water Carts will be sent to Brigade Transport park at 0800 on the 3rd instant. They will be met by horses of the R.A. at 0900 same day and drawn to the new camp.

4. BOVOUAC AREA. Bivouac areas at SURAFEND will be pointed out to Advance Parties on 3rd instant.

5. BILLETS. Such Billets as are allowed will be handed over to A/Town Major, SARONA. Billets and bivouac areas will be left clean when Units move out. Certificates will be rendered to this office by 1800 on the 4th instant that they were left in a clean, sanitary condition.

6. ADVANCE PARTIES. Advance Parties of 2 Officers per Battn. and 1 N.C.O. and 6 men per Company, plus Pioneers, Cooks and guides as necessary will proceed to SURAFEND, starting at 0600 on the 3rd instant. A mounted officer per Battalion will meet Staff Captain at Brigade Hqrs. in SARONA at 0730 on 3rd instant, in order to proceed to SURAFEND, when allocation of ground will be pointed out. Parties will be employed on arrival at SURAFEND in laying out the new area. The Officer in charge of each party will arrange for a hot meal to be ready on arrival of the Main Body of the Brigade.

7. 157th M.G.Coy. } Separate instructions will be issued for the
157th L.T.M.Bty. } move of the M.G.Coy and the L.T.M.Bty.

8. ACKNOWLEDGE.

[signature]

Captain,

a/Staff Captain, 157th Infantry Brigade.

P. T. O./ Issued at.

Issued at 1700 on 1st April 1918.

Copy No.1	Brigade Commander.
2	5th H.L.I.
3	6th H.L.I.
4	7th H.L.I.
5	5th A.&.S.H.
6	157th M.G.Coy.
7	157th L.T.M.Bty
8	Bde. Transport Officer.
9	Bde. Reserve S.A.A.
10	410th Field Coy. R.E.
11	A.D.S. 2nd L.F.A.
12	Bde. Supply Officer.
13	O.C. Divisional Train.
14	Bde. Water Officer.
15	A/Town Major, SARONA.
16	War Diary.
17	do.
18	File.

S E C R E T.   Copy No. 13

Appendix 3.

157th Infantry Brigade Administrative Instructions No.6
April 1918.

---

1. The 157th Infantry Brigade Group will be prepared to commence entrainment by 0700 on April 6th. Train timings will be communicated immediately they are received in this office.

2. 48 hours rations will be drawn on April 5th for consumption on April 6th and 7th.

3. On April 4th, 157th Infantry Brigade Group will transport all baggage, equipment and stores, which cannot be carried on the person when ~~tese~~ vehicles have been withdrawn, to LUDD Railway Station.
   A site for stacking these will be pointed out previously by the Staff Captain. They will be stacked by Units and under a Guard.

4. Subsequent to removing baggage, etc., all equipment special to the E.E.F. as detailed in list issued to you separately by D.A.D.O.S. and also all tents in use at SURAFEND Camp, will be returned to A.O.D. Depot, this will include 1 blanket per man and all bivouac sheets. All portable latrine equipment will also be returned. Subsequent to returning these articles, and on the same day, each Unit will draw 1 waterproof sheet per man and 1 Box Respirator from A.O.D. Depot LUDD.
   Compliance with each of above will be notified by wire to this office same day.

5. On April 5th all vehicles will be returned to a temporary A.O.D. Receiving Depot established near SURAFEND Camp.
   Subsequent to the return of vehicles, harness will be handed in to the same Depot.
   Animals will finally be led with head rope, head collar and nose bag to Field Remount Section, LUDD, and handed over.

6. Fanatis will be handed over to O.C. "D" Coy, C.T.C. by 1700 on the afternoon of 5th April.

7. Transport to move cooking utensils and any Officers kit to LUDD Station on day of entrainment may be obtained, but only the minimum number of camels will be provided. Number of camels required should be wired to Brigade Hqrs. by 1200 on 5th April. This baggage must be kept down to a minimum.

8. Loading Parties will be detailed for each Troop Train from the troops entraining previous to arrival at the Station.
   Provisionally a loading party per Battalion of 2 Officers and 40 Other Ranks, 1 Officer and 20 O.R. from Machine Gun Coy. and 1 Officer and 10 O.R. from Light Trench Mortar Battery should be detailed. These may, however, have to be re-told off when the distribution of trains and train timings are received. The loading parties detailed will not be changed until embarkation is completed. They will be responsible for unloading and re-loading at KANTARA EAST and WEST, and at port of embarkation.

9. Trains must be cleared of troops and baggage within 30 minutes of arrival at Station of detrainment without fail. A Representative of the Brigade Staff will meet troops on arrival at KANTARA EAST and arrangements for transport to KANTARA WEST will then be notified.

10. Arrangements have been made for Base Kits to be collected from Base Depot at KANTARA and proceed with Units from KANTARA WEST.
   The Brigade Group will probably entrain from KANTARA WEST during the night of April 7/8th.

P. T. O. // 11.

11. A Representative of the Brigade Staff will be at ALEXANDRIA on arrival of Brigade Group and will inform troops on arrival the arrangements for embarkation.

Instructions concerning returns to be rendered re embarkation will be forwarded later.

It should be clearly understood that O/C Ships is responsible for the compilation and rendering of these returns to the E.S.O.

12. All entrainments and embarkation must be carried out quickly and quietly. No talking to be allowed except by Officers and N.C.Os. when giving orders. Perfect discipline must be maintained. Commanding Officers and Company Commanders will carefully think out their arrangements beforehand. ~~In~~ All orders of entraining and ~~embarking~~ Embarkation Staff Officers must be carried out.

13. ACKNOWLEDGE.

Captain,

a/Staff Captain, 157th Infantry Brigade.

Issued at 0900 on 3rd. April 1918.

Copy No.1	G. O. C.
2	5th H.L.I.
3	6th H.L.I.
4	7th H.L.I.
5	5th A.&.S.H.
6	157th M.G.Coy.
7	157th L.T.M.Bty.
8	Bde. Transport Officer.
9	410th Field Coy. R.E.
10	~~H.Q.'s~~. 2nd L.F.A.
11	Bde. Supply Officer.
12	O.C. Divisional Train.
13	War Diary.
14	do.
15	File.
16	217 Coy. A.S.C.
17	219 Coy. A.S.C.

On His Majesty's Service.

"War Diary"
H.Q. 157th Inf Brigade
from 1st – 31st May 1918

Volume III

(Original Copy)

Vol. 2

31st May 1918

[signature] Major
Bde Major
157th Inf Bde

Confidential

Instructions regarding War Diaries and Intelligence Summaries are contained in F. S. Regs., Part II. and the Staff Manual respectively. Title pages will be prepared in manuscript.

Vol III

WAR DIARY
or
~~INTELLIGENCE SUMMARY.~~
(Erase heading not required.)

157th Infantry Brigade
May 1918

Army Form C. 2118.

M1

Place	Date	Hour	Summary of Events and Information	Remarks and references to Appendices
AIRE	1/5		Brigade Major returned from leave to the U.K.	
			G.O.C. visited the line the Brigade is to hold in case the order to "Man Battle Stations" is given.	
	2/5		Colonel Campbell Gord Highlanders lectured to the 5th 6th & 7th H.L.I. on bayonet fighting training etc. The lecture was very good indeed and appealed to the men.	
			Warning order for Div to be transferred to XVIII Corps.	
	3/5		G.O.C. & Bde Major rode out to see the country immediately in front of the line the Brigade is to hold in case of alarm (i.e. the BUSNES – STEENBECQUE line. Towards ST VENANT the country is unfavourable for a counter attack on our part but farther North it is more open and not so intersected with Canals and ditches.	
			75 Officers attended 2 Lectures in the Town Hall AIRE.	
			(a) by the O.C. 1st Army Infantry School – Notes on the recent operations	
			(b) by CRA 14th Division – Methods of organising for defence etc. Stressed close co-operation with Artillery & Infantry.	
			Warning order received that Division moves on 6th 7th & 8th May to relieve 1st Canadian Division on the VIMY ridge.	

A.W. Williams, Major

D. D. & L., London, E.C.
(A8004) Wt. W1771/M2031 750,000 5/17 Sch. 52 Forms/C2118/14

Instructions regarding War Diaries and Intelligence Summaries are contained in F. S. Regs., Part II. and the Staff Manual respectively. Title pages will be prepared in manuscript.

~~No~~ Confidential

Vol III

WAR DIARY
or
INTELLIGENCE SUMMARY.
(*Erase heading not required.*)

157th Inf Bde
May 1918

Army Form C. 2118.

M2

Place	Date	Hour	Summary of Events and Information	Remarks and references to Appendices
AIRE	4/5	-	G.O.C & Bde Major proceeded to VIMY to visit 11th Canadian Brigade which is the Bde we are to take over from. After going up into the line the G.O.C decides that 7th H.L.I & 5th A&SH would be in front Zone. 6th H.L.I in 2nd Zone & 5th H.L.I in 3rd Zone. Brigade Major collected what information he could on all G matters.	
			Capt Dras(?) a/Staff Captain ~~[illegible]~~ went down to VIMY to be attached to the 11th Canadian for a few days to get to know all about the Q arrangements. He took with him. The Intelligence Officer & R.Q.M.S & 6 Scouts per Battn.	
	5/5	1200	Bde Order No 97 issued to all concerned.	Appendix I
		1400	Conference of all COs at which the G.O.C explained the system of defence in the new Sector.	
	6/5	0908 & 0958	Brigade proceeded to MARDEUIL in 2 tactical trains. On arrival at MARDEUIL units detrained & marched to billeting areas which had been arranged for by Lieut Stewart who was sent on yesterday with the Billeting parties.	

[illegible signature] Major

D. D. & L., London, E.C.
(A8004) Wt. W1771/M2031 750,000 5/17 Sch. 52 Forms/C2118/14

Confidential

Instructions regarding War Diaries and Intelligence Summaries are contained in F. S. Regs., Part II. and the Staff Manual respectively. Title pages will be prepared in manuscript.

VOL III

WAR DIARY or INTELLIGENCE SUMMARY.

(Erase heading not required.)

457th Inf Bde

May 1918

Army Form C. 2118.

143

Place	Date	Hour	Summary of Events and Information	Remarks and references to Appendices
NEUVILLE ST VAAST	6/5		5th 6th & 7th HLI were billetted at NEUVILLE ST VAAST - 5th A&SH at MT ST ELOY. 155th LTM - MG Coy RE & Dets 2/FA at the former place also. It was unfortunate that the 5th A&SH should have been billetted at MT ST ELOY as they are for the front line and will consequently have a march of about 9 miles up to the front line tomorrow night.	
	7/5	0845	Batt: Commanders, with certain officers, Gas N.CO's & Signallers went up to view the new line. Guides were arranged to meet them up near Bde H.Q. The G.O.C. received information that the Boche is expected to attack at 0800 tomorrow morning. The whole morning and afternoon there was a perfect rush getting things organized for the relief. The 11th Canadian Brigade were very good in arranging for guides etc and helped us in every way. The Staff Captain arranged for the 5th A&SH to go up in the light railway, leaving MT ST ELOY at 1900. It was very difficult to get any definite information on the subject	Alws/ A.A. Williams Major

D. D. & L., London, E.C. (A8004) Wt. W1771/M2031 750,000 5/17 Sch. 52 Forms/C2118/14

Instructions regarding War Diaries and Intelligence Summaries are contained in F. S. Regs., Part II. and the Staff Manual respectively. Title pages will be prepared in manuscript.

Confidential

Vol III

WAR DIARY
or
INTELLIGENCE SUMMARY.
(Erase heading not required.)

15-3rd Inf Bde

May 17

Army Form C. 2118.

(M4)

Place	Date	Hour	Summary of Events and Information	Remarks and references to Appendices
NEUVILLE ST VAAST.	7/5	-	of the Q arrangements as the Brigade refilling point has been changed from that used by the Canadians so that it means there is will have to be an alteration in the routes the rations take on the light Railways.	
			Instructions were received during the morning that Battns proceeding into the line are to leave behind in their units transport lines all the personnel detailed to be left behind when a Battn goes into action and in addition to this Sections are not to go in more than 1 NCO & 6 men strong; this means that considering the front allotted to the Brigade we shall be very weak.	
		1900	Battns marched off from NEUVILLE ST VAAST to carry out the relief, Bde HQ moving at 2030.	
	8/5	0420	Relief completed. The relief was completed in the following order 5th HLI. 5th A&SH. 6th HLI & 7th HLI the latter was about one hour later than the slowest of the others, though the delay cannot be attributed to any special cause.	
			The day was spent in settling in and passed off very quietly.	
	9/5		Instructions received from Division ^ER 2/1/90^ that BILLIE BURKE trench is no longer to be held in any strength but only by posts at the point where BETTY CT and VESTA TILLEY CT join same. Copies of the defence scheme showing all the arrangements for the defence of this sector will be attached as [illegible] as completed	[illegible] - maps

D. D. & L., London, E.C. (A8001) Wt. W1771/M2031 750,000 5/17 Sch. 52 Forms/C2118/14

Instructions regarding War Diaries and Intelligence Summaries are contained in F. S. Regs., Part II. and the Staff Manual respectively. Title pages will be prepared in manuscript.

Confidential

Vol III

WAR DIARY
or
INTELLIGENCE SUMMARY.
(Erase heading not required.)

15th Inf Bde

May 1918

Army Form C. 2118.

(M6)

Place	Date	Hour	Summary of Events and Information	Remarks and references to Appendices
VIMY Ridge MAROEUIL & ST NAZAIRE Groove	13/5	1100	G.R. 17/4/2 received from Division instructing the Brigade to carry out an "Identification" raid on the night 14/15 May. 7th H.L.I. detailed to do this and as they are to be relieved the same night, they will leave the necessary number of men up to carry out the raid. Very wet all day & visibility very bad. 2 sections of the 412nd Field Co R.E. moved back from the neighbourhood of LA CHAUDIERE to the foot of the VIMY ridge near the LENS - ARRAS road.	
	14/5	0100	Relief of the 2 left Battns complete - vide appendix II. i.e. 6th H.L.I. relieved the 5th A&SH. 5th A&SH assumed correct positions necessary on adjustment of the defensive zones. Raid last night was carried through according to instructions. 2 platoons 7th H.L.I. entered the enemy front line at the junction of ABLAZE & ACHEVILLE trenches but unfortunately at this point the trench was unoccupied so no identification could be secured.	
	15/5		5th H.L.I. relieved 7th H.L.I. 0130. Artillery activity on the part of our Artillery & Enemy rather more marked than usual	

A.W. Williams Major

Bde Major 15th Bde

D. D. & L., London, E.C.
(A8001) Wt. W1771/M2031 750,000 5/17 Sch. 52 Forms/C2118/14

Instructions regarding War Diaries and Intelligence Summaries are contained in F. S. Regs., Part II. and the Staff Manual respectively. Title pages will be prepared in manuscript.

WAR DIARY
or
INTELLIGENCE SUMMARY.
(Erase heading not required.)

157th Inf Brigade
May 1915

Army Form C. 2118.

M705

Place	Date	Hour	Summary of Events and Information	Remarks and references to Appendices
LA FOLIE FARM. VIMY RIDGE	10/5		A very busy day for all. The G.O.C. was out all day looking round the trenches. We were informed that shortly we will have to carry out the organisation of the Sector instead of in breadth as it is at present. Patrols sent out ~~the~~ last night had nothing special to report. One officer accompanied by a few men got through the German wire but got no information of much value. 4 O.R. 7th HLI reported missing.	AWS
	11/5		The 4 men mentioned as being missing turned up at 10.20 pm last night having laid ~~at~~ out all yesterday in shell holes. Boche was very quiet all day. Preliminary instructions for relief sent out. Instructions sent out for tomorrow nights & the following nights relief.	AWS appendix II
	12/5		Letter received from the Division that all our surplus personnel left behind in the transport lines is to be sent tomorrow to a Training Camp at VILLERS. Leave has been opened for 1 Officer & 10 OR per Brigade per diem to the U.K. First party left yesterday. They are to have 14 days at home. All ranks are very delighted with the prospect of a few days at home	

A W [illegible] Major

D. D. & L., London, E.C.
(A8004) Wt. W1771/M2031 750,000 5/17 Sch. 52 Forms/C2118/14

Instructions regarding War Diaries and Intelligence Summaries are contained in F. S. Regs., Part II. and the Staff Manual respectively. Title pages will be prepared in manuscript.

Confidential

Vol III.

WAR DIARY or INTELLIGENCE SUMMARY.

(Erase heading not required.)

Army Form C. 2118.

152nd Inf Brigade

(147)

Place	Date	Hour	Summary of Events and Information	Remarks and references to Appendices
VIMY RIDGE S23c 1/20000			Orders received from the Division re the discharge of gas on our front on the night of the 16/17th May or first suitable night. Brigade Instructions issued Z/696.	Append IIIb
	16/5.		A quiet day. Patrols out last night were unable to get any definite information about anything. Orders received from Division that our own Light T.M.B are to come up here and relieve the 155 L.T.M. Battery.	
	17/5		Informed by Division that we will be relieved on the night of the 24/25th by the 155 Inf Brigade. The question of what numbers a Battalion is to go up into the front line is causing a great deal of talk. The only really definite information we have now is that the Officers must not exceed 22. As regards the Other Ranks. According to SS 143 and SS 135 the following are allowed. at Battn H.Q. 64 (fighting) 24 (Administrative); 4 Coy H.Q. at 22 (Incl 2 Coy S. Majors) 88; 16 Platoon H.Q @ 3 less 4 Sergts 44; 64 Sects at 7 448; 666. = 666. Other Ranks.	A.W. Williams Major

D. D. & L., London, E.C. (A8001) Wt. W1771/M2031 750,000 5/17 Sch. 52 Forms/C2118/14

Instructions regarding War Diaries and Intelligence Summaries are contained in F. S. Regs., Part II. and the Staff Manual respectively. Title pages will be prepared in manuscript.

Confidential

Vol III

WAR DIARY
or
INTELLIGENCE SUMMARY.
(Erase heading not required.)

157th Inf Bde

May 1918.

Army Form C. 2118.

(148)

Place	Date	Hour	Summary of Events and Information	Remarks and references to Appendices
VIMY RIDGE.	18/5		Finally decided that the HQ of the Right reserve Battn is to be established about S25 b 40.90. A party of Tunnellers from the 1st Canadian Tunnelling Company are coming up to carry out the work.	
			Last night a Test Artillery barrage was carried out, with the following result. Message handed in at Coy HQ 0119 hrs	
			" Received at Bde HQ 0122 "	
			" Received at Art: Bde HQ 0127 "	
			Guns fired at 0128½ "	
			The long delay of 5 minutes before the message could get through from Bde HQ to Art HQ was due to the fact that a "priority" wire was blocking the latters line & the RFA operators were not aware of the fact that a practice SOS call takes precedence over all "Priority" wires.	
	19/5		Memo from the Division to say that Corps Commander will visit our Section at 1030 tomorrow. GOC & Bde Major to go round with the Corps Commander & OC Battns to meet him at various places en route.	Appendix IV.
		2400	5th A&SH relieved 6th HLI	
	20/5	1030	Corps Commander arrived. He first held a small Pow-wow with GOC Bde, OC 6th & 7th HLI and his own Staff also Div Staff. Afterwards	

D. D. & L., London, E.C.
(A8004) Wt. W1771/M2031 750,000 5/17 Sch. 52 Forms/C2118/14

Instructions regarding War Diaries and Intelligence Summaries are contained in F. S. Regs., Part II. and the Staff Manual respectively. Title pages will be prepared in manuscript.

Army Form C. 2118.

(M9)

WAR DIARY
or
INTELLIGENCE SUMMARY.
(Erase heading not required.)

Confidential
Vol III

157th Inf Bde
May 1918

Place	Date	Hour	Summary of Events and Information	Remarks and references to Appendices
Vimy Ridge	20/5		Corps Commander went round the line. On the whole he seemed quite satisfied with what he saw. He complimented the 5th A&SH on the way in which they had their trench system arranged.	
		23.45	7th HLI relieved 5th HLI	
	21/5.		52nd Div GR/2/1/105 received instructing Brigade to arrange mutually with the 59th Bde on our left re the establishment of mutual posts to ensure touch being maintained.	
			These posts are to be 3 in number & the Bde Major in conjunction with the Brigade Major 59th Inf Bde fixed the following Posts:	
			Post A. 1 Sergt + 6 men of ours + 1 NCO & 6 men from 59th Bde. located at T2d 50.00	
			" B 1 NCO + 6 " " " + 1 Sergt + 6 men " " " " " T2c 20.40	
			" C " " " " " " " " " " " S12 b 8.4.	
			Post A to be under GOC 157th Bde.	
			Posts B & C " " " GOC 59 Bde.	
			All Battns warned that they must always have a raid scheme ready. (this applies to Battns in Reserve also.)	
			Brigade is to be relieved on the night 24/25 May. Representatives from Battns 153rd Inf Bde came round the line yesterday & also today.	[illegible] Major
			52nd Div Circular dealing with the S.O.S call received.	
	22/5.		Quiet day.	[illegible] Maj.

D. D. & L., London, E.C. (A8003) Wt. W1771/M2031 750,000 5/17 Sch. 52 Forms/C2118/14

Instructions regarding War Diaries and Intelligence Summaries are contained in F. S. Regs., Part II. and the Staff Manual respectively. Title pages will be prepared in manuscript.

Confidential

Vol III

WAR DIARY
or
INTELLIGENCE SUMMARY.
(Erase heading not required.)

157th Inf Bde
May 1918

Army Form C. 2118.

(14 pp)

Place	Date	Hour	Summary of Events and Information	Remarks and references to Appendices
VIMY Ridge S23c 3.4	23/5		Nothing of much interest to report. The Boche Artillery has been rather more active of late. Neighbourhood of VIMY was shelled quite heavily this afternoon	
		1300	Received the code word "ASTI" from Div - meaning gas beam will be discharged tonight vide appendix V	
			Bde Order No 100 re relief issued to all concerned	
			Defence scheme for left sector issued to all concerned	Appendix V
	24/5	0145	Gas beam successfully discharged.	
MT. ST ELOY	25/5	0030	Relief completed and Bde moved back into Divisional Reserve	
			The remainder of the 25th & the 26th May will be set aside for cleaning up & resting & then there will be 7 days training	Eloy
	26/6.		Relief of 157th L.T.M. Battery completed	
		1500	The G.O.C 52nd Div came round to inspect the billeting areas. He was horrified at the state of the Huts which certainly very dilapidated.	
	27/6	0900	G.O.C. went out to see the 5th H.L.I. training and to take one Company in platoon schemes	
			The object of these schemes is to try and teach the Officers & Sect leaders how to think out things for themselves & to make the training interesting for the men.	

A.L. Williams Major
Bde Major 157th Bde

D. D. & L., London, E.C.
(A8001) Wt. W1771/M2031 750,000 5/17 Sch. 52 Forms/C2118/14

Confidential

Vol III

WAR DIARY
or
INTELLIGENCE SUMMARY.
(Erase heading not required.)

Army Form C. 2118.

Instructions regarding War Diaries and Intelligence Summaries are contained in F. S. Regs., Part II. and the Staff Manual respectively. Title pages will be prepared in manuscript.

152nd Inf Bde

May 1918

(M1R)

Place	Date	Hour	Summary of Events and Information	Remarks and references to Appendices
MT ST ELOY	28/5.	-	GOC & Bde Major went out Training with the 7th HLI taking Platoons in small schemes.	
			Boche shelled MT ST ELOY Camping area with a long high velocity gun. The first shell which was fired at 0400 hit one of the huts of the 2nd Low. Fd Ambulance & killed 12 & wounded 17.	[illegible]
	29/5		~~Bde~~ GOC & Bde Major went out training with the 6th HLI Coys.	[illegible]
		1400	Bde Major & Bde I.O. took out representatives of Batts to reconnoitre routes in connection with Reserve Provisional Defence Scheme	Appendix VI
	30/5.		GOC & Bde Major went out training with 5th A&SH Coys.	
		1400	Bde Major made a reconnaissance of positions for Bde to take up under cover near VIMY in case the Bde is ordered up to Counter attack in the event of the Centre of the Divisional Sector being broken — Vide Provisional Defence Scheme	[illegible]
	31/5.		GOC & Bde Major went up to HQ to arrange about relief	
		0900	Div Order No 102 received } Both deal with the taking over by this Bde of the	
		2100	Bde Order No 102 issued. } Right (WILLERVAL) Section of 52nd Div Sector	
	30/5	1030	Demonstration in the use of Popham panel carried out practically with an Aeroplane. It was noted that Plane took short messages of 1 group of figures well but in the case of several groups of figures the plane did not wait to receive same. It is not known whether this was due to faulty sending or whether it was because the ~~Plane~~ observer thought the messages were finished	A Wilkie Major

A Wilkie Major

D. D. & L., London, E.C.
(A8001) Wt. W1771/M2031 750,000 5/17 Sch. 52 Forms/C2118/14

Instructions regarding War Diaries and Intelligence Summaries are contained in F. S. Regs., Part II. and the Staff Manual respectively. Title pages will be prepared in manuscript.

Confidential

Vol III.

WAR DIARY
or
INTELLIGENCE SUMMARY.
(Erase heading not required.)

157th Inf. Brigade

May 1918.

Army Form C. 2118.

(M 11)

Place	Date	Hour	Summary of Events and Information	Remarks and references to Appendices
MT ST ELOY.	31/5		Courses held during May	

Course	duration	Detail
Infantry Training	1 month	1 Officer & 1 N.C.O from each Battn.
Sniping Course	2 days	3 O.R. from each Battn.
"	19 "	1 N.C.O 5th H.L.I.
XVIII Corps Training Coy	45 "	4 O.R. per Battn.
Gas Course	4 "	1 Officer from 6th & 7th H.L.I.
"	7 "	2 O.R. 5th H.L.I. 1 Officer & 1 O.R. 5th A&SH. 1 O.R. 6th H.L.I.
"	7 "	1 Officer & 1 O.R. 5th H.L.I. 1 O.R. 6th H.L.I. & 5th A&SH
Lewis Gun Course	12 "	1 Officer 5th A&SH.
"	20 "	2 N.C.Os 5th H.L.I.
Musketry	14 "	1 N.C.O 7th H.L.I.
"	23 "	1 Officer & 1 N.C.O from each Battn.
Trench Mortar Course	17 "	1 Officer 157th L.T.M.B.
Cooperation with Aircraft	1 "	2 Signallers per Battn.
P.T. & Bayonet Course	6 "	1 Officer 7th H.L.I. 1 N.C.O 5th 6th H.L.I. & 5th A&SH

[signature] Major
157th Bde

D. D. & L., London, E.C.
(A8001) Wt. W1771/M2031 750,000 5/17 Sch. 52 Forms/C2118/14

Confidential

WAR DIARY
or
INTELLIGENCE SUMMARY.
(*Erase heading not required.*)

Instructions regarding War Diaries and Intelligence Summaries are contained in F. S. Regs., Part II. and the Staff Manual respectively. Title pages will be prepared in manuscript.

Vol III

157th Inf Brigade

May 1918

Army Form C. 2118.

M12

Place	Date	Hour	Summary of Events and Information	Remarks and references to Appendices
MT ST ELOY	31/5		Casualties for the period during which the Brigade was in the line were as follows:	

	Officers K	W	M	OR K	W	M
5th HLI	.	.	.	3	24	-
6th HLI	-	-	-	1	3	-
7th HLI	.	1	.	1	17	3
5th A&SH	.	.	-	.	4	
	.	1	.	5	48	3

Summary of strength 3/5/18

	(A) Strength excluding attached Officers	OR	(B) Not present with unit Officers	OR	(C) with unit Officers	OR
Bde HQ	7	67	1	-	6	67
5th HLI	43	1019	1	48	42	971
6th HLI	38	894	-	94	38	800
7th HLI	45	945	3	60	42	885
5th A&SH	40	1052	2	98	38	954
	173	3977	7	300	166	3677

Note 157th LTM Battery are not yet in the country

A Williams Major

D. D. & L., London, E.C.
(A8001) Wt. W1771/M2031 750,000 5/17 Sch. 52 Forms/C2118/14

Instructions regarding War Diaries and Intelligence Summaries are contained in F. S. Regs., Part II. and the Staff Manual respectively. Title pages will be prepared in manuscript.

Confidential

Vol III.

WAR DIARY
or
INTELLIGENCE SUMMARY.

(Erase heading not required.)

157th Inf Brigade

May 1918.

Army Form C. 2118.

(M13)

Place	Date	Hour	Summary of Events and Information	Remarks and references to Appendices
Mt St Eloy	31/5	-	Strength 25/5/18	

	(A) Strength excluding attached: Officers	OR	(B) Not present with unit: Officers	OR	(C) With unit: Officers	OR
157th Bde HQ	10	78	2	5	8	73
5th HLI	43	1016	7	158	36	858
6th HLI	44	868	12	149	32	719
7th HLI	43	940	11	178	32	762
5th A&SH	38	1005	12	150	26	855
157th LTMB	4	84	-	8	4	76
	182	3991	44	648	138	3343

A Williams Major

D. D. & L., London, E.C.
(A8004) Wt. W1771/M2031 750,000 5/17 Sch. 52 Forms/C2118/14

Appendix I

157th Infantry Brigade Order No. 97. Copy No........

=========================

Ref. Map Sheets MAROEUIL & ST.NAZAIRE RIVER 5th May, 1918.
Both 1/20,000.

1. (a) The 52nd Division will move from the neighbourhood of AIRE on the 6th, 7th & 8th inst., and take over the MERICOURT sector of the Line from the 4th Canadian Division from HUDSON Trench in square T.29.a & b., to the present northern boundary of the Canadian Corps Line at T.3.b.1.0. - a frontage of about 4,500 yards.

(b) The 157th Brigade Group consisting of 157th Infantry Brigade, 155th L.T.M. Battery, 413th Field Coy., R.E., and 2nd Lowland Field Ambulance will relieve the 11th Canadian Infantry Brigade in the line on the night of th 7/8th May.

The 156th Brigade will be in support about NEUVILLE, St. VAAST.

155th Brigade Group will be in reserve about St. ELOY.

Divisonal Headquarters will be at the CHATEAU ACQ, (W.30.b.2.4.)

2. (a) Personnel will proceed in tactical Trains on the 7th inst. to NEUVILLE ST.VAAST Camp according to attached schedule and instructions and thence by Route March to new area on the night of 7th/8th

(b) Transport and mounted personnel will move by road in accordance with instructions already issued.

3. (a) The 7th H. L. I., & 5th A & S. H.. will take over the front zone from the 87th Canadian regiment and the 102nd Canadian Regiment respectively. The 7th H. L. I., being on the right and the 5th A & S. H., on the left.

(b) The 6th H. L. I., will take over the second defensive zone from the 75th Canadian Regiment.

(c) The 5th H. L. I.. will take over the third defensive zone from the 54th Canadian Regiment (less two Companies)

(d) The 155th L. T. M. Battery will take over existing gun positions from the 11th Canadian L.T.M. Battery.

(e) Arrangements have been made for 2 guides per platoon other/

P. T. O.

other units in proportion to meet the Brigade at NEUVILLE ST. VAAST camp on the evening of the 6th inst. Those guides will remain with respective units for the night and following day, and will be available to guide them up on the night of 7th inst.

(f) Arrangements will be made for O.Cs. to visit their portion of the sector during the 7th inst.

(g) Details regarding relief will be arranged between C.Os. themselves. Units must not commence to cross the VIMY RIDGE until 2000 under relief must be complete by 0600 on the 8th inst.

(h) Defence schemes, Trench maps, existing communications, aeroplane photos, log books, trench and area stores, should be taken over.

(i) Completion of relief will be reported by Bab Trench Code to Brigade Headquarters by Priority Wire.

4. 413th Field Coy., R.E., with attached Infantry Pioneer Coy., will take over duties of the line and will come orders of G.O.C., 157th Infantry Brigade from 1700 on 6th inst. Details of this relief are being arranged by the C.R.E.

5. The 157th L.T.M. Battery is placed under orders of G.O.C. 155th Brigade from 0500 5th May.

6. Details regarding exact limits etc., of sectors to be held by units will be explained at to-day's conference.

7. Brigade Headquarters will be on the VIMY RIDGE in the LA FOLIE COPSE square S.23.c.

8. ACKNOWLEDGE.

[signature]
Major,
Brigade Major, 157th Infantry Brigade.

Issued at.......... on 5th May, 1918.

Copy No. 1 to	5th H. L. I.	7	2nd L. F. A.
2	6th H. L. I.	8	11th Canadian Inf. Bde.
3	7th H. L. I.	9	G.O.C.
4	5th A & S. H.	10	War Diary
5	413th Field Coy. R.E.	11	" "
6	155th L.T.M. Bty.	12	File.

appendix II

HEADQUARTER
No. Z/589
Date
157TH INFANTRY BRIG.

SECRET.

O.C. 5th H.L.I.
6th H.L.I.
7th H.L.I.
5th A.& S.H.

O.C. 52nd M.G.Battn.
242nd Bde. R.F.A.
155th L.T.M. Bty.
A.D.S. 2nd L.F.A.

In continuation of Z/520 of 11th inst. and Z/557 of 12th inst.

1. (a) On the night of the 13/14th May, 155th Inf. Bde. will take over a portion of the 52nd Division Left Section (157th Inf. Brigade.) of the line, so that the inter Brigade boundary will run for 155th Brigade ACHEVILLE Road - NEW BRUNSWICK Road, both inclusive as far as the Railway Embankment in T.26.a.3/9 (exclusive) - GRAND TRUNK Trench T.26.a.9.2. (inclusive) - thence to BOIS DU GOULOT at T.25.c.0.0. and so due West along the grid line.
(b) In order to obtain an even distribution of the front line system, the dividing line between the two Battalion Sections will be altered from the MERICOURT ROAD to the line VESTA TILLEY - PERRIE as far as square T.16.a.0.0. both of these trenches being inclusive to the Left Battalion Section.
The 7th H.L.I. will take over that portion of the 5th A.& S.H. line south East of this line, relief to be completed by the night of 13/14th May.
(c) The Northern boundary of the Brigade Section will remain as at present.

2. The present Second and Third lines i.e. the RED and BROWN Lines respectively, will be reorganised.
At present they are unsuitable for protracted defence, being organised in breadth instead of in depth.

3. From after the Relief of the 13/14th May, instead of one Battalion holding the RED LINE and one the BROWN, the whole area occupied by the two lines will be divided up into two areas in depth.

4. One Battalion will then hold the CHAUDIERE Area, the boundaries of which are as follows:-

On the NORTH

From square T.2.c.9.2. thence due WEST to T.1.d.3.3. thence along CYRIL TRENCH (exclusive) to S.11.c.0.4. - S.18. central - S.19.a. central.

On the EAST

The line of the Railway Embankment inclusive to the BOIS DE LA CHAUDIERE - thence along JULIA JAMES Trench (inclusive) to the junction of JULIA JAMES with GERTIE in square T.14.c.

On the SOUTH

An imaginary line from the junction of JULIA JAMES with GERTIE eastwards to the Railway junction (inclusive) in square T.13.d. - thence to square T.13.c. 0.0. - thence to the road junction in square S.24.c.4.8. PETIT VIMY - thence S.W. along the LENS - ARRAS road (inclusive).

5. The other Battn. will occupy the VIMY - NOVA SCOTIA area the boundaries of which are:-

On the NORTH

The southern boundary line of the CHAUDIERE area exclusive, the boundary line being continued S.E. from the junction of JULIA JAMES with GERTIE to T.14.a.0.0., thence Eastward to T.15. central.

On the EAST

From T.15.central due SOUTH to the junction of TOAST TRENCH with CANADA TRENCH.
(Note this means that the whole of [struck through] TOAST TRENCH between EMILE GERARD and CANADA Trenches is included in the area of the right front Battn).

On the SOUTH

Along/

Along the NEW BRUNSWICK ROAD (exclusive) to its junction with the Railway embankment (inclusive) to T.25.a.9.2. thence BOIS DE GOULOT at T.25.c.0.0. thence due WEST along the ~~RED~~ grid line.

6. H.Q., of the CHAUDIERE area will be at the present 5th. H.L.I. H.Q.
Co-ordinate S.24.a.2.0.
H.Q. of the VIMY - NOV A SCOTIA area in VIMY about squares T.25.a.5.8.

7. After relief on the night of the 13/14th the 5th A & S. H. will take over the CHAUDIERE area from the respective portions of the 5th H. L. I., & 6th H. L. I.
The garrison of the BROWN LINE in the area at present furnished by the 6th H. L. I., will take over that portion of the NOVA SCOTIA area at present held by the 6th H. L. I. in sufficient time to allow the 6th H. L. I., garrison to carry out its relief in the front line leaving a neucleus garrison in the BROWN LINE till the arrival of the 5th A & S. H. garrison.
As the H.Q. will not be vacated till the night of 14/15th the H.Q., 5th A & S. H. may be located for the one night in the present 6th H. L. I. H.Q.

8. After relief on the night of the 14/15th the 7th H. L. I. will take over the VIMY - NOVA SCOTIA Area from the 5th H.L.I.

9. During these reliefs the garrisons of the RED and BROWN Lines may be interchanged by day provided all movements are carried out by small parties and restricted to movements inside trenches and that there is no movement when hostile aeroplanes are overhead.
Similarly reliefs of the MAIN and ~~BROWN~~ RED lines may be carried out by day for such portions of the garrisons of the front line Battn. which are located BEHIND the ACTHESS - KHANE ZENDIR GERRARD - NEW BRUNSWICK Line.
The remainder must be done after dark.

10. Reliefs both on the nights 13/14th and 14/15th May, must be completed by 0300.
Details will be arranged mutually between O.Cs. concerned. A percentage of Scouts, L.Gunners and other specialists should be sent up in advance to look round by daylight. Relief completed will in all cases, be wired "Priority" in CODE to Bde. HQ.

11. Trench Stores, Existing communications, R.E. & Area Stores, Trench Diagrams, Defence schemes, and Log Books will be taken over.

A.C. Williams
Major,
Brigade Major, 157th Infantry Brigade.

12th May, 1918.

Appendix III.

Z/696

S E C R E T.

G. C. 95, 97 H. Battery

1. A "Gas beam" attack will be carried out on the XVIIIth Corps Front, from T.9.b., to N.28.b., on the night of May 16/17th, or the first night after upon which the wind is favourable.

2. In the 117th Infantry Brigade area there will be a Power Head situated at DORIS Dump, T.8.d.80.95., and the discharge point squares T.8.b.45.60., T.3.d.30.07.

3. A total of 4725 cylinders will be discharged of which 1875 will be discharged from the Brigade area.

4. Infantry parties will be required to assist in the arrangements for discharging the gas. These parties will be found from the 6th H.L.I., as many as possible being taken from that portion of the RED LINE held by the 6th H.L.I. and the remainder from their portion of the [illegible] LINE.

5. The cylinders will be transported to the Power Head (DORIS Dump square T.8.d.80.95) on the Light Railway in 78 trucks made up into trains as follows:-

7 trains of 10 trucks, &
1 train of 8 trucks.

6. From the Power Head (square T.8.d.80.95) trucks will be pushed up by the parties furnished by the 6th H.L.I., to the discharge point (squares T.2.b.45.60., to T.3.d.30.07).

7. The 6th H.L.I. will furnish a detachment of 300 men exclusive of Officers and N.C.Os. These men will be organised into 15 parties each of 20 men plus a Senior N.C.O., in charge of each party.

Every 2 parties will be under 1 Officer and the odd party will be also under an Officer.

The acting second in Command will be in charge of the whole/-

whole.

The total strength of the party to be furnished will therefore be:-

9 Officers (including the second in command) 15 senior N.C.Os. and 500 O.R.

These parties will parade at the Power Head (DORIS Dump square T.6.d.80.95), at 20 p.m. on the night of the discharge.

8. This party must be very carefully organised into the separate 15 parties of 1 N.C.O., and 30 men with 1 Officer to each 2 parties. and 1 Officer to the 15th Party.

Parties must be paraded beforehand, told off and numbered and steps taken to ensure that every N.C.O., and man knows to which party he belongs, the parties being numbered 1 to 15.

9. From the Power Station each party will push a group of 5 trucks up to the discharge point. Parties 1 to 14 will dispose of the 70 trucks comprising the first 7 trains, and party No. 15, will push up the 5 trucks of the last train.

Pushing and other parties will observe silence and the former must be careful on decline to check the pace of trucks.

1 O.R. Special Coy., R.E., will proceed with every truck.

In the event of a cylinder being hit by hostile fire, all ranks will adjust Respirators but will not sound KLAXON horns. The danger will, in any case be very local.

10. After unloading at the discharge point, parties will withdraw to a suitable trench in the vicinity and wait there.

The Divnl. Gas Officer will be asked to advise the O.C., detachment how far away he should take his party.

11. After the discharge of the gas the same parties as before will push the trucks back to the power head. The O.C. detachment Batts! ~~[illegible]~~ will ask the Officer i/c Special R.E. Party, for instructions as to when he will march his party away after their work is completed.

12. The outpost line between VESTA TILLEY Trench in square T.1.c. and N.25.a.0.4., also the troops in VESTA TILLEY Trench itself will be/

be withdrawn by ~~12 mid night~~ 2345 on the night of the discharge till after the discharge, and will return to their positions when the trenches and dug-outs are reported to be free from gas.

13. Troops forward of a line through M.11.c.9.0. - T.15.b.3.7. - T.1.b.8.9., will wear Box Respirators from 12 mid night on the night of the discharge until the orders for their removal is given by an Officer. This order should in no case be given until Zero plus 30, and then only if the trench system is reported clear of gas.

14. The Divnl. Gas Officer has been instructed by the Division to assist the Anti-Gas personnel of Units to make arrangements for

(a) Clearing Dug-outs by means of fires etc. immediately after completion of discharge.
(b) Clearing trenches, saps, etc., by means of Flappers etc.
(c) Troops should not re-occupy trenches etc., until qualified Anti-Gas personnel have declared them to be safe.

These points require most careful attention and C.Os. must satisfy themselves that the arrangements made by their Anti-Gas personnel are satisfactory, and issue orders that any instructions issued by the latter are to be carried out.

Special care must be taken to see that all blankets of protected dug-outs are let down prior to the discharge and that every dug-out in the danger area is carefully cleared of gas after the discharge. Company Commanders must work in co-operation with the anti-gas personnel, so that they may know when to give the orders for the removal of Box Respirators.

15. A decision will be given at 1 p.m. daily as to whether the operations will be carried out.

Code words will be used as follows:-

"Gas beam attack will take place to-night" ASTI.

No message will be sent at 1 p.m. if no attack is to take place.

To cancel Gas beam previously ordered the word "CHIANTI" will be sent.

16. Zero/

16. Zero hour will be at 12 mid night and, or as soon after as the trucks are reported to be in position.

17. All technical details regarding the discharge of gas are being arranged by a Special Unit R.E.

18. The O. C. ~~[illegible]~~ 5th A. & S.H., will arrange to keep the Brigade informed of the situation. An Officer should be detailed to be at the discharging point and he should have a few runners to take messages back to the nearest Fuller Phone.

19. The O.C. ~~[illegible]~~ 7th H.L.I., and ~~[illegible]~~ 5th A. & S.H., will arrange to re-occupy the lines of resistance and outpost on the first available opportunity reporting by "Priority" wire when this is done.

A. L. Williams

Major,
Brigade Major, 157th Infantry Brigade.

16th May, 1918.

O. C.,

[illegible]

Addendum No. 1 to 157th Bde. No. [illegible] dated 15th May, 1918

1. In continuation of Para [illegible]. Arrangements must be made for every man to have a label fixed on the front of his Box Respirator bearing the number of the Party to which he belongs.

2. In continuation of Para [illegible]. All men must be carefully warned that there must be no noise of any sort. The Trucks must be moved as silently as possible and there must be no talking or laughing. All orders must be whispered.

3. In continuation of Para [illegible]. All troops eastwards of a line drawn through [illegible] - [illegible] and [illegible] centrals, not ordered to wear Box Respirators should be ordered to be ready to adjust them at a moments notice from midnight onwards.

4. Reference Para [illegible] the Blankets or Curtains of all Protected Dugouts forward of the line through [illegible] - [illegible] and [illegible] Centrals should not be rolled up until the trench system is reported clear.

5. The O.C., [illegible] will arrange for a Lewis Gun under an Officer to be posted in [illegible] near the junction of this trench with VERA TRENCH. The Officer will, if he hears any noise made by the Trucks being moved, order a few short bursts of fire to cover same. Care must be taken that these bursts are not too long in case it may draw the enemy's attention to the fact that something unusual is on.

6. The O.C., [illegible] will arrange for an Officer with the necessary personnel and appliances for treating Gas cases to report to the O.C., Detachment [illegible] at DOREN DUMP and accompany the Party until latter has finished its task.

7. Separate instructions are being issued to the O.C., Detachment as to procedure to be adopted in case of an enemy attack.

A. Williams

Major,

Brigade Major, 107th Infantry Brigade.

18th May, 1918.

O. C.,

1. A Local Brigade Relief will take place as under:-

(a) Night 19/20th 5th A & S. H. will relieve 6th H. L. I.
(b) Night 20/21st 7th H. L. I. " " 5th H. L. I.

2. (a) Details regarding reliefs must be arranged mutually between the O.Cs. concerned.

(b) Relief of such portions of the front line Battns., which are located behind the ACTRESS - KEANE - TEDDIE GERRARD - NEW BRUNSWICK line may be carried out by day, provided all movements are carried out in small parties and restricted to movements inside trenches and that there is no movement when hostile aeroplanes are over head.

The remainder must be done after dark.

(c) Relief both on nights 19/20th and 20/21st May, must be completed by 0300 and notified by "Priority" wire in Code to Brigade Hqrs.

(d) Trench stores, communications, R.E., and Area stores, Trench diagrams, defence schemes and log books, will be handed over.

3. After relief in front line 5th H. L. I., will be located in the NOVA SCOTIA - VIMY area, and the 6th H. L. I., in the LA CHAUDIERE area.

Major,
Brigade Major, 157th Infantry Brigade.

18th May, 1918.

Appendix Va

HEADQUARTERS
No. 7/414
Date
157th INFANTRY BRIGADE

O. C.,

---

1. A Local Brigade Relief will take place as under:-

(a) Night 19/20th 5th A & S. H. will relieve 6th H. L. I.
(b) Night 20/21st 7th H. L. I. " " 5th H. L. I.

2. (a) Details regarding reliefs must be arranged mutually between the C.Os. concerned.

(b) Relief of such portions of the front line Battns., which are located **behind** the [illegible] - [illegible] - [illegible] [illegible] - [illegible] line may be carried out by day, provided all movements are carried out by small parties and restricted to movements inside trenches and that there is no movement when hostile aeroplanes are over head.

The remainder must be done after dark.

(c) Relief both on nights 19/20th and 20/21st May, must be completed by 0200 and notified by "Priority" wire in Code to Brigade Hqrs.

(d) Trench stores, ammunitions, S.A.A., and Area stores, Trench diagrams, defence schemes and log books, will be handed over.

3. After relief in front line 5th H. L. I., will be located in the [illegible] - VIMY area, and the 6th H. L. I., in the LA CHAUDIERE area.

A. Williams

Major,
Brigade Major, 157th Infantry Brigade.

19th May, 1918.

Office — Appendix V.

DEFENCE SCHEME.

MERICOURT SECTOR.

187th INFANTRY BRIGADE.

.-----------------------------

Index.

APPENDICES.

Maps.

157th Infantry BBrigade Defence Scheme.

MERICOURT SECTOR.

Ref. Map MAROEUIL and ST. NAZAIRE RIVER, 1/20,000.

1. BOUNDARIES.

On the SOUTH.

The ACHEVILLE ROAD (exclusive) - NEW BRUNSWICK ROAD (exclusive) up to its junction with the BROWN LINE in square T.20.•.50. thence down to the junction of the BROWN LINE with GRAND TRUNK Trench (inclusive) thence through Cemetry (exclusive) in square T.25.d. - BOIS DE GULOT at square T.25.c.0.0. thence due WEST along the grid line.

On the NORTH.

Junction of BILLIE BURKE and BETTY Trenches (inclusive) WESTWARD along the grid line to T.2.c.3.0. - T.1.d.7.3. - junction of RED Trench with the LENS - ARRAS Road (inclusive) along RED Trench and CYRIL Trench (both exclusive) - S.11.c.0.4 - S.15.central - thence to LA TARGETTE - SOUCHEZ Road at S.19.a.5.0.

2. GENERAL DESCRIPTION OF AREA.

The VIMY RIDGE, which runs generally N.W. and S.E. is the dominatinf tactical feature in the Area.
The Eastern slope of the Ridge is very steep, and from it two distinct spurs run out into the plain below, causing the trench area to be divided into twp spurs and three valleys.
The two spurs are :-
(a) The VIMY BASTION which merges Eastwards into the NOVA SCOTIA Spur.
(b) The LA CHAUDIERE Spur.

An advance along either of these spurs would afford the enemy support for an advance on similar spurs on either flank, and so increase his chances of success in operation against the VIMY RIDGE.
Both Spurs have been strongle organised.
Our Outpost Line is situated East of the foot of the Ridge and at a distance of about 600 yards from it, while the enemy's front line varies from about 1200 yards on the Right, to 2000 Yards in the centre, and about 800 yards on the Left from our Outpost Line.

3. ORGANIZATION OF SECTOR.

The Sector is divided into four Areas in depth.
These Areas are as follows:-the boundaries being shewn in Appendix 1. and Map "A"

(a) TOAST AREA. The RIGHT half of the front line garrisoned by "A" Battalion.
BETTY AREA LEFT half of the front line garrisoned by "B" Battalion.

(c) VIMY - NOVA SCOTIA Area. garrisoned by "C" Battalion.

(d) CHAUDIERE AREA. garrisoned by "D" Battalion.

4. ZONES OF DEFENCE.

There are two Zones of Defence, which together contain three LINES of RESISTANCE, each of which must be held to the last.

(a) First ZONE of DEFENCE.
The TOAST and BETTY Areas constitute the FIRST ZONE which consists of:-
(i) An Outpost Line.

(ii) The Main Line of Resistance.

~~(b)~~ MAIN LINE of RESISTANCE. is the NEW BRUNSWICK - T EDDIE G ERRARD - KEANE - ACTRESS Line (BLUE LINE).
The garrison of this line will fight to the last. There will be no retirement from it, nor will it be re-inforced except by the Outposts falling back on it.

The OUTPOST LINE consists of the MONTREAL - QUEBEC - LILY ELSIE- VESTA TILLEY Trenches; the role of the garrison of this line is to hang on as long as possible so as to break up the enemy's infantry attack, and then to fall beck on the MAIN LINE of RESISTANCE.

The OUTPOST LINE is again covered by a series of "LOOK - OUT" Posts, located at TOT Trenchm TWELFTH AVENUE, junction of TORQUAY and TOTNES Trenches, junction of TOAST and TOTNES Trenches, at the junction of VESTA TILLEY and BILLIE BURKE, and the junction of BETTY and BILLIE BURKE. The role of these "LOOK-OUT" Posts is to give warning of the hostile infantry attack and then to fall back to the Outpost Line.

(b) SECOND of DEFENCE.
This Zone comprises the VIMY - NOVA SCOTIA and the CHAUDIERE Areas.
In this Zone there are two LINES of RESISTANCE, i.e.

(i) The RED LINE, otherwise known as the BAILLEUL - WILLERVAL - CHAUDIERE - HIRONDELLE Line.

(ii) The BROWN line and VIMY BASTION.

The garrisons of the RED LINE consist of half "C" Battalion and half "D" Battalion.

In the event of the enemy having overwhelmed the First Zone, battle will be given in this line, the garrisons of which will fight to the last. There will no retirement.

The other line of resistance in this Zone is the BROWN LINE ~~of~~ and the VIMY BASTION, the latter being a defended locality for all round defence (the NORTHERN and part of the EASTERN face of it being a portion of the BROWN LINE).
The allround defences are not yet completed.
The garrisons in this third line of resistance must fight to the last. There will be no retirement.

5. PRINCIPLES of DEFENCE.

The principles of defence in this Sector :-

(a) Distribution in Depth.

(b) Offence, i.e. Local counter attacks to restore the situation.

In order to prevent local penetration developing into a break through, it is not only considered necessary to be distributed in depth, but also to have rear lines and systems permanently garrisoned during the fight, so that the penetration may be localised and prevented from spreading.

The best method to effect this is to allot to each Battalion an area, which the Battalion Commander must be prepared to hold at costs with his own Battalion, without assistance from outside. In other words he must fight it out to the last in that area with his own resources. Each Battalion Commander will in turn sub-divide his area into Company and platoon areas.

If one of these areas id overwhelmed the enemy ought not to be able to make any headway, so long as the localities in rear and on either flank hold out. The enemy will thus find himself in a pocket and can be dealt with later.

The Defence of each of these areas or localities must be active and every Commander, from the Battalion to the Platoon Commander must keep some portion of his force in reserve for this purpose.

There will be no re-inforcing from a rear locality to a forward one, otherwise rear lines will be depleted of their garrisons and a further penetration may take place.

Each area must be defended in depth, with successive lines of resistance facing to the normal front, but area commanders must, in addition, be prepared to defend either flank.

6. TROOPS.

The troops available for the defence of the Sector are:-

1 Infantry Brigade. (4 Battalions).
1 Light Trench Mortar Battery.
2 Sections Field Coy. R.E.

in addition, but not under the immediate orders of the Brigade Commander are:-

3	6" Newton Mortars.
24	Machine Guns under Divisional Machine Gun Officer.
1	Composite Brigade R.F.A. (consisting of:- 4 18 pdr. Batteries. and 2 4.5 How. Batteries)
2	Heavy Batteries. (60 pdrs.)
4	Siege Batteries.

7. DISPOSITION of TROOPS.

Shewn on attached map A. B.

8. MACHINE GUNS.

8. MACHINE GUNS.

These (24) are under Divisional orders. 4 of the guns however being in reserve at the disposal of the G.O.C. Sector, at Machine Gun Left Group H.Q.
Guns are distributed in depth and placed in pairs os nests situated generally in open emplacements.

For detailed dispositions see Map B. C
The Machine Gun barrage is under alteration & will be shewn on Map C later.

9. LIGHT TRENCH MORTARS.

For positions see Map B. C

10. The S . O . S .

(a) The signal is a number 32 Rifle Grenade GREEN over RED over GREEN.

(b) The following are the arrangements for sending up and repeating the S.O.S. Signal:-

Authority for sending up the S.O.S. rocket has been delegated to platoon and section Commanders.

The sentry on duty in each group in the "LOOK-OUT" Line, in advance of the Outpost Line is armed with a ~~nu~~ No. 32 Rifle Grenade S.O.S. Rocket.

When the hostile attack is seen approaching the section commander orders the rocket to be fired and at the same time sends a runner back to a relay post which carries the message to Coy. H.Q., from where it is transmitted by telephone, to Battn. and Brigade H.Q. and the Artillery. Runners from Coy. H.Q. also take the message to Battn. H.Q. Battalion Headquarters repeat the message over the buried c cable to Brigade Headquarters.

The sentries at Coy. H.Q. and all Battn. H.Q. in rear, on seeing the S.O.S. rocket fired from the "LOOKOUT" Line repeat it by firing their rockets so that except in very misty weather, these signals should be seen by the Artillery look-outs on VIMY RIDGE.

(c) There is a possibility that the "LOOK-OUT" Line might be surprised and overwhelmed, and thus be unable to send up the S.O.S. Signal. It must therefore be made quite clear to sentries in rear, that should they see the hostile infantry advancing in force, that they must cause the S.O.S. rocket to be fired without waiting to see it fired from the front.

(d) The buried cable runs right up to the "LOOK-OUT" Line in TOTNES Trench (Square T.17.a.7.6.) where it ends in a deep dugout. A small post has been located here, from where the S.O.S. rocket can be sent up, and at the same time the S.O.S. message sent straight to Brigade Headquarters abd the Artillery along the buried cable.

(e) The S.O.S. Signal can thus be transmitted as ubder:-

(i) By S.O.S. rocket from the "LOOK-OUT" Line.
(ii) By wire over the buried cable. from the "LOOK-OUT" Line.
(iii) By runner from the "LOOKOUT" Line to Coy. H.Q. and

10. (contd.)

(iii) / and by runner and telephone from Coy. H.Q. to Battn. H.Q.
(iv) By wire over the buried cable from Battn. H.Q. to Brigade H.Q.
(v) By power buzzer to Brigade H.Q. and the Artillery.
(vi) By S.O.S. sentries at Coy. H.Q. in case the "LOOK-OUT" Line is surprised and overwhelmed before it can send up the S.O.S. Signal.

(f) All ranks must be cautioned that the S.O.S. Signal is not to be sent up when a bombardment or Barrage comes down but only when the hostile infantry attack approaches.

ARTILLERY 11. The following Artillery is covering the front of the Sector with it's fire:-

R.F.A. 242nd A.F.A. Bde. ~~(242 Bde.~~

(242nd Brigade. (A/242, B/242, C/242,
(D/242
(1 18 pdr. Battery.
(4.5 How. " both
(attached from 56th Bde. R.F.A.

Heavy Artillery.

23rd	Heavy Battery.	(60 pdrs.)
146th	Heavy Battery.	(60 Pdrs.)
280th	Siege Battery.	(6 inch.)
204th	" "	(6 ")
234th	" "	(8 ")
19th	" "	(9.2 ")

X ⟶

S . O . S.

The Barrage line runs as follows and is shewn in Map A.

YELLOW BARRAGE. T.17.b.70.20. - T.10.central - T.4.c.0.6.
This barrage will come down on above line for 2 minutes, after which it will drop back on to

RED BARRAGE. T.17.c.95.25. - T.17.a.10.25. - T.10.a.00.00. - T.9.central - T.3.d.00.00.
In the event of the Barrage S.O.S. BLUE being sent to the Artillery, guns will drop back to the

BLUE BARRAG E. T.17.c.1.0. - T.16.d.54.90. -T.9 .c.45.68. - T.3.c.45.00.

HOWITZERS. The 4.5 Howitzers fire on selected points along the whole front. These points in the case of all three barrages approximately 150 yards to 200 yards forward of the 18 pdr. Barrages.

Note. It will thus be seen that the Artillery Barrage is very thin.

12. ACTION in Case Of ATTACK.

(a)/

The F.A. Brigades supply a Liaison Officers with Battn. H.Q. of the Front Line Battalions, and the F.A. and Heavy Artillery each send a Liaison Officer to Brigade H.Q.

12. ACTION IN CASE OF ATTACK.

(a) When an attack is considered imminent "TAKE UP BATTLE POSITIONS" willbe sent out to all concerned, when working parties will be cancelled and any troops not in their actual Battle Positions will move to them.

(b) In case of surprise attack, working parties will report themselves to the nearest infantry Commander, who should inform Brigade H.Q. of the presence of these parties.

(c) Permanent garrisons of the three lines of resistance are to figh it out to the last.
The ground between the systems is to be fought for just as much as the systems themselves. Every inch of ground in the area is to be fought for.

(d) Localities are not to be given up because their flanks have been turned.
If local penetration takes place and garrisons of other parts of the line hold out, the enemy will only find himself in a pocket and can be dealt with later.

13. PROBABLE LINES OF ENEMY APPROACH.

(a) It is unlikely that the enemy will make a direct attack against the front of this position in the initial stage of an offensive, but should he obtain any success either North or South of this area, he would probably try to confirm his success by pushing against our front.

(b) A possible line of advance is up the valley between the HIRONDELLE and LA CHAUDIERE Spurs.

(c) Penetration might be attempted via the low ground between NOVA SCOTIA and HUDSON Spurs, and so to get behind our various systems of defence, from the South.

14. ACTION TO MEET ABOVE POSSIBLE LINE OF APPROACH.

(a) Should the enemy meet with successes on the North or South of this Area, and try to confirm it by a direct attack, then the garrisons of the various lines of defence will carry out their roles as laid down inpara 4.

(b) To meet a hostile advance up the valley between the HIRONDELLE and LA CHAUDIERE Spurs flank positions have been arranged along the PICTOU -CENTRE - GLACE and BLIGHTY Trenches
(CENTRE Trench and GLACE Trench are to a certain extent indisrepair and not properly firestepped, though this work is in hand, but the trenches are fightable in their present condition.)
In addition to the defensive line of trenches the ground in this neighbourhood is entirely in our favour, and could be fought without trenches.

(c) To protect our RIGHT flank in case penetration has taken place SOUTH of our Area, the Right Battalion in our front Line will occupy TOAST Trench which has been firestepped (work not yet quite complete) to the SOUTH. Also CANADA Trench from it's junction with TOAST Trench to its junction with PEGGIE is being turned into a defended locality with all round defences.

15. COMMUNICATIONS.

Vide Appendix II.

16. POLICY of WORK.

As time and labour permit, the following are to be turned into Defended Localities with all round defence and wired in all round.

(a) The CANADA and KURTON Trenches from junction on the RIGHT with TOAST Trench to their Junction with PEGGIE on the LEFT.

(b) The GLADYS - DORIS and HAYTER (to its junction with JULIA JAMES) Trenches.

(c) YARMOUTH - PICTOU - HALIFAX and that portion of BLUENOSE which lies between YARMOUTH and HALIFAX.

(d) The Quarries (T.16.c.9.3.)

(e) JULIA JAMES (that postion between CANADA and HAYTER) - GERTIE, and that portion of HAYTER between JULIA JAMES and GERTIE.

17. MEDICAL ARRANGEMENTS.

Vide Appendix III.

18 Administrative Arrangements to be added later.

C D Hamilton Moore

Brigadier General,
Commanding, 157th Infantry Brigade.

APPENDIX I.

BOUNDARIES OF AREAS.

1. TOAST AREA.

ON THE SOUTH. ACHEVILLE - NEW BRUNSWICK ROAD, exclusive, to its junction with CANADA TRENCH.

ON THE NORTH. VESTA TILLEY exclusive to its junction with TEDDIE GERRARD thence South West to T.15.a.0.0 .

ON THE WEST. From T.15.a.0.0. due East to T.15.central, then due SOUTH to the junction of TOAST and CANADA TRENCHES (exclusive).

2. BETTY AREA.

ON THE SOUTH. VESTA TILLEY inclusive to its junction with TEDDIE GERRARD, thence North West along TEDDIE GERRARD (inclusive) to its junction with PEGGY, thence South West along PEGGY (inclusive) to T.15 .a.0.0., thence S.S.W. to the junction of JULIA JAMES with GERTIE (inclusive). That portion of PEGGY running S.W. of square T.15.a .0.0., being exclusive of this area.

ON THE NORTH. From junction of BETTY with BILLIE BURKE inclusive to square T.3.c.0.0., thence due WEST to RAILWAY Embankment exclusive along the Railway Embankment at T.2.c. 8.0. (exclusive).

ON THE WEST. From the Railway Embankment at T.2.c.8.0., S .S.W. along the Railway Embankment exclusive to the junction of the latter with JULIA JAMES, thence along JULIA JAMES exclusive to its junction with GERTIE.

3. VIMY - NOVA SCOTIA AREA.

ON THE SOUTH. NEW BRUNSWICK ROAD (exclusive) to its junction with the BROWN LINE square T.20.c.5.0. thence down to the junction of the BROWN LINE with the GRAND TRUNK Trench (exclusive), thence through the CEMETRY (exclusive) in square T.15.d. - BOIS DEGULOT, at square T.15.c.0.0., thence due WEST along the GRID LINE.

ON THE NORTH. T.15.central - T.15.a .0.0. thence S.S.W. to junction of JULIA JAMES with GERTIE (exclusive) thence WESTWARD to the junction of the two railway embankments (exclusive) in square T.13.d. - thence to road junction square S.24.c.4.8. - PETIT VIMY thence South West along the LENS - ARRAS Road inclusive.

ON THE EAST. From T.15.central due SOUTH to junction of TOAST C.T. with CANADA Trench (inclusive) thence to NEW BRUNSWICK Road (exclusive).

4. CHAUDIERE AREA.

ON THE NORTH. Railway Embankment, square T.2.c.8.0. (inclusive)/

ON THE NORTH (Contd)

(inclusive) to T.2.c.3.0 - T.1.d .7.3. - Junction of RED TRENCH with the LENS - ARRAS Road (inclusive) - along RED TRENCH and CYRIL Trench (both exclusive) - S.11.c.0.4. - S.15.central - Thence to LA TARG ETTE - SOUCHEZ Road at S.19.a.5.0.

ON THE SOUTH. Junction of JULIA JAMES (inclusive) - junction of the Railway embankments in T.13.d. (inclusive) - thence to Road Junction S.24.c.4.8. - PETIT VIM Y - thence South West along the LENS - ARRAS Road (exclusive)

ON THE EAST . From the Railway Embankment square T.2.c.8.0. to the junction of the Railway Embankment with JULIA JAMES (inclusive) - thence along JULIA JAMES (inclusive) to its junction with GERT IE (inclusive)

Appendix II

Communications.

Reference :-
(MAROEUIL 1/20,000
(Attached Diagram.
(" Line Records.
(containing pair numbers and routes of all buried lines in
(use as by Brigade and Units in this Sector.

The communications in this Sector depend almost entirely on :

BURIED CABLE.

The buried cable routes are put down 7 feet deep, with deep dugouts at frequent intervals, through which cable is led on to racks for testing purposes and for joining up H.Q. of units to the system.

The number of spares in the main route averages about 80, and in the branch routes 25, so that there are sufficient lines for all requirements in this sector.

1. FIRST LINE OF DEFENCE.

On looking at the attached diagram, it will be seen that the Main buried route runs from Brigade Headquarters (Test Box S.V.) situated at Brigade Headquarters) to H.Q. of Left Battn. in Front Line (Test Box T.D. T.8.d.5.7.) along behind the First Line of Defence to H.Q. of Right Battn. in the Line (Test Box T.J. T.18.d.1.8.) from there to H.Q. to H.Q. of Left Front Battn. of Brigade on Right (Test Box T.T. T.27.d.4.8.) and thence through Right B.H.Q., (Test Box A.J. A.3.a.8.1.) backwards. Thus so long as the first line of defence is held, the enemy can in no way interfere with, or cut off communications either to the Rear, or laterally, by intercepting the Buried Route at an intermediate point or Test Box, except by a shell burst which penetrates 7 feet down and direct on the cable route. Should enemy occupy our Outpost Line any buried routes running from Battalion H.Q., forward that happen to be joined up, can be disconnected at T est Boxes at Battalion H.Q. This also applies to lateral communications in the RIGHT and LEFT should they fall back.

2. SECOND LINE OF DEFENCE.

Should the First Line of Defence be overwhelmed, a branch route from Test Box T.E. (T.15.b.5 .6.) runs behind the Second Line of Defence to H.Q. of Right Battalion holding the Second Line of Defence (Test Box T.O. T.25.a-9.4.) and from there to junction box T.Q. (T.28.d.5. 4.) where it joins the forward route back to Advance Divisional H.Q. Through this junction box communication is also maintained with Left Rear Battalion of Right Brigade (Test Box T.S. T.26.d.1.8.). The Left Battalion of Second Line of Defence is connected to Buried Route at Test Box S.L. (S.24.a.1.1.) . As all company lines for Battalions in the Second Line of Defence are in buried routes behind their Defence Line, all lines forward can be disconnected at Test Boxes T.E. and T.S. thus ensuring that in event of First Line being captured no working lines run forward into enemy territory.

4 3. DETAIL OF BURIED LINES./

5. DETAIL OF BURIED LINES.

A. ------------- BRIGADE ---------------

1. Brigade to Division.

The Brigade has two lines to Division, both of which are in the buried route. One of these is used for FULLERPHONE and the other for telephobe working. There is a third line joined up in Brigade Office which is ear-marked for use in Divisional Defence Scheme, which could be used in case of necessity.

2. Brigade to Lateral Brigades.

There is a line in buried route to Brigade on Right and Left. Both these lines are behind the Second Line of Defence.

3. BRIGADE to Battalions.

There are two lines from Brigade H.Q., to each Battalion in Front Line, following line of buried Cable route mentioned in para 1 , and one line to each of the Battalions in rear, running as mentioned in para 2. Buried Cable. All these lines are in the Buried Route.

4. Brigade to M.G. Companies.

Both M.G. Coys. allotted to this Sector are in touch with Brigade H.Q., by buried Lines, extended by ground line to their H.Q.

5. Brigade to L.T.M. Battery.

No line on buried route could be allotted solely for this unit, but an instrument is in circuit at their H.Q., on line from Left rear Battalion, to their # Company in BLUENOSE Trench which can be used in case of emergency.

6. Brigade to Artillery.

Brigade is connected with Artillery Group R.F.A. covering it's Front, by buried line to Group H.Q., Corps Heavy Artillery can be got through Divisional Advanced Station and Heavy Artillery Liaison Officer is in direct communication with his Battery and O.P.

B. -----------BATTALIONS ......

1. Battalions to Brigade.

Each Battalion in the front line has two circuits Brigade H.Q. One line for FULLERPHONE, working the other spare. To ensure that the spare line is frequently teste it is kept joined up to an instrument on exchange at eith end, so that it can be proved O.K. at any time.

These 4 lines terminate in Test Boxes, which in t case of Left Battalion, is in the same dugout as Battalio H.Q., and in the case of Right Battalion, at the N.E. end of tunnel leading to QUARRY. Thus no interruption betw end of buried cable and Battalion H.Q. is possible.

Each Battalion holding the Second Line of Defenc has one line to Brigade H.Q. The Left rear Battalion H are beside the Test Box at which it's line terminates. The Right rear Battalion however, is somedistance (400

1. Battalions to Brigade (contd.)

from the buried route, and, in event of heavy shelling the extension from Test Box to Battn. H.Q. is unlikely to prove serviceable. In this event the Battn. Signal Office would be moved into Test Box and messages delivered from it by runner. (The burying of extension from buried route to Battn . H.Q. would do away with this difficulty.)

2. Battalions to Lateral Battalions.

Both Front Line Battalions are joined to Battalions on Right and Left, and to each other laterally.

All circuits being in the buried route, and running behind the First Line of Defence.

3. Battalions to Companies.

In the case of Front Line Battalions the only buried lines to their Companies are between H.Q. Battalion, and a Test Box T.M. (T.15.a.1.8.) from which point, a ground expension to the Right Company of the Left Battalion, and the Left Company of the Right Battalion has been run.

The Left Rear Battalion has a line to it's Companies in the RED LINE running in buried route to T.O. Test Box (T.7.d.9.8.) and extended from there to Company H.Q. route to The Right Rear Battalion has a circuit in the buried route to Test Box T.L. (T.20.a.2.1.) expended by trench line to Coy. H.Q., near junction of GERTIE AND PEGGIE Trenches.

From the Right Front Battalion, a branch route runs to TOMMIES Trench (Test Box T.K. T.17.a.7.8.) A."D.3" will be kept joined up to one of the lines in this route for S.O.S. purposes only.

In the event of a heavy bombardment the company Signal Offices would be moved to the Test Dugout, and should it be impossible to keep exyension through, work direct from cable head.

4. Battalions and Artillery.

An Artillery Liaison Officer is at each fron Battn. H.Q., and is in direct communication by buried cable with his battery and Brigade. These lines are maintained and work by the R.F.A. personnel.

II GROUND LINES.

\- -

1. BRIGADE.

Except for extensions of buried circuits to Right Rear Battalion H.Q., (vide para B sub-para 1 , Buried Cable) and M.G. Coys., all lines from Brigade to Units are in the buried system.

2. Battalions.

Ground lines from Battalions to their Companies, were taken over and maintained. These lines are laid in the trenches and "D.3s" are joined up to these solely for S.O.S. work. It is unlikely however, that they will withstand any heavy bombardment, and no great reliance can be placed on them.

III VISUAL.

A Visual Station is situated at S.23 c.3.2. which is in touch by visual with all four Battalions in this Sector, and with the Left Front Battalion of Brigade in Right Sector.

IV. (A) RUNNERS. (Brigade to Units.)

Owing to the long distances between Brigade and unit H.Q. a system of relay posts for runners has been installed in two chains, each post consisting of four runners.

These posts are normally used for carrying sealed packets or messages to Battalions, and units who have no FULLERPHONE. They will, in case of an attack be used to supplement or replace cable and visual communication should necessity arise.

(i) The Left Chain. (Posts 1,2,and 3.) work from Brigade H.Q.d to Left Front Battn. H.Q. dealing en route with messages for L.T.M.Bty., whose H.Q., are beside No.2 Post.

No.1 Post is at T.24.a.9.6. and is manned by left REAR Battn.
No.2 Post is at T.13.b.5.2. and is manned by Left FRONT Battn.
No.3 Post is at Left Front Battn. H.Q. and is manned by Left Front Battalion.

(ii) The Right Chain. Consists of 5 relay Posts, A , B , C , D, & E. Three of which A , D & E. are at the H.Q. of Right Front, Right Rear and Left Rear Battalions respectively.

"A" Post is at Right Front Battalion H.Q., and is manned by Right Front Battalion.
"B" Post is at T.21.d.9.8. and is manned by Right Front Battalion.
"C" Post is at T.20.c.6.0. and is manned by Right Rear Battalion.
"D" Post is at Right Rear Battalion H.Q., and is manned by Right Rear Battalion.
"E" Post is at Left Rear Battalion H.Q. and is manned by Left Rear Battalion.

Thus each Battalion maintains two Relay Posts of 4 men each, and is responsible for their proper working.

The average time taken to get from one Post to another is as follows:-

Post 2 - 3 20 minutes.	Post 1 ro Bde. Hqrs. 15 minutes.
Post 2 - 1 14 minutes.	

Total for run 49 minutes.

Post A - B 18 Minutes.	Post D - E 18 minutes
Post B - C 21 Minutes.	PBst E to B.H.Q. 18 "
Post C - D 23 "	

Total for Run 98 minutes.

These timings will have to be increased during wet weather or at night, and can be cut down in fine weather when th going is good.

Runners to other units such as field Coy., and Advanced Dressigfstation are sent direct from B.H.Q., but sealed packets for M.G. Coy., at 126 a.7.3 are delivered from D Relay Post.

(B) Runners. BATTALIONS.
= = = == ==== = = = = = = = =

Each Battalion has a Battalion and Coy. H.Q., runners who know location of all neighbouring units and B Company Headquarters.
Owing to the restriction in the use of "D.3s" , runner is the normal means of inter-communication within a Battalion, and in the event of hostile attack, Relay Posts would be established at selected spots.

5. PIGEONS.

2 pigeons are sent up daily to each Battalion in the Front Line for use in emergency.
If no such emegency arises, the birds are released with a practise message on arrival of fresh pair.

6. WIRELESS.

A wireless station is in position beside Brigade H.Q., working to Divisional Headquarters.

7. POWER BUZZER & AMPLIFIER.

Not yet in possession but expected shortly .

APPENDIX III

Medical Arrangements.

1. Locations.

2nd Lowland Field Ambulance

Main Dressing Station.	AUX RIETZ	A.8.c.5.5.
Advanced Dressing Station	VIMY	T.25.a.9.4.
" " "	LA CHAUDIERE	S.18.c.9.3.

Relay Posts T.13.b.7.8.

T.20.b.2.7.

T.26.a.3.9.

2. Wounded.

Normally all wounded will be evacuated from Regimental Aid Posts through the Relay Posts to one or other of the Advanced Dressing Stations - by hand, wheeled stretcher or trolleys according to circumstances.

3. Walking Wounded.

During heavy fighting when there are a number of walking of wounded, the Advanced Dressing Station, 3rd Lowland Field Ambulance, (A.8.c.8.8.) will be used as a walking wounded Collecting Centre, and walking cases will be evacuated from this place by Light Railway or motor lorry.

4. Lying and Sitting Cases.

Lying and sitting cases will be evacuated from the Advanced Dressing Station to the Main Dressing Station by hand, wheeled stretcher, ambulance wagons or light railway, according to circumstances.

APPENDIX ~~III~~ IV

* * * * * * * * * * * * * * * * * * *

List of Co-ordinates.

Ref. MAROEUIL 1/20,000.

187th Infantry Brigade H.Q. S.24.c.3.4.

Area.	Battn. H.Q.	Company H.Q.
TOAST.	T.16.c.2.3.	T.16.d.4.3.
		T.16.a.2.2.
		T.15.b.5.7.
		T.16.c.9.4.
BETTY.	T.8.d.35.28.	T.15.a.9.8.
		T.8.d .2.3.
		T.8.b.2.6.
		T.8.a.7.1.
VIMY-NOVA SCOTIA.	T.25.d.2.8.	T.20.b.8.0.
		T.20.a.9.7.
		T.19.d.9.6.
		T.19.c.3.7.
CHAUDIERE	S.24.a.9.0.	T.8.c.0.8.
		T.8.c.1.7.
		S.18.a.9.0.
		S.24.a.5.3.

\- - - - - - - - -

187th Light Trench Mortar Battery.	T.13.b.5.0.
R.F.A. Left Group Brigade Headquarters.	S.27.b.0.6.
M.G. Battalion, Left Group Coy. H.Q.	S.27.b.7.6.
2 Sections 413th Field Coy. R.E.	A.5.b.9.3.
2nd Lowland Field Ambulance.	
Main Dressing Station.	A.7.d.

List of Co-ordinates. (contd.)

2nd Lowland Field Ambulance.	
A . D . S .	S.18.c.2.5. T.25.d.2.4.
Transport Lines.	F.11.b.
Brigade Details Camp.	X.19.

- - - - - - - - - - - -

Appendix VI

Reserve Brigade Provisional Defence Scheme.

1.

(a) The fighting portion of the Reserve for the 52nd Division consists of the following:-

157th Infantry Brigade (including 157th L.T.M. Bty.) and 1 Company 52nd M.G. Battalion.

(b) The role of the Divisional Reserve in case of the enemy penetrating our line is dependent on the extent and direction of the enemy penetration, but roughly it may be required to :-

(i) Form a Defensive Flank to the SOUTH.
(ii) Form a Defensive Flank to the NORTH.
(iii) Counter attack to restore a broken centre.

2. The following general principles are laid down to meet the three contingencies mentioned above :-

(a) In the event of the enemy breaking through S. of WILLERVAL, the Battalion in the NEUVILLE ST. VAAST area will move at once to occupy the ECURIE SWITCH from THELUS POST (exclusive) to the THELUS Trench in A.17.b., Battalion H.Q. being established at A.6.a.5.0. the present location of the Right Brigade H.Q. The remainder of the 157th Infantry Brigade, billetted at MONT ST. ELOY will move to NEUVILLE ST. VAAST area about A.3.d. marching in the following order:-

Brigade Headquarters.
5th H.L.I.
7th H.L.I.
6th H.L.I.

Brigade Headquarters, will be established in the vicinity of the Test Box at A.3 .d.70.60.
Battalions will be disposed as follows :-

5th H.L.I.	SOUTH EAST	of Bde. H.Q. about A.4.C.0.4.
6th H.L.I.	NORTH ~~of~~	of Bde. H.Q. about A.3.d.5.9.
7th H.L.I.	WEST	of Bde. H.Q. about A.3.d.4.6.

The 157th L.T.M. Battery will join the remainder of the 157th Infantry Brigade and will be located with the 7th H.L.I. WEST of Brigade Headquarters.

The Reserve Company 52nd M.G. Battalion will act as follows :-

2 guns will be sent to each of the following positions

JERUSALEM M.G. POST	A.17.c.20.60.
RAILWAY POST	A.11.d.40.40.
JORDAN "	A.12.c.45.40.
TAPE "	B.7.c.15.45.
THELUS "	B.7.a.85.00.

The remainder of the Company will move to NEUVILLE ST. VAAST area in A.3.d. and will be located in rear of the 7th H.L.I. WEST of Brigade Headquarters.
M.G. Battalion Headquarters will be at A.6.a.50.00.

(b) In the event of the enemy breaking through from the NORTH, the 157th Infantry Brigade will concentrate in the neighbourhood of

2. (b) contd.

of HILL 130.

5th A.&.S.H. and 157th L.T.M.Bty. will proceed to this place direct from NEUVILLE ST. VAAST. The remainder of the 157th Infantry Brigade will march from MONT ST. ELOY in the order mentioned in 2 (a) above, proceeding by route (not marked on reference Map, but which will be reconnoitred by Battalion Intelligence Officers under Brigade I.O.) FRASER CAMP - X.28.d.0.0 - F.3.a.8.2. - F.4.c.5.5. - F.4.d.8.4. - S.25.b.9.1. through F.5.central - along the ARRAS - BETHUNE ROAD to S.25.b.8.6. to S.26.a.1.9. - S.19.d.7.9. - ~~20~~ S.20.c.5.2. Brigade Headquarters, will be in the vicinity of the Test Box at S.20.a.40.00.

Other units of the 157th Infantry Brigade will be disposed as ~~fol~~ follows :-

5th H.L.I.	about point	S.20.d.50.60.
6th H.L.I.	about point	S.20.a.90.50.
7th H.L.I.	about point	S.20.a.20.50.
5th A.&.S.H.	about point	S.20.c.50.20.
157th L.T.M.B.	" "	S.20.c.70.90.

Reserve M.G. Company will send guns to the following positions:-

1	gun T.R.25.	S.22.d.62.82.
1	gun T.R.24.	S.22.d.70.75.
2	guns MAPLE	S.22.a.82.49.
2	guns BEACH	S.22.a.42.94.
2	guns ELM	T.16.c.35.25.

The remainder of the Company will be located in close proximity to the 7th H.L.I. about S.20.a.40.20.

(c) In the event of penetration into our front line, the 157th Inf. Bde. will in the first place concentrate at NEUVILLE ST. VAAST in the neighbourhood of A.3.d. as already detailed in para 2 (a). except that the 5th A.&.S.H. will " Stand To " in their present camp (HANSON CAMP).
The Reserve Company 52nd M.G. Battalion will stand to in their present camp (CUBITT CAMP).

Subsequently the whole of the 157th Inf. Bde. with the Reserve Coy. 52nd M.G. Battalion will cross the VIMY RIDGE and concentrate under cover of VIMY; being distributed as follows :-

5th H.L.I.	S18.d.80.00 (under cover of railway embankment)
6th H.L.I.	S24 c 60.40
7th H.L.I.	S24 c 00.20
5th A.&.S.H.	S30a 40.50
157th L.T.M.Bty.	In rear 5th A&SH.
Reserve ~~52nd~~ Company 52nd M.G. Battalion.	In rear 7th HLI.

Note. Orders for this march will be issued when the time comes.

Brigade Headquarters, after this move, will be established at the ~~present~~ old H.Q. of the Left Brigade, S23 c 30-40 with an Advanced Centre at S24 a 20.00

3.

(a) Allunits must be prepared to move one hour after the receipt of the order "STAND TO".

(b) When on the move there will be an interval of 400 yards between Battns. and/

3. (b) Contd.

and 20 yards between Platoons and Companies.

29th May, 1918.

Br. General,
Commanding, 157th Infantry Brigade.

SECRET.

Copy No. 9

157th Infantry Brigade Order No. 101.

1. (a) The 157th Infantry Brigade with the Reserve Coy., of the 52nd Division M.G. Battn., is now in Divisional Reserve.

(b) The role of the Divisional Reserve in case of the enemy penetrating our line is dependendent on the extent and direction of the enemy penetration, but roughly it may be required to form a defensive flank, either (a) to SOUTH or (b) to NORTH or (c) counter attack to restore a broken centre.

(c) All Units will be prepared to move 1 hour ~~before~~ after receipt of the order "STAND TO".

2. (a) In the event of the enemy breaking through SOUTH of WILLERVAL, the Battn., in the NEUVILLE ST. VAAST area will move at once to occupy the BROWN SWITCH from THELUS POST (exclusive) to the THELUS TRENCH in A.17.b.

The remainder of the 157th Infantry Brigade and the Reserve Company, 52nd Division M.G. Battn., will move to NEUVILLE ST. VAAST AREA about A.3.d.

(b) In the event of the enemy breaking through from the NORTH the 157th Infantry Brigade and the Reserve Company 52nd Division M.G. Battn., will concentrate in the neighbourhood of HILL 135 about S.30.b., ready to support the 2nd Canadian Infantry Work Battalion, manning the GREEN LINE from its junction with PADDOCK SWITCH in S.29., to its junction with the BULLY SWITCH in ~~[illegible]~~ M.20.d.

(c) In the event of a penetration into our front line, the 157th Infantry Brigade with the Reserve Coy. 52nd Division M.G. Battn., will concentrate about NEUVILLE ST. VAAST in A.3.d., cross the RIDGE by night and assemble under cover of VIMY in the re-entrant at S.24.d., to attack next morning S.E. or E. as required.

3. Definite orders regarding "Forming up" places for Units, routes to same, position of Brigade Hqrs., etc., will be issued as soon as the G.O.C., has made a personal reconnaissance.

In the meantime, the C.O., 5th A & S. H., will reconnoitre in detail with his Officers the positions mentioned in 2 (a) above, and the best routes for getting to same from his Camp.

In addition he will reconnitre with his Officers routes to HILL 135 and S.24.

All other Commanding Officers will reconnitre with their Officers routes to the following places, HILL 135, A.3.d., and S.24.d., The routes to be followed should as far as possible be off the main roads.

Battns., of the 156th Infantry Brigade are, on relief, handing over a Map of the "Rearward Defences", which shows all the positions mentioned in these Orders.

4. ACKNOWLEDGE.

A.W. [illegible]

Major,

25th May, 1918. Brigade Major, 157th Infantry Brigade.

Issued at 1100 on 25th May, 1918.

Copy No. 1	Brigade Commander.	No. 6	Reserve Coy. M.G. Bn.
2	5th H. L. I.	7	File.
3	6th H. L. I.	8	War Diary.
4	7th H. L. I.	9	War Diary.
5	5th A & S. H.	10	157th L.T.M. Bty.

On His Majesty's Service.

Vol 3

"War Diary"

H Q 157th Inf Bde

From 1st - 30th June 1918

Volume III

(Original Copy)

June 30th 1918

[illegible] Capt
a/ Brigade Major
157th Inf. Bde

Confidential

Vol III

WAR DIARY
or
~~INTELLIGENCE SUMMARY.~~
(Erase heading not required.)

Army Form C. 2118.

Instructions regarding War Diaries and Intelligence Summaries are contained in F. S. Regs., Part II. and the Staff Manual respectively. Title pages will be prepared in manuscript.

141st Inf Bde

June 1918.

J1

Place	Date	Hour	Summary of Events and Information	Remarks and references to Appendices
MT ST ELOY	1/6		Nothing unusual to report. For about 1 hour in the morning the Boche put over a good many high velocity shells into the neighbourhood of MT ST ELOY village but apparently without doing any damage.	Alw
VIMY RIDGE (Willerval Section)	2/6	0930	The Brigade relieved the 156 Bde in the Willerval (Right) section of the Drome Sector. Relief was carried out by day. Troops taken by bus from Mount St Eloy to Canadian Monument and from there by comm. trenches to line. 5th & 6th HLI in front line 5th HLI on right, each batt. three coys. in front line. 7th HLI Right sub-section reserve and 5th A&SH left, 2 coys of latter batt. stationed in camp at Maroeuil St Vaast. All troops had debussed by 1745 and relief completed by 1900.	Mhd
	3/6	0800	Patrols have nothing of interest to report no enemy patrols being seen. Bde informed that 152nd Bde of 51 Div on right will be relieved on night of 3rd/4th June by 153rd Bde of same Division. Orders are issued for reorganization of Bde Section. Blue line or line of Resistance is withdrawn to Yukon Trench, Nome Trench and Montreal Trench. Line in front of this to be Outpost Line. Reorganization to be completed by 5th June. Divn. instruct that wiring of Blue, Red & Brown Line to be put in hand at once and this wiring given priority of all other work. Enemy artillery moderately active – they shelled Vancy comm. trench during morning. 5 minutes bombardment carried out by our guns on small portion enemy's line at 1200; field guns firing intense salvies rapid.	Mhd
	4/6		Machine Guns in Brigade Section were relieved by guns of their own (52nd Div) Batt. last night without incident. 5 minutes bombardment carried out at 1720 on same lines as previous day. Enemy artillery moderately active during day.	Mhd

A. Mor Dray Capt

D. D. & L., London, E.C. (A8005) Wt. W1771/M2031 750,000 5/17 Sch. 52 Forms/C2118/14

Instructions regarding War Diaries and Intelligence Summaries are contained in F. S. Regs., Part II. and the Staff Manual respectively. Title pages will be prepared in manuscript.

Confidential

Vol III

WAR DIARY
or
~~INTELLIGENCE SUMMARY.~~
(Erase heading not required.)

157th Inf. Bde

June 1918

Army Form C. 2118.

(52)

Place	Date	Hour	Summary of Events and Information	Remarks and references to Appendices
Vimy Ridge (Willerval Section)	5/6		A raid was carried out by Divn. on our left last night. Hostile artillery active throughout day at counter battery work but no damage done. 5 minutes bombardment of enemy lines carried out at 11.00 by our guns. Patrols out during night could find no signs of enemy patrols	AOD
	6/6		Brigade Order No 103 issued to all concerned for Interbattalion relief (vide Appendix I). Hostile artillery again active by day at counter battery work.	Appendix I AOD
	7/6		Information received from Corps via Division that the enemy was expected to make an attack in this part of the line any time after the 8th. Order received from Division that patrols are to be cut down to a minimum and every available man to be used for wiring	AOD
	8/6		Inter-battalion relief carried out by day without incident. Instructions received from the Division that the reorganization of the line to be completed by 2400 on 9th June. Brigade Order No 104 issued detailing such reorganization (vide Appendix II)	Appendix II AOD
			Enemy still shows no activity with his patrols and nothing seen of them by our patrols. GOC Bde attended conference at Div. Hqrs	AOD
	9/6		Artillery on both sides more active otherwise nothing of interest to report.	AOD

A. McDeas Capt

D. D. & L., London, E.C. (A8001) Wt. W1771/M2031 750,000 5/17 Sch. 52 Forms/C2118/14

Instructions regarding War Diaries and Intelligence Summaries are contained in F. S. Regs., Part II. and the Staff Manual respectively. Title pages will be prepared in manuscript.

Confidential **WAR DIARY** *or* **INTELLIGENCE SUMMARY.** (*Erase heading not required.*)

157th Inf. Bde

June 1918

Vol III

J 3

Army Form C. 2118.

Place	Date	Hour	Summary of Events and Information	Remarks and references to Appendices
Vimy Ridge (Willerval sector)	10/6		Raid carried out by left Brigade of Division entered enemy trenches during previous night but did not succeed in securing identifications as enemy had evacuated.	
		0400	Brig. Gen. J. D. Hamilton Moore C.M.G. D.S.O. proceeded on 14 days leave to U.K. followed by 3 days Senior Officers Machine Gun Course at Grantham. Lt. Col. J. Anderson C.M.G. D.S.O. took over command of the Brigade.	
			Brigade informed that in accordance with orders from Higher Command a daylight raid would be carried out by us probably in conjunction with Divisions on either ~~flank~~. It was arranged that one company 5th B.L.I. should carry out the raid. Scheme for a proposed raid was forwarded to the Division and is being considered.	A.D.
	11/6		Report received that 51st Div. did not consider that mutual [illegible] posts mentioned in Appendix II para 4(i) were satisfactory. Capt. Deas accompanied G.S.O. II 51st & 52nd Div. round posts and slight alterations were made. (a) & (e) remained the same positions of remainder are now as follows (b) B 9 b 9.0 (c) (d) B 9 c. 3.1. It was arranged that sections from each Division would lie in adjacent bays and the double sentry at night would be provided by one man from each Div.	A.D.
			Hostile artillery was active throughout day in FARBUS area ~~[illegible]~~ from early morning till midday 140 5.9 and 4.2 shells were thrown in	

D. D. & L., London, E.C. (A5004) Wt. W1771/M2031 750,000 5/17 Sch. 52 Forms/C2118/14

[Signature] Capt.

Instructions regarding War Diaries and Intelligence Summaries are contained in F. S. Regs., Part II. and the Staff Manual respectively. Title pages will be prepared in manuscript.

Confidential

Vol III

WAR DIARY
or
~~INTELLIGENCE SUMMARY.~~
(Erase heading not required.)

157th Inf Brigade

J 4

Army Form C. 2118.

Place	Date	Hour	Summary of Events and Information	Remarks and references to Appendices
Vimy Ridge (Willerval Section)	11/6		close proximity to FARBUS POST. The THELUS Ridge line was also heavily shelled.	
			A 3 minute bombardment of points in enemy lines was carried out at 9 p.m. and 11 p.m. by field guns and heavies (60 pdrs & 6" hows) both firing intense.	[illegible]
			A daylight relief was carried out in left section of Divisional Sector the 156th Brigade relieving the 155th Bde.	
	12/6		A test S.O.S. was carried out last night the time taken from Bty Hqrs in the line till the first gun fired was 6 minutes it is realized, however, that owing to fact that watches cannot be synchronised with the gunners and the difficulty of an officer in the line knowing when the first burst takes place the exact time taken cannot be definitely ascertained.	
			Orders were issued for an interbattalion relief to take place by daylight on the 14th June (see Appendix III). Each battalion will then return to the position it occupied when we came into this section on the 2nd June.	Appendix III
			Orders were also issued for a small raid to be carried out by the 5th A&SH without artillery as owing to the fact that not more than 2 platoons were to take part in the raid it was considered by this means a surprise was more likely to be effected (see Appendix IV)	Appendix IV

[illegible] Capt

D. D. & L., London, E.C.
(A8003) Wt. W1771/M2031 750,000 5/17 Sch. 52 Forms/C2118/14

Confidential

WAR DIARY
or
~~INTELLIGENCE SUMMARY.~~
(Erase heading not required.)

Army Form C. 2118.

157th Inf Bde

Vol III

(J 5)

Instructions regarding War Diaries and Intelligence Summaries are contained in F. S. Regs., Part II. and the Staff Manual respectively. Title pages will be prepared in manuscript.

Place	Date	Hour	Summary of Events and Information	Remarks and references to Appendices
Vimy Ridge (Willerval Section)	13/6.		Verbal warning was received that the section of the Quinl Sector would probably be reorganized again the Main Line of Resistance being withdrawn to the Post-Beehive Line. The object of this withdrawal is to bring our line of Resistance back out of range of the enemy's Trench Mortars as it was found in the recent operations that the garrisons of the forward trenches were absolutely blotted out and their trenches flattened by a 3 hour Trench Mortar barrage. In view of this possibility another line of Posts between the present Red and Brown lines were sited.	MHD
			Field and Heavy Guns carried out two 3 minute intense bombardments of enemy trenches in ARLEUX LOOP during day.	
			Showing our command of No Man's Land no trace of enemy patrols has as yet been found by our night patrols.	
	14/6		Raid mentioned in Appendix IV ~~last night~~ was carried out last night by 2 platoons 5th A&S.H under Lt. G R Thomson but they did not succeed in reaching enemy line. About 500 yds from our line they came upon ~~out~~ the first line of enemy wire which was found to be made up of exceptionally thick strands of wire. The line was made up of six apron fences very close together and about 15 yds in width. After great difficulty a gap	MHD

M McDougall Capt

D. D. & L., London, E.C. (A5001) Wt. W1771/M2031 750,000 5/17 Sch. 52 Forms/C2118/14

Instructions regarding War Diaries and Intelligence Summaries are contained in F. S. Regs., Part II. and the Staff Manual respectively. Title pages will be prepared in manuscript.

Confidential

WAR DIARY
or
~~INTELLIGENCE SUMMARY.~~
(Erase heading not required.)

Vol III

157th Inf. Bde

(J 6)

Army Form C. 2118.

Place	Date	Hour	Summary of Events and Information	Remarks and references to Appendices
Vimy Ridge (Willerval Sector)	14/6		was cut in the wire and an officer's patrol was sent out to reconnoitre the rear line of wire and here again a gap could not be found although the wire was searched for a distance of 300 yds. The party having then been out from 11 p.m. till 2 a.m. it returned not having attained its object owing to the large quantity of thick wire discovered.	
			Field and Heavy Artillery carried out a 5 minutes destructive shoot on the wire in front of ARLEUX LOOP at 3.5 p.m. 5th H.L.I. were instructed to send out an officer's patrol at night to ascertain the damage done.	
			Two bursts of 5 minutes were carried out by Field guns and Heavies on Arleux Loop.	[initials]
	15/6		Patrol reports show that all patrols sent out during night could find no trace of enemy in No Man's Land.	
			An operation undertaken by the 153rd Brigade on our immediate right last night was unsuccessful. The plan was as follows. At zero hour a smoke cloud was to be sent over from the 153 Bde lines towards the enemy lines, at the same time cylinders were to be let off giving the impression that gas was being sent over although none was to be used. The smoke cloud was to be followed by four fighting patrols who were to enter the enemy lines and inflict casualties and obtain	

D. D. & L., London, E.C. (A8001) Wt. W1771/M2031 750,000 5/17 Sch. 52 Forms/C2118/14

[signature]

Instructions regarding War Diaries and Intelligence Summaries are contained in F. S. Regs., Part II. and the Staff Manual respectively. Title pages will be prepared in manuscript.

Confidential

Vol III

WAR DIARY

~~or~~

~~INTELLIGENCE~~ SUMMARY.

(Erase heading not required.)

157th Inf. Bde

(87)

Army Form C. 2118.

Place	Date	Hour	Summary of Events and Information	Remarks and references to Appendices
Vimy Ridge (Willerval Sector)	15/6		identification. No Man's Land was found to be too wide however and the smoke lifted before it reached the enemy lines and patrols were forced to return without achieving their object.	
			Enemy shelled Brocon Line and Embankment in vicinity of 2 companies of Battalion (5th A&S.H.) in MERSEY Area. No casualties were caused. He also shelled the junction of MERSEY ALLEY with railway embankment but it is believed this was intended for guns behind the railway	AWD
	16/6		Heavy Artillery fired during day on enemy wire in front of ACHEVILLE Road in continuation of wire cutting shoots which are now in progress. Enemy artillery activity on Brigade sector was particularly quiet.	
			Orders received from Division that the 155 Bde would relieve the Brigade in present Section on 20th June. Relief to be carried out by daylight as far as possible. Arrangements made with 155 Bde. that the complete relief would be carried out by day.	AWD
	17/6	0600	A day patrol under 2Lt. K.A. Macintosh sent out by 6th H.L.I. all day yesterday and which returned last night succeeded in obtaining valuable information regarding the block formed by the enemy in HUDSON TRENCH in T 26 b 25.85. On receipt of this 6th H.L.I. decided to attack this block with bombs tomorrow at dawn. The Post cannot be entered on account of [illegible] were	

[illegible] Capt.

D. D. & L., London, E.C. (A8004) Wt. W1771/M2031 750,000 5/17 Sch. 52 Forms/C2118/14

Instructions regarding War Diaries and Intelligence Summaries are contained in F. S. Regs., Part II. and the Staff Manual respectively. Title pages will be prepared in manuscript.

Confidential

Vol III

WAR DIARY
or
~~INTELLIGENCE SUMMARY.~~
(Erase heading not required.)

157th Inf. Bde.

(T 8)

Army Form C. 2118.

Place	Date	Hour	Summary of Events and Information	Remarks and references to Appendices
VIMY RIDGE (WILLERVAL)	17/6		but it can be bombed and sentries sniped from 20 yds range.	
			A patrol of 5th H.L.I. under 2Lt. E.D. TURNER went out at 11.30 p m last night to ascertain damage done to enemy's wire by our artillery during bombardment yesterday. Party did not get any further than the ARLEUX-WILLERVAL ROAD when it was challenged by a strong German patrol and owing to danger of being cut off our patrol withdrew.	
			Orders for relief were issued today (Appendix) Relief was to be completed by day as far as possible. If relief is completed by day command will pass on relief if not then at 0900 on 21st June.	Appendix V
			Artillery continue bombardment of enemy wire on Brigade front.	AB
			Enemy artillery very active against Corps artillery in THELUS. Over 300 heavy shells during day were put over in close proximity to one battery – no casualties and no material damage to guns.	
	18/6		Harassing fire was carried out by Field guns last night as from patrol reports of the previous night it was suspected that the enemy was holding his front line in strength and also had several large patrols in No Man's Land.	

[signature] Capt.

D. D. & L., London, E.C.
(A6001) Wt. W1771/M2031 750,000 5/17 Sch. 52 Forms/C2118/14

Instructions regarding War Diaries and Intelligence Summaries are contained in F. S. Regs., Part II. and the Staff Manual respectively. Title pages will be prepared in manuscript.

Confidential

Vol III

WAR DIARY
or
INTELLIGENCE SUMMARY.
(Erase heading not required.)

157th Inf. Bde

(39)

Army Form C. 2118.

Place	Date	Hour	Summary of Events and Information	Remarks and references to Appendices
Vimy Ridge (Willerval Sector)	18/6		One company of Battalion (5th A & S H) in Mersey Area moved from their position behind the Embankment near Grand Trunk C.T. to THELUS Post after morning stand-down on account of enemy shelling previous day by which they suffered 2 men killed & 10 wounded.	
			Patrol of Lieut. J. W. England M.C. and 2 sections 6th H.L.I with a L.G. went out to examine wire but found it unbroken. Patrol of Lieut. Gilchrist with 2 sections 5th H.L.I also examined wire and found it badly broken in places and pitted with fresh holes and would offer little obstacle.	
			Bombing party of 6th H.L.I after ascertaining Beaver Block was occupied by enemy threw 9 bombs into post all landing on enemy side of block.	AAD
	1	1500	Brigade Transport was inspected by G.O.C. Division and was complimented on its very smart turnout	
	19/6		Patrol activity last night was small. Enemy was heard to be wiring but owing to patrolling of enemy's wire by his patrols our patrol could not get close up.	
			Enemy fired a few gas shells in close vicinity to Brigade Hqrs last night but did no damage.	AAD
			Nothing else of interest to report.	

M. McDiarmid
Capt

D. D. & L., London, E.C.
(A8004) Wt. W1771/M2031 750,000 5/17 Sch. 52 Forms/C2118/14

Instructions regarding War Diaries and Intelligence Summaries are contained in F. S. Regs., Part II. and the Staff Manual respectively. Title pages will be prepared in manuscript.

Confidential

Vol III

WAR DIARY
or
~~INTELLIGENCE SUMMARY.~~
(Erase heading not required.)

157th Inf Bde

J10

Army Form C. 2118.

Place	Date	Hour	Summary of Events and Information	Remarks and references to Appendices
Vimy Ridge (Willerval Sector)	20/6		155 Bde relieved the Brigade in the line today. Relieving Brigade came up in busses to a point about 200 yds W. of Canadian monument from where a ~~the~~ chain of guides was provided. First battalion arrived at Debussing Point at 0845 and all units of the relieving Brigade had passed down the C. T's by 1230. Relief was completed by 1630. Our own battalions with the exception of the 5th H.L.I who were going to NEUVILLE St VAAST being taken to Mont St ELOY by the busses that brought up the 155 Bde. All battalions were in their new areas by 2030. The command did not pass today the Brigade Commander and Brigade Major remaining in the line.	[initials]
Mt St ELOY	21/6		Command of WILLERVAL SECTION passed to G.O.C. 155 Bde at 0900 this morning. Shortly after arrival here Brigade Commander & Brigade Major together with 140 officers from the Brigade proceeded to WAVRANS near St. POL to witness a demonstration of Tanks. All sorts & types of tanks were seen and their cooperation with infantry was explained and shewn on the ground with skeleton troops. Previous to proceeding the Brigade Commander went round the camps with the Staff Captain. Defence Scheme for the Brigade whilst in reserve was issued to all concerned (Appendix VI)	Appendix VI [initials]
			[signature] Major	

D. D. & L., London, E.C. (A8003) Wt. W1771/M2031 750,000 5/17 Sch. 52 Forms/C2118/14

Confidential

WAR DIARY
or
~~INTELLIGENCE SUMMARY.~~
(Erase heading not required.)

Army Form C. 2118.

15th Inf Bde

Vol III *J 11*

Instructions regarding War Diaries and Intelligence Summaries are contained in F. S. Regs., Part II. and the Staff Manual respectively. Title pages will be prepared in manuscript.

Place	Date	Hour	Summary of Events and Information	Remarks and references to Appendices
Mt St Eloy	22/6		A new defence scheme was received from the Division to come into force at midnight tonight. The Brigade Commander and Brigade Major visited Camblain Range this morning and watched the 7th H.L.I firing. In the afternoon G.O.C. Division inspected all camps in the Brigade. During conversation he stated he did not wish any work done in the afternoon whilst the Brigade was in reserve.	[illegible]
	23/6		Brigade Commander, Brigade-Major and Lt Col Wilson 5th H.L.I visited Corps School FRESSIN and were away all day.	[illegible]
	24/6		Brigade Commander inspected platoon 6th H.L.I that returned today from Corps School FRESSIN. A very good report on their smartness etc. was received and a letter of congratulation was received from the G.O.C. Division. Instructions received from the Division to the effect that the Brigades were to be reduced to three battalions. G.O.C. phoned Brigade Commander that the 5th A&S.H were to be taken out of this Brigade and were to be ready to go in the course of two or three days.	[illegible]
	25/6		Orders were received from the Division that the 5th A&SH along with 5th KOSB and 8th Scottish Rifles would leave for the 30th Division to which Division they had been posted to on the 26th June. Brigade Commander and Brigade Major visited the training area and ranges during the morning and saw the various Batts. training.	[illegible]

[signature] Capt.

D. D. & L., London, E.C. (A8004) Wt. W1771/M2031 750,000 5/17 Sch. 52 Forms/C2118/14

Instructions regarding War Diaries and Intelligence Summaries are contained in F. S. Regs., Part II. and the Staff Manual respectively. Title pages will be prepared in manuscript.

Confidental

WAR DIARY
or
INTELLIGENCE SUMMARY.
(Erase heading not required.)

Vol III

157th Infantry Bde

J 12

Army Form C. 2118.

Place	Date	Hour	Summary of Events and Information	Remarks and references to Appendices
Mt. St. Eloy	26/6		Corps Commander arrived at Bde. Hqrs at 1030 and went round the various training areas and inspected the troops at work. The 5th A & SH paraded for inspection as a Batt. at Le Pendu Camp. The Corps Commander inspected the Batt. and afterwards gave them an address on the subject of their leaving the Division.	
			Orders were received from the Division that the 157 Bde. would relieve the 156 Bde in the Left Section of the Divnl Sector on the 29th June. Relief to be completed by 0600 on 30th June but command to pass on the afternoon of the 29th. Warning order issued to Batts that relief was taking place on day named and that batts would go into line as follows. 7th HLI to Right Subsection, 6th HLI to Left Sub section & 5th HLI in reserve.	AHD
	27/6		Brigade Major visited 156 Bde in the morning in order to get details of relief. Brigade Commander visited Batt. training areas. Brigade Sports were held in the afternoon at which G.O.C. Division attended.	AHD
			Brigade Order No 108 for the relief was issued to all concerned (Appendix VII)	Appendix VII
	28/6		5th A.&S.H. embussed at 10.15 and proceeded to BAMBECQ to join the 34th Division and not 30th Div. as previously ordered. Transport also	AHD

[signature]

D. D. & L., London, E.C. (A8001) Wt. W1771/M2031 750,000 5/17 Sch. 52 Forms/C2118/14

Instructions regarding War Diaries and Intelligence Summaries are contained in F. S. Regs., Part II, and the Staff Manual respectively. Title pages will be prepared in manuscript.

Confidential

Vol III

WAR DIARY
or
INTELLIGENCE SUMMARY.
(Erase heading not required.)

157th Inf. Bde

J 13

Army Form C. 2118.

Place	Date	Hour	Summary of Events and Information	Remarks and references to Appendices
Mt St Eloy	28/6		started this morning to proceed by road Brigade Commander visited the Battalion before leaving.	
		1030	G O C Division met the Officers, Platoon Sergeants & C S M of a Company of the 6th H L I near Berthonval Farm to give them a tactical scheme without troops.	
			New Defence Scheme received from the Division and Defence Scheme for action of Reserve Brigade issued to all concerned forthwith (Appendix VIII)	Appendix VIII
			In the afternoon Brigade Commander visited section of Divnl Sector to be taken over on 29th from 156th Bde	
			Between 11 p m and 12 midnight enemy aircraft flew over Mt St Eloy and dropped 4 bombs in the vicinity but no damage done	
	29/6	0900	Battalions at Mt St Eloy commenced to proceed by lorry to the line the battalion in Neuville St Vaast marching up. The 2 Batts at Mt St Eloy had all left by 12.30 p m. Relief was effected without incident and with no enemy interference. Completion of relief was wired to Division at 5 p m.	
		2300/ 1am	Information received from a deserter indicated that the Division opposite our front the 119th German Division was in course of relief tonight by 52nd Division. Intense harrassing fire was carried out by field Artillery from 11 p m to 1 a m a proportion of gas shells	

D. D. & L., London, E.C. (A8001) Wt. W1771/M2031 750,000 5/17 Sch. 52 Forms C2118/14

[signature]

Instructions regarding War Diaries and Intelligence Summaries are contained in F. S. Regs., Part II. and the Staff Manual respectively. Title pages will be prepared in manuscript.

Confidential

Vol III

WAR DIARY
or
INTELLIGENCE SUMMARY.
(Erase heading not required.)

157th Inf Bde

J 14

Army Form C. 2118.

Place	Date	Hour	Summary of Events and Information	Remarks and references to Appendices
Nr. St. Eloy	29/6		being put over at the trench junctions. The enemy did not retaliate. Batts were informed that active patrolling was to be carried out with a view to making better acquaintanceship with our opposite number. 2 patrols of Right Battalion took up defensive positions to wait for	[initials]
	30/6		enemy patrols last night but none were seen. A patrol of 6th HLI under 2Lt J. Craig took up defensive position at 2250. A patrol of enemy estimated to number 10 was seen approaching our patrol's left flank about 100 yds away. Our patrol altered position to engage it but enemy detected movement and made off. 157th L T M Batty relieved 156 L T M Batty today relief being completed by 4 p.m. Brigade Commander visited all three batt Hqrs during course of morning	[initials]
			[signature] Capt	

D. D. & L., London, E.C.
(A8001) Wt. W1771/M2031 750,000 5/17 Sch. 52 Forms/C2118/14

Instructions regarding War Diaries and Intelligence Summaries are contained in F. S. Regs., Part II, and the Staff Manual respectively. Title pages will be prepared in manuscript.

Confidential

Vol III

WAR DIARY
or
INTELLIGENCE SUMMARY.
(Erase heading not required.)

157th Inf Bde
June 1918

Army Form C. 2118.

J 15

Place	Date	Hour	Summary of Events and Information	Remarks and references to Appendices
Vimy Ridge Maddiere Sector	30/6		Casualties for the period during which the Brigade was in the line were as follows.	

	Officers K	Officers W	Officers M	O.R. K	O.R. W	O.R. M
5th H L I	–	–	–	1	10	
6th H L I	–	–	–	2	11	
7th H L I	–	–	–	–	9	
5th A & S H	–	–	–	3	16	
157 L.T.M. Batty	–	–	–		1	
	–	–	–	6	47	

Summary of Strength 1/6/18

	(A) Strength excluding attached: Officers	O.R.	B. Not present with Unit: Officers	O.R.	With unit: Officers	O.R.
Bde Hqrs.	4	31	–	3	4	28
5th H L I	42	977	10	180	32	797
6th H L I	44	860	13	173	31	687
7th H L I	43	905	15	182	28	723
5th A & S.H	40	1007	12	185	28	822
157 L.T.M. Batty.	5	104	2	14	3	90
	178	3884	52	737	126	3147

[illegible signature]

D. D. & L., London, E.C.
(A8004) Wt. W1771/M2031 750,000 5/17 Sch. 52 Forms/C2118/14

Instructions regarding War Diaries and Intelligence Summaries are contained in F. S. Regs., Part II. and the Staff Manual respectively. Title pages will be prepared in manuscript.

Confidential

Vol III

WAR DIARY
or
~~INTELLIGENCE SUMMARY.~~
(Erase heading not required.)

157th Inf Bde
June 1918

Army Form C. 2118.

(J 16)

Place	Date	Hour	Summary of Events and Information	Remarks and references to Appendices
Vimy Ridge ([illegible])	30/6		Strength 29/6/18	

	(A) Strength excluding attached		(B) Not present with unit		(C) With Unit	
	Officers	O R	Officers	O R	Officers	O R
~~157 Bde Hqrs~~						
5th H L I	43	958	11	148	32	810
6th H L I	42	890	14	139	28	751
7th H L I	39	884	12	158	27	726
	124	2732	37	445	87	2287

[illegible] Capt

D. D. & L., London, E.C.
(A8001) Wt. W1771/M2031 750,000 5/17 Sch. 52 Forms/C2118/14

Instructions regarding War Diaries and Intelligence Summaries are contained in F. S. Regs., Part II. and the Staff Manual respectively. Title pages will be prepared in manuscript.

Confidential

WAR DIARY or INTELLIGENCE SUMMARY.

(Erase heading not required.)

Army Form C. 2118.

Vol III

157th Inf Bde

June 1918

J 17

Place	Date	Hour	Summary of Events and Information	Remarks and references to Appendices
Vimy Ridge (Willerval Sector)	30/6		Courses held during June	

Course	Duration	Detail
Pigeon Course	3 days	1 OR per Batt.
Gas	1 week	1 off 6th HLI 2 NCO's 5th & 7th HLI
Power Buzzer	21 days	2 ORs each 6th & 7th HLI
Snipers	18 "	1 NCO 6th HLI
Platoon Commanders	5 weeks	2 offs each batt.
Gas	1 week	1 off 7th 1 NCO per batt.
Lewis Gun Class A	26 days	1 off 5 A&SH 1 NCO 5-6-7 HLI
" " " B	26 days	2 ORs per Batt.
Infantry	10 days	1 platoon 6th HLI
Lewis Gun Class A	8 days	1 off 5 HLI
" " " B	16 days	2 NCO's 6 HLI
Signalling Course (beginners)	6 weeks	7 ORs 5 & 6 HLI 8 ORs 7 HLI & 5 A&SH
Light Trench Mortar	18 days	1 NCO 157 LTMB
Gas	1 week	1 off 5 A&SH 1 NCO per Batt.
Signalling (Officers Beginners)	3 weeks	1 off 5 A&SH
Rifle Grenade Dischargers	3 days	1 NCO per Batt.

[signature] Capt

D. D. & L., London, E.C.
(A5001) Wt. W1771/M2031 750,000 5/17 Sch. 52 Forms/C2118/14

Instructions regarding War Diaries and Intelligence Summaries are contained in F. S. Regs., Part II. and the Staff Manual respectively. Title pages will be prepared in manuscript.

Confidential

Vol III

WAR DIARY
or
~~INTELLIGENCE SUMMARY.~~

(Erase heading not required.)

Army Form C. 2118.

157th Inf Bde

June 1918

J18

Place	Date	Hour	Summary of Events and Information	Remarks and references to Appendices
Vimy Ridge (Chaufdrière)	30/6		Courses held during June (continued)	

Course	Duration	Detail
Musketry	25 days	1 off 5-6 HLI 5 ASH 1 NCO 5-6-7 HLI
Observer	~~2~~	1 private 7 HLI
Infantry	5 weeks	1 off 6-7 HLI 5 ASH 2 ors each batt
Signalling (Instructor)	6 weeks	1 off 6 HLI 1 or 5-7 HLI
" " (Dunstable)	9 weeks	1 or 6 HLI
Gas	1 week	1 off 6 HLI 1 NCO 5-6 HLI 2 NCOs 7 HLI

J. W. Deas Capt

D. D. & L., London, E.C.
(A5001) Wt. W1771/M2031 750,000 5/17 Sch. 52 Forms/C2118/14

S E C R E T. *Appendix I*

No. .....

157th Infantry Brigade Order No. 103.

6th June, 1918

1. The following reliefs will be carried out on 8th June, 1918.

(a) 7th H. L. I. will relieve 5th H. L. I.
(b) 5th A & S. H. " " 6th H. L. I.

After relief 5th H. L. I. and 6th H. L. I. will take over same dispositions as 7th H. L. I. and 5th A & S. H. respectively.

2. As musch of relief as possible will take place during day light . Not more than 2 Platoons of each Coy. of the relieving Battns should be on the move at the same time (This does not apply to Companies at NEUVILLE ST VAAST)

Companies moving from NEUVILLE ST VAAST to the Eastern foot of VIMY Ridge and vice versa will do so in Sections at not less than 100 yards interval.

3. Relief will be completed by 2300.

4. Details of relief will be arranged by Os.C, concerned. A percentage of observers, scouts etc, of reserve Battns should proceed to the line 24 hours in advance.

5. All trench maps, stores, etc., will be handed over.

6. Completion of relief will be wired "Priority" to Bde Hqrs using the code word "GUM".

7. ACKNOWLEDGE.

Major,
Brigade Major 157th Infantry Brigade.

Copies No. 1 to 5th H. L. I.
2 6th H. L. I.
3 7th H. L. I.
4 5th A & S. H.
5 157th L. T. M.BTY.
6 Hqrs. 155th Inf. Bde.
7 Hqrs. 52nd Division.
8 Artillery Hqrs.
9)
10) War Diary.
11 File.
12 153rd. Inf. Bde.

Appendix II
Copy No.

SECRET

157th Infantry Brigade Order No. 104.

8th June, 1918.

1. (a) The Right (WILLERVAL) Section of 52nd Divisional Sector will be reorganised on the 9th June, by bring back the Main Line of Resistance i.e. the BLUE LINE to the YUKON - NOME - OTTAWA - NEW BRUNSWICK line, with an observation line in PLUMER, MONTREAL trenches.

The outpost line as such is to be abolished both in the RIGHT and LEFT Sectors and what was formerly the outpost line i.e. PLUMER - MONTREAL - QUEBEC - LILY ELSIE, will now become an observation line only. Both the RIGHT and LEFT Sections are therefore now organised on the same principles.

(b) The RED LINE i.e. the POST LINE - BEEHIVE TRENCH including the POSTS DURHAM, SUBURB, FOVANT, BARNSLEY, WAKEFIELD, SHEFFIELD and CANADA will remain the same.

(c) The BROWN LINE will also remain the same.

2. The whole section will be divided into 4 Battn Areas, each organised in depth. The names and limits of these areas are as given below.

(a) YUKON area for RIGHT FRONT Battn. is bounded on
- (i) South by TIRED ALLEY (inclusive) to its junction with POST LINE (inclusive)
- (ii) WEST by POST LINE - BEEHIVE TRENCH (all inclusive) to the junction of latter with WESTERN road.
- (iii) NORTH by WESTERN road (inclusive) as far back as its junction with BEEHIVE

(b) OTTAWA area for LEFT FRONT Battn is bounded on
- (i) SOUTH by WESTERN Road (exclusive) as far back as its junction with BEEHIVE
- (ii) WEST by BEEHIVE Trench (inclusive) from its junction with WESTERN Road Northward to its junction with GRAND TRUNK C.T. (inclusive) - thence Westward along GRAND TRUNK C.T. (inclusive) to point T.21.c.40.10. and thence due North to the NEW BRUNSWICK - ACHEVILLE Road (about T.21.c.40.60.).
- (iii) NORTH by NEW BRUNSWICK - ACHEVILLE Road (inclusive) from point T.21.c.40.50. Eastwards.

(c) FARBUS area for the RIGHT REAR Battn. is bounded on:-
- (i) EAST by POST LINE - BEEHIVE Trench (both exclusive) to the junction of latter with WESTERN Road.
- (ii) SOUTH by TIRED ALLEY (inclusive) from its junction with POST LINE Westwards.
- (iii) NORTH by WESTERN Road (exclusive) from its junction with BEEHIVE TRENCH as far as Embankment then through B.2.central to N.E. corner of STATION WOOD and thence along the track B.2.c.6.9. - B.2.c.0.5. - B.1.d.6.0. - B.7.central.

(d) MERSEY area for LEFT REAR Battn is bounded on:-
- (i) EAST by BEEHIVE Trench (exclusive) from its junction with WESTERN Road NORTHWARD to its junction with GRAND TRUNK C.T. (exclusive) - thence Westward along GRAND TRUNK C.T. (exclusive) to point T.21.c.40.10. thence due North to the NEW BRUNSWICK - ACHEVILLE Road about point T.21.c.40.60.
- (ii) SOUTH by WESTERN Road (exclusive) from its junction with BEEHIVE TRENCH as far as Embankment then through B.2.centre & Westward along the NORTHERN BOUNDARY of the FARBUS AREA.
- (iii) NORTH by NEW BRUNSWICK - ACHEVILLE Road (inclusive) from about point T.21.c.40.60. Westwards to the junction of GRAND TRUNK Trench and BROWN Line (exclusive) thence just North of the CEMETRY in T.25.d. to BOIS DE GULOT about poi[nt] T.25.c.00.00.

3. Each of the above AREAS will be garrisoned by one Battn. Garrisons will be distributed as under :-

(a) YUKON

(i) The Main Line of RESISTANCE will be divided into 3 Coy areas each Coy having 3 platoons in the main Line(each platoon furnishing 1 section for the observation line by night and 2 observers by day) and 1 platoon in the hands of the Coy Commanders in the Support Trench behind the BLUE LINE.

(ii) The remaining Coy will furnish the garrisons of the RED LINE Posts i.e. SUBURB - DURHAM - FOVANT & BARNSLEY (1 Platoon in each)

(iii) The Battn Commander is thus left with no reserve except his Hqrs Details.

These details will afford protection to Battn Hqrs.

(b) OTTAWA Area

(i) The Main Line of RESISTANCE will be divided into 3 Coy areas, each Coy having 3 Platoons in the Main Line (each platoon furnishing 1 section for the observation line by night and 2 observers by day) and 1 Platoon in support.

(ii) The remaining Coy will furnish the garrison of the RED LINE Posts i.e. WAKEFIELD, SHEFFIELD & CANADA & a portion of the BEEHIVE Trench between the two former.

(iii) The Battn Commander would have no reserve in his hands other than Battn H.Q. Details which would form protection for Battn H.Q.

(c) FARBUS AREA

(i) 2 Coys in BROWN LINE with supports behind the Railway Embankment.

(ii) 1 Coy finding garrisons for SPUR, FARBUS, TAPE & BORDER POSTS (1 Platoon in each).

(iii) 1 Coy in small "BLOB" Posts to be constructed West of the Railway Embankment near the foot of the VIMY RIDGE. Until those posts are completed this Coy will be located behind the Embankment. The Posts have already been selected and will be dug by this Battn.

(d) MERSEY AREA

(i) 2 Coys in BROWN LINE with supports behind the Railway Embankment.

(ii) 1 Coy in small "BLOB" Posts on slopes of VIMY RIDGE. Until these posts have been completed this Coy will be located behind the Railway Embankment.

(iii) Battn H.Q. and 1 Coy in THELUS POST. This Coy less 1 Platoon to remain for the present at NEUVILLE ST VAAST.

4. (i) The flank defences on the Right of the Brigade Area, i.e. Along TIRED ALLEY, consists of a series of 5 combined posts of 2 sections each. The position of these are as follows.

(a) B.10.a.6.5.
(b) B.9.b .9.0.
(c) B.9.d.5.8.
(d) B.9.c.2.3.
(e) B.13.b.8.9.

Of these (a), (c) & (e) are commanded by N.C.Os. of 51st (H) Division and (b) & (d) by N.C.Os. of the Brigade holding the WILLERVAL Section.

(ii) Personnel for Posts (a), (b) & (c) will be supplied by the YUKON Battn. That for (d) & (e) being supplied by the FARBUS Battn.

(iii) Units will supply a Lewis Gun Section for the Posts commanded by their own N.C.Os., and for the other Posts they will supply a rifle section.

5. (a) The role of the observation line requires special mention. It is an observation line purely and not an outpost line.

(i) Every effort is to be made to make the enemy think that this is our/

our real line of Resistance. With this end in view each Coy in the BLUE LINE, in addition to the 3 Observers per platoon will send each platoon one at a time daily up into the observation line to fire its 5 rounds practice. Arrangements should be made also for some of these men to throw up some earth occassionally to deceive the enemy into thinking that work is still being done on the line.

(ii) The object of the sections which are in the observation line by night and the observers by day is simply to afford immunity from surprise, their role is not in any way a fighting role. By night in the event of a hostile bombardment commencing the sections will withdraw to the Main Line of Resistance directly the bombardment begins, each section leaving 2 men behind with S.O.S. Rockets, which will be put up as soon as the enemy Infantry is observed to be advancing. The 2 men after giving the alarm will withdraw with all speed.
By Day the 3 observers posted from each platoon will withdraw to the Main Line of Resistance as soon as they have sent up the S.O.S. Rocket on seeing the hostile Infantry advancing.

(b) With regard to the supporting platoons for the BLUE LINE.
Where accommodation for these does not already exist and until such time as the necessary support trenches can be completed these supporting platoons will be located in the BLUE LINE itself. Commanders of these Platoons must however, reconnoitre for suitable shell holes or broken ground behind the BLUE LINE in rear of their Coy Areas to which they can lead their platoons immediately the hostile barrage lifts and from which they can carry out their role as supporting platoons.
The enemy usually endeavours to make a small break in our front line and through this break his Infantry will endeavour to penetrate and at once extend outwards before passing on to attack the next line. The one Platoon per Coy in support will therefore be in support not as one complete platoon, but in 4 section posts covering the rear of the Coy front so as to be able to bring fire on any part which may be penetrated.

6. (a) In order to prevent local penetration developing into a break through, it is not only considered necessary to be distributed in depth, but also to have rear lines and systems permanently garridon during the fight, so that the penetration may be localised and prevented from spreading.
(b) With this end in view each Battn has been allotted an area which the Battn Commander must be prepared to hold at all costs without any outside assistance. There will be no reinforcing from a rear locality to a forward one. Otherwise rear lines will be depleted of their garrisons and a further penetration may take plac

7. Reference to para 3 sub paras (c) (iii) and (d) (ii).
The one Coy in each of the FARBUS and MERSEY Areas which are to occupy "BLOB" Posts West of the Embankment cannot occupy these posts by the 9th inst, they will however, be located behind the Railway Embankment so as to be available for work on these posts.
To make room for them 2 Platoons from each of 3 Coys in each of the areas will be at once located in the BROWN LINE with the 2 remaining Platoons per Coy in support behind the Embankment (the third Platoon per Coy to be moved up to the BROWN LINE as soon as accommodation is available) There will thus be room in the MERSEY Area for the 3rd Coy to be behind the Embankment.
The 4th Coy (less 1 Platoon) will remain at NEUV ILLE ST VASST until accommodation is available in THELUS POST.
Battn H.Q. for MERSEY AREA will move up to THELUS POST to-morrow unde separate instructions to be issued.

8. Reorganisation as indicated above must be completed by 2400 on 9th June. Battns will report completion by code word "KIYA".

9. A/

9. A LA TARG ETTE sketch shewing the 4 areas will be forwarded to B attns as soon as possible.

M ajor,
B rigade Major, 157th Infantry B rigade.

Issued at ....

Copies No. 1 to 5th H. L. I.
2 6th H. L. I.
3 7th H. L. I.
4 5th A & S. H.
5 157th L. T. M. Bty.
6 Hqrs. 52nd Division.
7 Hqrs. 52nd Divn. M.G. B attn.
8 Hqrs. Artillery.
9)
10) War Diary.
11 File.

Appendix III

S E C R E T.

No. 11 ....

157th Infantry Brigade Order No. ~~104~~ 105.

12th June, 1918.

1. The following reliefs will be carried out on 14th June, 1918.

(a) 5th H. L. I. will relieve 7th H. L. I.
(b) 6th H. L. I. " " 5th A & S. H.

After relief 7th H.L.I. & 5th A & S. H. will take over same dispositions as 5th H. L. I. and 6th H. L. I. respectively.

2. As much of relief as possible will take place during day light. Not more than 2 Platoons of each Coy of the relieving Battns should be on the move at the same time.
(This does not apply to Platoons at NEUVILLE ST VAAST.)
Platoons moving from NEUVILLE ST VAAST to the Eastern foot of VIMY Ridge and vice versa will do so in Sections at not less than 100 yards interval.

3. Relief will be completed by 2300.

4. Details of relief will be arranged by Os.C. concerned. A percentage of observers, scouts etc., of reserve Battns should proceed to the line 24 hours in advance.

5. All trench maps, stores, etc., will be handed over.

6. Completion of relief will be wired "Priority" to Bde Hqrs. using the code word "Pemberton".

7. ACKNOWLEDGE.

A. W. Wilkins [signature]
Major,
Brigade Major, 157th Infantry Brigade.

Issued at ....

Copies No. 1 to 5th H. L. I.
2 6th H. L. I.
3 7th H. L. I.
4 5th A & S. H.
5 157th L. T. M. Bty.
6 Hqrs. 52nd Division.
7 Hqrs. 156th Inf. Bde.
8 Hqrs. 155rd. Inf. Bde.
9 Artillery Hqrs.
10)
11) War Diary.
12 File.

Appendix IV

SECRET

157th Infantry Brigade Order No.106.

12th June, 1918.

Reference Map Sheets MAROEUIL & St. NAZAIRE River 1/20,000

1. The 5th A. & S. H. will carry out a raid on the enemy trenches on the night of 13/14th June, 1918.
The point to be raided will be the enemy trench about square T.23.d.7.2.

2. The object of the raid will be to:-
(a) Obtain identifications.
(b) Inflict casualties.
The raiders are not to stop for (b) when they have once obtained (a)

3. Strength of party not to exceed 2 Platoons. If 2 Platoons are employed, 1 will be in support.

4. No artillery will be employed, as a surprise is more likely to be effected by a silent raid. Artillery will be standing by in case help is wanted for the withdrawal.

5. Personnel taking part in the Raid will not carry identification marks such as letters, pay books, identity discs, or Regimental badges

6. Live prisoners are required and anything which will establish the identity of the Units opposite to us, should be brought away such as enemy shoulder straps, packs etc.

7. The following code will be used between Brigade and Battn. Hqrs:-

Raid will take place ...	... ...	... BLOOD.
Raid will not take place	... ...	... RAT.
Raiding party returned	... ...	... GLASGOW.
Casualties in raiding party	(State number)	... HEROES.
Prisoners taken	...(State number)	... BLIGHTERS.
Estimated German Casualties	(State number)	... DUDS.

8. Zero hour will be notified later. The reference hour will be 10 p.m. Thus if the raid is to take place at 11 p.m. a wire will be sent as follows:- "BLOOD plus 60". If the raid is to take place at 1-30 a.m. on the 14th the wire will read "BLOOD plus 210".

9. Every effort must be made to bring back a ny casualties which may be suffered on our side during the raid.

10. An Officer from Brigade Hqrs. will be at the 5th A & S. H. Hqrs about 6-30 p.m. to synchronise watches.

A. Wells[signature]
Major,
Brigade Major, 157th Infantry Brigade.

Issued at ....

Copies No. 1 to	5th H.L.I.	Copy No. 8.	A.D.S. 3rd. L.F.A.
2	6th H.L.I.	9	Hqrs. 52nd Division.
3	7th H.L.I.	10	Hqrs. 153rd. Bde.
4	5th A & S. H.	11	Hqrs. 156th Bde.
5	157th L.T.M. Bty.	12	B.G.C.
6	M.G. Commander Right Group.	13, 14	War Diary.
7	412th Fd. Coy. R.E.	15	File.

SECRET. Copy No. 12..

157th Infantry Brigade Order No. 107. *Appendix V*

Reference map MAROEUIL 1/20,000

1. 157th Infantry Brigade will be relieved by 155th Infantry Brigade in the WILLERVAL Section on the 20th & 21st June.

2. Reliefs will be carried out in day light and will be as follows:-

June 20th . 5th H.L.I. will be relieved by 5th R.S.F. in YUKON Area.
6th H.L.I . will be relieved by 4th R.S.F. in OTTAWA Area.
7th H.L.I. will be relieved by 5th K.O.S.B. in FARBUS Area.
5th A & S. H. will be relieved by 4th K.O.S.B. in MERSEY Area.
Relief to be completed by 6 a.m. on 21st June.
June 21st 157th L.T.M.Bty will be relieved by 155th L.T.M. Bty, relief to be completed by 6 a.m. on 22nd June.

3. Details of relief will be arranged between Os.C. concerned.

4. Communications, Trench Maps, Maps of No Man's Land, Defence Schemes, Log Books and Notes on Work on Progress and Trench Stores will be handed over.
Lewis Gun Magazines may be exchanged by mutual arrangement.

5. Advance parties from 155th Inf. Bde., are going into the line on the 19th June. Guides will be arranged as follows:-

5th H. L. I . 1 Guide to take party to Batt'n Hqrs at 2 p.m. at 157th Bde. Hqrs.
6th H. L. I . 1 Guide to take party to Batt'n Hqrs at 2-15 p.m. at 157th Bde. Hqrs.
7th H. L. I . Guides for all Posts and Companies at Bde. Hqrs at 2-45 p.m .
5th A & S. H. Guides for all Posts and Companies at 3 p.m. at 157th Bde. H qrs.

6. Relieving troops for the BROWN LINE and EAST thereof will be guided to the point at which the Railway crosses TIRED ALLEY and MERSEY ALLEY, respectively, under Brigade Arrangements as shewn below. Beyond these two points and for the Posts WEST of the BROWN LINE arrangements will be made between Os. C. concerned.
The relieving troops will arrive by Bus. Debussing point will be on NEUVILLE ST. VAAST - LES TILLEULS Road at a point which will be notified later.
7th H. L. I., will provide a chain of picquets under an Officer (who will be stationed at debussing point) along th e tracks from the NEUVILLE ST VAAST - LES TILLEULS Road to the junction TIRED ALLEY - THELUS Ridge Line. 5th A & S. H. will provide a similar chain under an Officer along the tracks from NEUVILLE ST VAAST - LES TILLEULS Road to the end of MERSEY ALLEY, thus avoiding CANADIAN M onument. These chains will be in position by 9-30 a.m. and will remain till all relieving troops have passed up.
Units of 155th I nfantry Brigade will be directed as follows:-

5th R. S. F. by TIRED ALLEY.
4th R. S. F. by MERSEY ALLEY.
5th K.O.S.B. by TIRED ALLEY.
4th K.O.S.B. by MERSEY ALLEY.

7. Outgoing troops on leaving the communication trenches will move in sections at not less than 100 yards interval.

8. On relief units will move into Camps as follow s:-

5th H.L.I.	HILLS Camp, NEUVILLE ST VAAST.
6th H.L.I.	FRASER Camp, MONT ST. ELOI.
7th H.L.I.	OTTAWA CAMP " " "
5th A & S. H.	LE PENDU Camp " " "
157th L.T.M.B.	CUBITT CAMP NEUVILLE ST VAAST

9. Units may send in advance a party of not more than 5 Officers in all and 10 O.R. per Coy., to take over Camps.

10. Details at RISPIN Camp will rejoin their Units at the Camps shewn above on day of relief.

11. Completion of relief and arrival in Camp willbe reported by the code words " DORIS" and "KEANE" respectively.

12. The time at which Command will pass will be notified later. At this hour Brigade Headquarters will close at THELUS MILL and re-open at MONT ST ELOI at the same hour.

13 Acknowledge.

A.Wolley(?)
Major,
Brigade Major, 157th Infantry Brigade.

Issued at ....

Copies No. 1 to	5th H. L. I.	No. 8 to	Artillery Hqrs.
2	6th H. L. I.	9	Hqrs. 156th Bde
3	7th H. L. I.	10	Hqrs 154th Bde.
4	5th A. & S. H.	11	G.O.C.
5	157th L.T.M. Bty.	12	) War Diary.
6	Hqrs. 52nd Division.	13	)
7	155th Inf. Brigade.	14	File.

Amendment to Brigade Administrative Instructions No. 103.

Para 3 Supplies is cancelled and the following substituted.

3. Supplies.

From 20th June inclusive, rations for all Units of the Bde. will be drawn from BLACKPOOL SIDING A.7.d.4.8.

H. M. Hewison
Captain,
Staff Captain, 157th Infantry Brigade.

18th June,

S E C R E T.   Copy No. 11

157th Infantry Brigade Administrative Instructions No. 103.

Issued with reference to Brigade Order No. 107 of 17/6/18.

Reference Sheet 51c. N.E.

1. Relief.

5th H. L. I.	relieved by	5th R. S. F.	Will proceed to	HILLS CAMP, NEUVILLE ST. VAAST.
			Will proceed to	FRASER CAMP.
6th H. L. I.	"	4th R. S. F.	"	" OTTAWA CAMP.
7th H. L. I.	"	5th K. O. S. B.	"	" LE PENDU.
5th A & S. H.	"	4th K. O. S. B.	"	" CUBITT CAMP.
157th L.T.M. Bty.	"	155th L.T.M. Bty	"	

2. Transport.

Under Orders of the Brigade Transport Officer Transport will move from the present lines to lines occupied by the relieving Battns. Relief will be completed by 1400 on 20th inst. Arrangements will be made direct between Brigade Transport Officers.

Relief of Duties. Battns will arrange to hand over to relieving Battns the water point duties furnished in this area.

3. Supplies.

Rations for 21st will be drawn as at present from LEADLEY SIDING and sent to the camps which Units are to occupy.

Rations for consumption from 22nd, From BLACKPOOL SIDING for Units in ST. ELOI Camps.

From LEADLEY SIDING for 5th H. L. I., & L. T. M. Battery. The 5th H. L. I. will provide transport for L.T.M. Bty.

4. Water.

Water is laid on in the camps. Strict supervision must be exercised to prevent wastage.

5. Lorries.

The motor lorries which bring up the relieving Battns will be available to convey the Battns of this Brigade to ST. ELOI.

Embussing Officer Lt. D.B. LOCKHART.

6. Area and Trench Stores.

Soyers stoves, Food Containers, Petrol Tins and all Trench stores will be handed over and receipts obtained.

The pro-forma issued with Q.198/5 will be used and the instructions laid down carefully complied with. The duplicate will be sent to Brigade Headquarters by 1800 on 21st. This will be returned if required

7. Billet Improvements.

Units of the 155th Brigade will hand over to the relieving Units their scheme of work for Billet sanitation and minor improvements and a schedule of the work in progress. This will include the construction of ovens, anti-aircraft protection etc.

8. Duties.

Battn on duty 21st, 7th H. L. I.

Next for Duty 6th H. L. I.

The following Guards and Picquets will be furnished by Battn on

Duty/

8. Duties (Contd)

duty and will mount as shewn:-

No.	Duty	Strength	Location	Time
(1)	Bde. Hqrs Guard.	1 N.C.O., 6 Men	Brigade Hqrs.	1700.
(2)	Picquet.	1 N. C. (3 men (3 men	F.15.a.0.7. F.14.a.3.5.	1500 - 2130.
(3)	Picquet.	1 Officer 2 N.C.O. & 12 Men.	F.13.b.8.6.	1500 - 2130.
(4)	Picquet.	1 N.C.O. 3 Men	F.13.a.2.7.	1500 - 2130.
(5)	Picquet.	1 N.C.O. 3 Men	F.1.a. 4.2.	1500 - 2130.
(6)	To be held in readiness if called on. Officer will report at Bde Hqrs.	1 Platoon.		1800 - 2200.
(7)	Divnl. Canteen.	1 Sergt.	OTTAWA Camp	1715 - 2030.
(8)	Camp construction Party.	120. [redacted] Men exclusive of Offrs. & N.C.Os. ½ Picks, & ½ shovels	R.E. Dump FRASER Camp.	0800 - 120 1300 - 170

9. Duties to be furnished by Battalions.

By 5th H. L. I .

No.	Duty.	Strength	Location	Time to report.
(9)	P.P. Compound.	1 Sgt. 1 L/Cpl. 6 Men.	AUX RIETZ Caves A.8.c.6.8. (Ref. MAROEUIL Map)	N.C.O. i/c Compound at 0900 on 20th & daily there after.
(10.)	Ammunition Dump.	1 N.C.O.& 3 Men	HILLS Camp.	0900 on 20th
(11.)	Forward Battle Stragglers station.	1 N.C.O. & 5 men	A.11.b.1.8.	When called on see A.I. No. A.F.9 of 25/5/18
(12.)	Prisoners of War Cage.	1 N. C. O. & 12 Men.	A.8.c.3.7.	When called on See A.I. No. A.F.9 of 25/5/1

The names of men detailed for 11 and 12 will be sent direct to A.P.M.

No.	Duty	Strength	Location	
(13.)	Water Picquets.	1	(A.8.a.1.5. (A.8.a.3.6 .	Horses. "
		1	A.8.a.3.8.	Drinking.
		1	A.8.b.6.5.	Horses.
		1	(F.11.b.1.2. (F.11.b.6.3.	" "
		1	(F.12.a.1.4. (F.12.a.2.1.	" Drinking.
		1	(F.12.a.6.2. (F.12.a.4.6.	Horses. Taps.
		1	(F.12.a.3.6. (F.12.a.6.9.	" "
		1	(A.7.d.7.6. (A.7.d.9.2.	Tank. Horses.

Men detailed for Water Duty will report at 0900 on 20th to Battn Hqrs of Battn which is to be relieved.

9. (Contd)

By 6th H. L. I.

No.	Duty.	Strength	Location.	
(14.)	Water Picquet.	1 Man.	(F. 8.a.8.2. (F.8.b.3.1.	Drinking. Horses.
		1 Man.	(F.9.c.9.1. (F.9.d.4.3.	Horses. Drinking.
		1 Man.	(F.9.c .9.4. (F.9.c. 9.5.	" ~~Drinking~~. Horses

Men detailed for duty will report at 0900 on 20th to Battn Hqrs of Battn which is to be relieved.

By 7th H. L. I.

No.	Duty.	Strength.	Location.	
(15.)	Water Picquet.	1 Man 1 Man	F.2.a.28. F.2.c.14.	Drinking. "

Men detailed for duty will report at 0900 on 20th to Battn Hqrs of Battn which is to be relieved.

By 5th A.& S. H.

No.	Duty.	Strength	Location.	
(16)	Water Picquet.	1 Man	(F.8.c. 5.9. (F.8.c.5.6.	Tank. Drinking.
		1 Man.	(F.4.d.1-2. (F.4.d.2-1	Horses. Drinking.
		1 Man.	(F.10.d.1-4. (F.10.d.1-8.	Tank. Horses.

Men detailed for duty will report at 0900 on 20th to Battn Hqrs of Battn which is to be relieved.

Divisional Chaff Cutting Depot. To be furnished by Battn on Duty each day.

No.	Duty.	Strength	Location.	Time.
(17.)	Chaff Cutting.	1st Shift 2 Sections 2bd Shift 2 Sections.	Blackpool Sdg. A.7.d.4.8.	0730 - 1130 1400 - 1800

Men detailed will report to N.C.O. i/c Divisional Chaff-Cutting Depot five Minutes before their shift is due to start.

Water Picquets.

(a) Chloride of Lime is required for all water tanks and is provided by the M.O. of the unit finding the water picquet.
(b) The duties of water picquets are detailed in 52nd Divnl Circular Administrative Instructions No. 7 dated 24/5/18.

Orders in writing will be handed over by all picquets being relieved.

The Brigade Transport Officer will detail one Water Cart daily for the Signalling School, VILLERS AU BOIS. The cart will be left at the Camp.

10. Discipline.

N.C.Os and Men are forbidden to leave the Divisional Area.

BOOIVRES and other villages in the 51st Divn Area (i.e. South of an East and West Line through Cross Roads F.14.b.10.6.) are strictly out of bounds for all units of the Brigade.

11. Bounds.

The bounds for the Brigade are marked by 52nd Divnl Boards at the following points.

F.15.a.1 .7.
F.14.a.8. 7.
F.13.b.8.6.
F.13.a.9.9.
F.1.d.5.2.

No N.C.O. or man is allowed outside these Points without a pass signed by his Commanding Officer and bearing the office stamp.

Battalion bounds will be marked by Battn Boards which have been issued.

No man will leave the area of the three camps at ST. ELOI or the Camp area at NEUVILLE ST VAAST without a belt.

It must be impressed on all men that they must be properly dressed and tidely dressed when going out of camp area.

Steps will be taken to see that this is carried out.

12. Baths.

Baths are allotted to Units as under:-

NEUVILLE ST VAAST, Baths.

60 men each half hour.

21st	5th H.L.I.	0900 to 1200	=	360 men.
	"	1300 to 1700	=	480 "
				840
22nd	L.T.M. Bty.	0900 to 1000	=	120 Men.

Berthonval Baths.

60 men each half hour.

21st	6th H.L.I.	0800 tp 1200	=	480
	"	1300 to 1700	=	480
				960

St. ELOI, Baths.

40 men each half hour

21st	5th A & S. H.	0800 to 1200	=	320
	"	1300 to 1700	=	320
22nd	"	0800 to 0900	=	80
				780
22nd	Brigade Hqrs.	0900 to 1030	=	120.

VILLER AU BOIS Baths.

40 men each half hour.

21st	7th H. L. I.	0800 to 1200	=	320
	"	1300 to 1700	=	320
				640

13. Area Stores.

Area stores taken over should be carefully checked and a copy

of/

13 Area Stores (Contd)

of the receipt sent to Brigade Hqrs by 1800 on 21st.

14. ACKNOWLEDGE.

H M Hewison

Captain,
Staff Captain, 157th Infantry Brigade.

Issued at ....5 p.m. 18/9/18....

Copies No. 1 to 5th H. L. I.
2 6th H. L. I.
3 7th H. L. I.
4 5th A. & S. H.
5 157th L. T. M. Bty.
6 Bde. Transport Officer.
7 Hqrs. 155th Inf. Bde.
8 Hqrs. 52nd Division.
9 G.O.C.
10 (War Diary.
11 (
12 File.

Action of Reserve Brigade.

= = = = = = = = = = = =

Appendix VI

Reference Map MAROEUIL 1/20,000

1. (a) The Divisional Reserve consists of
One Infantry Brigade
One Coy. 52nd Divn. M.G. Battn.

(b) The role of the Divisional Reserve in case of the enemy penetrating our line is dependent on the extent and direction of the enemy penetration, but roughly it may be required to
(i) Form a defensive flank to the SOUTH
(ii) Form a defensive flank to the NORTH
(iii) Counter attack to restore a broken centre.

2. The following general instructions are laid down to meet the three contingencies mentioned above.

(a) In the event of the enemy breaking through South of WILLERVAL the NEUVILLE ST VAAST Battn will move at once on the order "MAN ECURIE" to occupy the ECURIE SWITCH from THELUS POST (exclusive) to the THELUS Trench in A.17.b., Battn Hqrs being established at A.6.a.50.00, the present location of the Hqrs Right Section. The remainder of the Brigade will move to the NEUVILLE ST VAAST Area, marching in the following order:- Brigade Hqrs, OTTAWA Battn, FRASER Battn, LE PENDU Battn, and assemble as follows:-

OTTAWA Battn.	Between LICHFIELD Post No. 1 (A.430.10.60) and ZIVY DUMP (A.9.b.70. 60).
FRASER Battn.	N. W. Lichfield Post No. 1 at about A.3.d.50.90.
LE PENDU Battn.	About 300 yards WEST of Brigade Hqrs

O.C. L.T.M. Bty will detail 2 Sections to come under the orders of the O.C. NEUVILLE ST VAAST Battn, for the defence of the ECURIE SWITCH.

L.T.M. Bty (less 2 sections) will assemble at LICHFIELD Post No. 1

Bde Hqrs & Hqrs OTTAWA & FRASER Battns will be at A.E. Test Box LICHFIELD Post No. 1.

Hqrs LE PENDU Battn. will be at old CANADIAN Battn Hq. about A.3.d.70.60.

The Reserve Coy. 52nd Divn M.G. Battn. will act as follows:-

2 Guns will be sent to each of the following positions:-

JERUSALEM Post	A.17.c .20.60.
RAILWAY "	A.11.d.40.40.
JORDAN "	A.12 .c.45.40.
TAPE "	B.7.c.15.45.
THELUS "	B.7.a.85.00.

The Coy (less 10 guns) will move into reserve at LICHFIELD Post No. 1.

52nd M.G. Battn H.Q. will be established at A.J. Test Box, A.6.a.50.00.

(b) In the event of the enemy breaking through from the NORTH the Brigade will, on the order "CONCENTRATE HILL 130" concentrate in the neighbourhood of Hill 130 ready to support the 2nd C.I.W. Battn, manning the GREEN LINE from its junction with the PADDOCK Switch in S.29 to its junction with the BULLY SWITCH in M.20.d. H.Q. of the 2nd C.I.W. Battn will be at SOUCHEZ. The NEUVILLE ST VAAST Battn and the L.T.M. Bty will proceed to this place direct. The remainder/

2 (b) Contd.

remainder of the Brigade will march from MONT ST ELOI in the order mentioned in 2 (a) above, proceeding by route (not marked on map which must be reconnoitred by Battn Intelligence Officers under Brigade I. O. both by day and by night)

FRASER Camp - X.28.d.00 - F.3.a.8.2. - F.4.c.5.5. - F.4.d.8.4. - S.25.b.9.1. - through F.5. central along the ARRAS - BETHUNE Road to S.25.b.8.8. - S.26 .a.1.9. - S.19.d.7.9. - S.20.c .- S.20.a.40.00.

Brigade Hqrs willbe at S.P. Test Box,	S.20.a .40.00
NEUVILLE ST VAAST Battn about point	S.20.c.50.20.
FRASER Battn.	S.20.a.20.50.
OTTAWA Battn.	S.20.d.50.60.
LE PENDU Battn .	S.20.a.90.50.
L.T.M. Bty.	S.20.c.70.90.

The Reserve M.G. Coy.

Will send guns to the following positions:-

1 Gun T.R. 25.	S.22.d.82.82.
1 " T.R. 24.	S.22.d.70.50.
2 " MAPLE	S. 22.a.82.49.
2 " BEACH	S. 22.a.42.84.
2 " ELM.	S.16.c.35.25.

The M.G. Coy. less 10 guns , will move to Hill 130 and be located in rear of NEUVILLE ST VAAST Battn.

(c) In the eventof penetration into our front line, the NEUVILLE ST VAAST Battn will move at once on the order "MAN BONVAL" to occupy that portion of the GREEN LINE between S.23 .d.60.00 and A.5.b.70.20 pushing forward posts well down the Eastern slopes of VIMY Ridge to cover the BONVAL - REENTRANT and the LENS - ARRAS Road. Battn H.Q. will be at Test Box S.Q. at S.28.c.50.50.

2 Sections L.T.M. Bty will come under the orders of O.C. NEUVILLE ST VAAST Battn for defence of GREEN LINE. The remainder of the Brigade will move as detailed in para 2 (a).

M.G. Coy. will send 2 guns to each of the following positions:-

HOW M.G. Post.	S.30 .d.48.70.
THISTLE Post	S.30.a.63.34.

The Coy less 2 sections will stand by in CUBITT Camp sending an Officer to report to Brigade Headquarters at A.E. Test Box.

3. In view of the possibility of the Brigade being ordered to occupy ~~certain trenches~~ after arriving at the various positions of assembly, the necessary reconnaissances will be carried out by Officers of the Battns named, of the several trench systems with which their Battn is concerned.

In 2 (b) The Battn in OTTAWA and 2 Sections L.T.M. Bty will be prepared to man the ECURIE SWITCH from the THELUS Trench S.W. to BILLE Redoubt (A.17.c.20.60) (inclusive). Bde. Hqrs will remain at A.E. Test box (LICHFIELD POST No. 1).

In 2(b)

The Brigade will be prepared to support the 2nd C.T.W. Battn, (Colonel McKinnery, D.S.O.) who will be manning the GREEN LINE from its junction with the PADDOCK Switch. In this case Battns will be disposed as follows:-

OTTAWA Battn. From junction of GREEN LINE and PADDOCK Switch in S.29 . to junction GREEN LINE and BLIGHTY in S.22.a.

LE PENDU Battn. Thence to GEORGE S.15.a.20.70.

FRASER Battn. BOIS EN HACHE (S.2 .c.) inclusive.

NEUVILLE ST VAAST Battn. In reserve at position of assembly.

L.T.M. Bty/

3. Contd.

L.T.M. Bty . will detail 2 Mortars to come under the Orders of each Battn in the GREEN LINE. The Battery (less 3 sections) remaining in reserve near Bde. H.Q.
Bde. H.Q. will remain at S.J. Test Box S.20.a.40.20.

I n 2 (c)
(i) The LE PENDU Battn will be prepared to m an the GREEN LINE from A.5.b.7.3 . to THELUS POS T (exclusive).
Bde. H.Q. will remain at A.E . Test Box.
(ii) The Brigade less NEUVILLE ST VAAST Battn will beprepared to move by night across the VIMY Ridge and concentrate about the following positions

OTTAWA Battn.	S.18.d .80.00.
L E PENDU "	S.24.c .60.40.
FRASER "	S.24.c.00.90.
L.T.M . Bty. (less ½ B ty)	
& M.G. Coy (less 8 guns)	S.30.a.40.50.

Bde. Hqrs will move to with advanced H.Q.
at

4. All units must be prepared to move 1 hour after the receipt of the order "STAND TO"

5. When on the move the re will be a distance of 650 yards between Battns and 20 yards between Platoons and Coys.
Main Roads must be avoided as musch as possible.

Major,
Brigade Major, 157th Infantry Brigade.

19th J une, 1918.

Operation Orders
by
Major T.R. Blair
Comdg 1/7th Bn The Cameronians (Sco. Rifles).

18th June 1918.

1. The Battalion will be relieved by 1/4th Royal Scots on 20th inst. After relief Coys will move back to positions occupied by Coys. of 4th Royal Scots as follows:–

"B" Coy. 7th S.R. to position of "B" Coy. 4th R.S. in CANADA LINE.
"C" Coy. 7th S.R. " " " "C" Coy. 4th R.S. "
"A" Coy. 7th S.R. " " " "A" Coy. 4th R.S. BROWN LINE
"D" Coy. 7th S.R. " " " "D" Coy. 4th R.S. "

2. Coys should send representatives to new areas today to get a general idea of defence scheme etc.

3. Care must be taken that no Battn Stores are handed over to incoming unit as Trench Stores – (N.B. Periscopes, and Very Lights are Battn. Stores.) – unless special instructions to that effect are issued.

Lewis Gun magazines and boxes will be handed over.

4. Receipts for Trench Stores handed over will be forwarded to Battn. H.Q. at S.24.a.3.0. by 9 p.m. on 20th inst.

Receipts for Trench Stores taken over in new areas will be forwarded to Battn. H.Q. by 9 p.m. on 20th inst.

Usual sanitary certificates will be obtained from incoming unit & forwarded with trench receipts.

5. Relief will be notified by code word "CAPT. APSIMON" and arrival at new areas by code word "R.A.M.C." The latter will be sent to new Battn. H.Q.

6. Precedence will be given to 4th Royal Scots troops moving up.

7. No. 9 Platoon (2nd Lieut. D. Lenton) will proceed, on relief, to Bde. H.Q. (S.27.b.0.5.) where they will report to Staff Captain who will allot them a bivouac area.

(Sgd) Hector C. Maclean
Capt & Adjt.
1/7th Cameronians (Sco. Rifles).

APPENDIX VIa

APPENDIX VII.

Operation Order
by
Major R. Blair
Comdg. 5th Bn. The Cameronians (Scottish Rifles)

27th June 1918.

1. The Battn. will be relieved by daylight on 29th June by 1/5th H.L.I. and will move back thereafter to OTTAWA Camp where Coys. will be disposed as formerly.

2. Communications, log books, trench stores, etc. will be handed over to incoming unit and receipts (in duplicate) handed to Orderly Room by 8 a.m. on 30th inst.

3. A list of trench stores which will be handed over will be sent to Orderly Room by 8 a.m. on 28th inst.

4. Coys. will move back on relief by platoons at 400 yards interval as follows:–

A & D Coys. by BROWN LINE and HUMBER to barrier at S.28.d.8.8. and thence by motor.

B & C Coys. by GLACE and BLIGHTY to CAMPBELL Rd (S.28.a.3.8.) and thence by motor.

5. Strict march discipline must be maintained in moving back and on no account will there be any straggling or crowding together of platoons.

6. All Lewis Gun magazines and tin boxes will be handed over with the exception of 4 magazines per A.A. gun. Drums will be handed over.

7. Periscopes and Very Pistols are Battn. stores and will not be handed over.

8. Relief will be notified by code word "WHISKEY" and arrival at new area by code word "BILL".

9. Sanitary certificates will be obtained from incoming unit & forwarded with trench store receipts.

10. Guides will be provided for incoming units as under.

(A) For Advance Party on 28th inst. at barrier (S.28.d.8.8) at 3 p.m. 1 N.C.O. per Coy. These N.C.Os. will report at Battn. H.Q. at 1 p.m.

(B). For Main Body on 29th inst. 1 Officer per Coy. and 1 Other Rank per platoon of A & D Coys. at barrier (S.28.d.8.8) at mid-day. 1 Officer per Coy. and 1 Other Rank per platoon of B & C Coys. at CAMPBELL Rd (S.28.a.3.8). at mid-day.

P.T.O.

APPENDIX VII

11. 2nd Lieut. J. W. Strathearn will be Embussing Officer for this Bde. at S.28.d.8.8. on 29th inst. and will report to Battn. H.Q. at 10 a.m. on that day for orders.

(Sgd) Hector C. Maclean
Capt. & Adjt.
Cameronians
(Sco. Rifles)

Appendix VII

SECRET. Copy No.......

157th Infantry Brigade Order No. 108.

27th June, 1918.

Ref. Map MAROEUIL 1/20,000

1. The 157th Infantry Brigade will relieve the 156th Infantry Brigade in the LEFT (CHAUDIERE) Section on the 29th - 30th June as under:-

29th June.
7th H.L.I. relieve 4th R.S. in front line RIGHT SUB-SECTION
6th H.L.I. " 7th R.S. in front line LEFT SUB-SECTION
5 th H.L.I. " 7th S.R. in RESERVE.
30th June.
157th L.T.M.B. relieve 156th L.T.M.B.

2. (a) Battns billetted at MONT ST. ELOI will move by Motor Lorry as follows:-

7th H.L.I. to Barrier on LA FOLIE FARM Road at S.28.d.8.8. starting at 9 a.m.
6th H.L.I. via the ARRAS - SOUCHEZ Road - CAMPBELL Road to S.28.a.3.8. starting at 9 a.m.
(b) (i) H.Q. & 2 Coys 5th H.L.I. will proceed by route march from MILLS Camp to the barrier on the LA FOLIE Farm Road the leading platoon arriving there at 1215 p.m.
(ii) 2 Coys will proceed via the ARRAS - SOUCHEZ Road - CAMPBELL Road to S.28.a.3.8. leading platoon arriving at 1215 p.m.

3. (a) Guides, 1 Officer and 1 O.R. per Battn Hqrs, 1 Officer per Coy and 1 O.R. per platoon will meet units as follows:-
6th H.L.I. on CAMPBELL Road, S.28.a.3.8. at 9.15 a.m.
7th H.L.I. at Barrier, S.28.d. 8.8. at 9.15 a.m.
5th H.L.I. for 2 Coys & Hqrs at Barrier S.28 .d.8.8. at 1215 p.m.
& for 2 Coys on CAMPBELL Road, S.28.a.3.8. at 1215 p.m.

4. (a) 7th H.L.I. & H.Q. & 2 Coys 5th H.L.I. will move by HUMBER, PEGGY, & TOAST Trenches.
6th H.L.I. & 2 Coys 5th H.L.I. will move by BLIGHTY, CLACE. & HALTER Trenches (latter for 6th H.L.I. only).
(b) Up to the VIMY Ridge movement will be by Platoons at 200 yards distance, after that it will be by Groups of 2 Sections at 100 yards distance.

5. (a) 7th H.L.I. & 6th H.L.I. will arrange for their own debussing officers.
(b) An Officer of the Brigade Staff will superintend the embussing at MONT ST. ELOI.

6. (a) Advanced parties consisting of Battn Intelligence Officer, & 1 Officer per Coy., 1 N.C.O. per platoon, Coy Gas N.C.Os. & a proportion of Lewis Gunners, Signallers, Scouts and runners will go into the line on 28th June.
3 Motor Lorries have been arranged for, to take above up. Busses will be at MONT ST. ELOI (entrance to FRASER Camp) at 2 p.m. and are allotted 1½ to each of 6th & 7th H.L.I. 5th H.L.I. advanced party will march up.
(b) Guides for advance parties have been arranged as follows:-
5th & 7th H.L.I. at Barrier S.28.d. 8.8. at 3 p.m.
6th H.L.I. on CAMPBELL Road at S.28 .a.3.8 at 3 p.m.

7. 157th L.T.M.B. will proceed up to the line on 30th June by route march. O.C., L.T.M.Bty will make his own arrangements re routes & guides.

8. Communications, trench maps, maps of No Man's Land, Defence Scheme, Log Books, and Trench Stores will be taken over.

9. All other details re, relief will be arranged between C.Os. concerned.

10. In the event of Alarm during relief, Units will send an Officer to the nearest Battn Hqrs. to report their position to the Battn H.Q. in whose area they happen to be and also to Bde H.Q.

11. Personnel of units to be left out of the line will proceed to Divisional Details Camp arriving there by 3 p.m. 29th June.

12. Between the completion of the Infantry and L.T.M. Bty relief, the 157th L.T.M.Bty will come under the orders of G.O.C. 156th Infantry Brigade.

13. Completion of reliefs will be reported to Bde. Hqrs by the code word "CHAUDIERE".

14. Command will pass on comple tion of the Infantry Relief. Brigade Headquarters will close at MONT ST. ELOI at 4.30 p.m. on 29th June, and open at S.27.b. 0.5. at same time.

15. ACKNOWLEDGE.

A. Williams

Major,
Brigade Major, 157th Infantry Brigade.

Copies No. 1 to 5th H. L. I.
2 6th H. L. I.
3 7th H. L. I.
4 157th L. T. M. Bty.
5 Hqrs. 52nd Division.
6 Hqrs. 156th Inf. Bde.
7 Hqrs 155th Inf. Bde.
8 52nd M.G. Battn.
9 H.Q. 52nd Divnl. Artillery.
10 B.G.C.
11 (War Diary.
12 (
13 File.

SECRET. Copy No. 12

157th Infantry Brigade Administrative Instructions
No. 105.
Issued with reference to Brigade Order No. 108 of 27th June. 1918.
= = = = = = = = = = = = = = = = = = =

27th June, 1918.

Ref. Map MAROEUIL 1/20,000

1. MOVE.

The Brigade less 5th H.L.I. and L.T.M.B. will be conveyed on June 29th by motor lorries from MONT ST. ELOI to relieve the 156th Bde.

7th H.L.I. to Barrier at LA FOLIE FARM, S.28.d.8.8.
6th H.L.I. by CAMPBELL ROAD to S.28.a.3.8.
The motor lorries will be parked on the main road at 0900.
Lorries for 6th H.L.I. will be at the entrance to FRASER CAMP.
Lorries for 7th H.L.I. at entrance to OTTAWA CAMP.

2. RELIEF.

5th H.L.I. will relieve 4th R.S.,
6th H.L.I. will relieve 7th R.S.
7th H.L.I. will relieve 7th S.R.

3. TRANSPORT.

Transport will be brigaded in ROSS & DALLY CAMPS.
Units will take over the lines of the battalions which they relieve.
Arrangements for the move will be made between the Brigade Transport Officers.
The move will be completed by 1400 on 29th.

4. RATIONS.

Refilling point from 29th June inclusive will be LEADLEY SIDING (A.2.c.5.9.)
Rations will be drawn at 0730 daily.
Rations are forwarded to units from the Transport lines as follows:-

Right Line Battalion.

For 4 Companies.	By Light Railway to CANADA DUMP, T.20.b.6.3.	
Battn. Hqrs.	~~Rail.~~ NEW BRUNSWICK, T.19.d.8.2. VICTORIA DUMP (T.18.b.3.2)	

LEFT LINE BATTALION
SUPPORT ~~Left Line~~ Battalion.

2 Companies.	By light Railway to CAYUGA DUMP	S.24.c.6.8.
1 Company.	NEW BRUNSWICK	T.19.d.8.2
1 Company.	BORDER	T.25.a.4.8
Battn Hqrs.	By rail to CAYUGA or by Limber.	

L.T.M. Bty. VICTORIA DUMP.

5. WATER SUPPLY.

MONT FOREST System.

T.15.b.7.6.	3	400 Gallon Tanks.
T.16.c.6.8.	3	" " "
T.16.c.9.2.	1	" " "
T.16.d.3.7.	3	" " "
T. 16.b.9.1.	3	" " "

GIVENCHY MAIN.

S.12.b.9.6.	1	W.B.F. 12 Taps.
S. 12.b.8.5.	2	400 Gallon Tanks.
T.8 .a.0.0.	1	" " "
T.8.a .7.8.	4	" " "
T.8.d. 5.6.	4	" " "

VIMY.

S.18.c .9.3.	2	S.P.
S.24.b.2 .9.	2	200 Gallon Tanks.
T.20.c.3. 1.	2	" " "

6. WATER PICQUETS.
The following picquets will relieve those found by the 156th Bde by 1400 on 29th.

Right Line Battn.
1 N.C.O. & 5 men for MONT FOREST System.

Left Line Battn.
1 N.C.O. & 2 men for GIVENCHY.
T.8.a.00. T.8.a.7.8. T.8.d.5.6.

Reserve Battn.
1 N.C.O. & 4 men for GOODMAN MAIN & VIMY (T.20.c.3.1.)
1 N.C.O. & 3 men for GIVENCHY (S.12.b.9.6.) (S.12.b.8.5.)
& VIMY (S.18.c.9.3.) (S.24.b.2.9.)

7. AMMUNITION SUPPLY
The Brigade ammunition dumps are situated as follows:-

Main Dump	Cayuga	S.24.c.8.5.
Forward Dumps.	Culvert	T.20.c.2.1.
	PEGGIE	T.19.b.7.8.
	NANAIMO	T.13.a.2.4.

8. RESERVE RATIONS.
Reserve rations will be taken over by Battalions as follows:-

		Biscuits	Meat.
Right Line Battn.	T.16.c.9.5.	700	690
Left Line Battn.	T.8.d.3.7.	750	768
Support Battn.	S.24.d.1.2.	750	756
	T.7.d.9.5.	1,350	1,336
	T.21.a.3.3.	600	576

9. R.E. MATERIAL
Will be supplied on demand through Brigade from ZIVY Dump and will be sent up by Light Railway.

10. SALVAGE.
All salvage will be collected and sent to VICTORIA, CAYUGA or PEGGY Dump.
The Reserve Battn will detail 2 Sections to report at 1000 on 30th at VICTORIA Dump for salvage duty.

11. MEDICAL.
Main Dressing Station, AUX REITZ. A.8.c.5.5.
A. D. S. LA CHAUDIERE S.18.c.9.5.

12. BURIAL.
An advanced collecting post is established at T.19.b.8.4. Units will send bodies there and will wire to Divnl Burial Officer who will remove these and arrange for burial.

13. STRAGGLER'S POSTS.
Stragglers posts are established at following points and are manned by personnel found by A.P.M.
S.11.d.4.2. S. 18.c.9.2. S.24.b.4.6. T.19.c.2.5.

14. BILLETS.
(a) All billets and Camps must be left scrupulously clean.
(b) A list of Area Stores handed over to incoming units will be forwarded to Brigade Hqrs., on 30th June by 12 noon.
(c) Certificates will be obtained from the Area Commandant that there are no outstanding claims for damage to Government property.

15. TRENCH STORES.
List of Trench Stores taken over will be furnished as per schedule to reach Bde Hqrs, not later than 1200 on 1st July.

16. ACKNOWLEDGE.

H M Hewison

Captain,
Staff Captain, 157 th Infantry Brigade.

Issued at ..20-30....24/6/18..

Copy No. 1 to 5th H. L. I.
2 6th H. L. I.
3 7th H. L. I.
4 Bde. Transport Officer.
5 Area Commandant.
6 Hqrs. 156th Inf. Bde.
7. Hqrs. 52nd Divn.
8. 157th L.T.M.Bty.
9. 2 nd Lowland Field Amb.
10. B.G.C.
11. (War Diary.
12 (
13. File.

War Diary

Appendix VIII

Please cancel Circular Memorandum ~~BB~~"Action of Reserve Brigade" dated 19th June, and substitute the attached.

[illegible signature]

Major,

Brigade Major, 157th Infantry Brigade.

28th June 1918.

* O.C., L.T.M.Bty will detail 2 Sections to come under the orders of the O.C., NEUVILLE ST. VAAST Battn for the defence of the ECURIE SWITCH.

L.T.M.Bty. (less 2 sections) will assemble at LICHFIELD POST No.1.

Bde Hqrs. & Hqrs OTTAWA & FRASER Battns. will be at A.E. Test Box, LICHFIELD POST No.1.

Provisional Defence Scheme.

1. (a) The Divisional Reserve consists of
One Infantry Brigade.
One Coy. 52nd Divn M.G. Battn.

(b) The role of the Divisional Reserve in case of the enemy penetrating our line is dependent on the extent and direction of the enemy penetration, but roughly it may be required to

(i) Form a defensive flank to the SOUTH
(ii) Form a defensive flank to the NORTH
(iii) Counter attack to restore a broken centre.

2. The following general instructions are laid down to meet the contingencies mentioned above.

(a) In the event of the enemy breaking through S. of WILLERVAL or in anticipation thereof, the Battalion at NEUVILLE ST. VAAST will move at once on the order "MAN THELUS" to occupy the ECURIE SWITCH from THELUS POST (inclusive) to the THELUS trench in A.17 .b. - one company in THELUS POST, 2 Coys in the SWITCH and 1 Platoon each in SPUR, FARBUS, BORDER and TAPE POSTS.

Battn Hqrs will be established at A.6.a.50.00, the present location of the Hqrs Right Section. The remainder of the Brigade will move to the NEUVILLE ST VAAST Area, marching in the following order:-

Brigade Headquarters,
OTTAWA Battalion,
FRASER Batt alion.
~~LE PANDU Battalion~~,
and assemble as follows:-

OTTAWA Battn. Between LICHFIELD Post No.1 (A.4.c.10.60) and ZIVY Dump (A.9.b.70.60.)
FRASER Battn. N.W. Lichfield Post No.1 at about A.3.d.50.90.

*(b) In the event of the enemy breaking through from the N. or in our centre, or in anticipation thereof, the Brigade will, on the order "~~Counter attack~~ Concentrate NEUVILLE ST. VAAST" move to the area about A.3.d.

Battns from MONT ST. ELOI will move as directed in (a) above.

The NEUVILLE ST VAAST Battn & 157th L.T.M.Bty will stand to in their own billeting area and will each send an officer to report to Brigade Hqrs at LICHFIELD Post No.1.

From here the Brigade will act according to circumstances. It may reinforce the BROWN LINE, one Battn going into VIMY Village and one Battn into PETIT VIMY and the BROWN LINE N. of that place or, the Brigade may cross the Ridge and assemble under cover in the re-entrant about S.24 .c. to counter attack next morning S.E. or E.

3. In view of the possibility of the Brigade being ordered to occupy certain trenches after arriving at the various positions of assembly the necessary reconnaissances will be carried out by Officers of the Battns named, of the several trench systems with which their Battn is concerned.

<u>In 2 (a)</u> The OTTAWA Battn and 2 Sections L.T.M .B. will be prepared to man the ECURIE SWITCH from the THELUS TRENCH S.W. to LILLE Redoubt (A.17.c.80.60. inclusive)

<u>In 2 (b)</u> (i) The OTTAWA Battn with 1 Section L.T.M.B. will be prepared to proceed to VIMY to assist in the defence of that place.

The FRASER Battn with 1 Section L.T.M.B. will be prepared to proceed to PETIT VIMY to assist in the defence of that Locality and the BROWN LINE to the NORTH.

(ii) The Brigade will be prepared to move by night across the VIMY Ridge and concentrate about the following positions:-

OTTAWA Battn.	...	...	...	S.18.d.80.00.
FRASER "	...	...	...	S.24.c.00.20.

3. In 2 (b) (ii) Contd.

NEUVILLE ST. VAAST. Battn.	... ...	S.24.c.60.40.
L. T. M. Battery.	... ...	S.30.a.40.50.

Bde H.Q. will move to S.V. Post Box S.23.c.2.2.
with Advanced H.Q. at S.L. Post Box S.24.a.2.0.

4. The action of the M.G. Coy will be,

In 2 (a) send 2 guns to each of the following positions.

Jerusalem M.G. Post	... ...	A.17.c.20.60.
Railway Post.	... ...	A.11.d.40.40.
Jordan "	... ...	A.12.c.45.40.
Tapo "	... ...	B.7.c.15.45.
Tholus "	... ...	B.7.a.85.00.

The Coy (less 2½ sections) will move into reserve at LICHFIELD POST No.1.

In 2 (b) The Coy (less any guns specially detailed by Divn H.Q.) will stand to in CUBITT Camp, sending an officer to report to Brigade H.Q. at LICHFIELD POST. If the Brigade crosses the VIMY Ridge for the purpose of making a counter attack, orders will be issued to M.G. Coy to follow the Brigade and to select a covered site about S.30.a.40.50. alongside the L.T.M.Bty.

5. All units must be prepared to move 1 hour after the receipt of the order "Stand To".

6. When on the move there will be a distance of 400 yards between Battalions and 20 yards between Platoons and Companies.
Main roads must be avoided as much as possible.

7. Acknowledge.

A Williams
Major,
Brigade Major, 157th Infantry Brigade.

28th June, 1916.

H.Q 157 Infy Bde
Vol 4

On His Majesty's Service

SECRET

D. A. G.,

3rd Echelon,

Base.

111/34 3 A

111/20 3 A

War Diary

H. Q. 157th Inf Bde

from 1st – 31st July 1918

Vol III

Original Copy

July 31st 1918

J. W. Deas Capt
for Brigade Major
157th Inf Bde

Instructions regarding War Diaries and Intelligence Summaries are contained in F. S. Regs., Part II. and the Staff Manual respectively. Title pages will be prepared in manuscript.

Confidential
Vol III

WAR DIARY
or
INTELLIGENCE SUMMARY.
(Erase heading not required.)

15[7]th Inf Bde

Army Form C. 2118.

(H1)

Place	Date	Hour	Summary of Events and Information	Remarks and references to Appendices
Vimy Ridge (Chalk ...)	1/7		Defensive patrols were sent out last night by both batts but no enemy were seen or heard. Harrassing fire was carried out by artillery and 6" T. M's last night.	
			Instructions regarding Field Artillery barrage and Heavy Artillery S O S points were issued to all concerned together with position of Light Trench Mortars and location and barrage of 6" Newtons (Appendix I)	Appendix I
			Brigade Major appointed G S O 2 30th Division and instructed to join this Division forthwith. Captain A C Deas 3rd A&SH takes on the duty temporarily of acting Brigade Major.	
	2/7		Daylight patrol of 6th H L I under 2 Lt P A E. McCracken and 1 Scout left our lines at 1600 on 30th June and took up a position on the face of the ridge about T22 c. 2 2. Good observation into the enemy line was obtained. Information gained:- Enemy wire - single wire about 200 yds in advance of front line in T4a with trip wire at intervals. 2 or 3 belts immediately in front of trench - outer belt in good condition and very thick inner belts seemed in bad repair. Wire in front of support line beyond the embankment appeared to be good. Patrol returned at 2145 on 1st July	

A C Deas Capt

D. D. & L., London, E.C.
(A8001) Wt. W1771/M2031 750,000 5/17 Sch. 52 Forms/C2118/14

Instructions regarding War Diaries and Intelligence Summaries are contained in F. S. Regs., Part II. and the Staff Manual respectively. Title pages will be prepared in manuscript.

Confidential

Vol III

WAR DIARY
or
INTELLIGENCE SUMMARY.
(Erase heading not required.)

Army Form C. 2118.

157th Inf. Bde

(H 2)

Place	Date	Hour	Summary of Events and Information	Remarks and references to Appendices
Vimy Ridge (Aberdeen Sector)	2/7	2315 1/7	Patrol of 7th H.L.I left our lines at 2315 under 2 Lt. McCormick with 12 men. Enemy patrol of 20 was encountered. Our patrol opened rapid fire killing 8 wounding 5 and taking 2 prisoners.	
		0110	Small raiding party believed to be same as mentioned above attacked one of our posts in T.1? Central. Attack was repulsed. Officer i/c party killed and body brought in and 2 OR taken prisoners wounded one of which has since died. Prisoners belong to 119th Division so relief of the Division believed to have taken place on 30th was incorrect.	MB
			Brig Gen C. D. Hamilton-Moore CMG DSO returned today from leave to U.K and took over command of Brigade Lt Col Anderson CMG DSO returning to 6th H.L.I.	
			Orders were issued for the relief of 6th HLI in Left Sub sector by 5th HLI on 5th July (Appendix II)	Appendix II
	3/7		Patrol went out to try and find and bring in German dead killed last night but found 2 German patrols watching this point and our patrol was forced to withdraw.	
			Orders received from Div that Gas Beam Attack would take place on whole of 1st Army front on night of 5th June if wind favourable. 2000 cylinders to be discharged from the Brigade Sector. Brigade Orders issued on the subject (Appendix iii)	Appendix III

Instructions regarding War Diaries and Intelligence Summaries are contained in F. S. Regs., Part II. and the Staff Manual respectively. Title pages will be prepared in manuscript.

Confidential

Vol III

WAR DIARY
or
INTELLIGENCE SUMMARY.
(Erase heading not required.)

157 Bde Hdqrs

H 3

Army Form C. 2118.

Place	Date	Hour	Summary of Events and Information	Remarks and references to Appendices
Vimy Ridge ([illegible])	4/7		Patrols last night saw no enemy and have nothing to report. Artillery activity normal. Capt. C. S. Sterling-Cookson M.C. K.O.S.B. took over appointment of Bde Major from today.	[illegible]
	5/7		Patrols last night have nothing to report. Owing wind being in wrong direction Gas-Beam attack was postponed. Inter-battalion relief was completed by 1 p.m.	[illegible]
	6/7		Patrols were active last night but could find no trace of the enemy. About 4 p.m. 2 deserters of the 46th R.I.R. came into our lines having crawled across "No Mans Land". They stated they were Poles and were fed up. The Gas Beam attack was again postponed on account of wind being unfavourable.	[illegible]
	7/7		Nothing of interest to report. The usual patrolling took place during the night.	[illegible]
	8/7.		Patrolling as usual, nothing to report.	

D. D. & L., London, E.C.
(A8001) Wt. W1771/M2031 750,000 5/17 Sch. 52 Forms/C2118/14

Army Form C. 2118.

Instructions regarding War Diaries and Intelligence Summaries are contained in F. S. Regs., Part II. and the Staff Manual respectively. Title pages will be prepared in manuscript.

WAR DIARY
or
INTELLIGENCE SUMMARY.
(*Erase heading not required.*)

157th Inf. Bde – (H. 4.)

Place	Date	Hour	Summary of Events and Information	Remarks and references to Appendices
VIMY RIDGE (Chaudiere Section.)		9/7	Usual patrols went out from dusk till dawn, otherwise nothing to report occurred.	[illegible]
		10/7	Nothing to report. Patrols were out as usual by night.	[illegible]
		11/7	Nothing to report. Patrols were out as usual. The wind being favourable ~~the "GAS BEAM ATTACK" took place. There was no retaliation by the enemy.~~ The 6th H.L.I. relieved the 7th H.L.I. in the front line right-subsector	[illegible] ~~App. III~~ App. IV
		12/7.	The Corps Commander Gen. Hunter-Weston visited the Bde. area proceeding to the line at 10.20 am. and leaving the line at 7.45 pm. The "GAS BEAM" took place tonight without any difficulty or retaliation on the part of the enemy – Heavy showers during the day & night –	App. III. [illegible]
		13/7	Nothing to report. The patrols were out as usual – Weather stormy, heavy showers at intervals –	[illegible]
		14/7.	There is nothing of importance to report. Patrolling was carried out as usual. Heavy showers during the night –	[illegible]
		15/7	Patrols were out as usual. Very heavy rain and thunderstorm during the night. Nothing to report –	[illegible]

D. D. & L., London, E.C. (A8001) Wt. W1771/M2031 750,000 5/17 Sch. 52 Forms/C2118/14

Instructions regarding War Diaries and Intelligence Summaries are contained in F. S. Regs., Part II. and the Staff Manual respectively. Title pages will be prepared in manuscript.

WAR DIARY
or
INTELLIGENCE SUMMARY.
(Erase heading not required.) 157th Infy. Bde. H.Qrs. (H.5)

Army Form C. 2118.

Place	Date	Hour	Summary of Events and Information	Remarks and references to Appendices
MERICOURT SECTOR - (chantier) VIMY RIDGE	16/7		Patrols were out as usual, otherwise nothing to report. Showers during the day & night.	
	17/7		The Bde. was relieved by the 155th Bde. in the line. The 157 Bde withdrawing to billets in the Reserve area at St. ELOI. Relief completed by 5.30 pm.	App. V.
MONT ST ELOI.	18/7		Units spent the day bathing and cleaning up.	
"	19/7		Training. Gen. HUNTER-WESTON visited the 5th & 6th H.L.I. at training during the forenoon. Orders received that the Divn. would be relieved starting on 20th by 8. Divn.	
AUCHEL AREA.	20/7		The Bde. was relieved by 23rd Infy. Bde. & moved to AUCHEL AREA, coming into G.H.Q. Reserve, attached XVII Corps for administration, & billeted in XIII Corps area.	App. VI.
"	21/7		Church parades. Reconnoitring of training areas.	
"	22/7		Training.	
"	23/7		Training. The Brigade ordered to hold itself in readiness to move by bus or rail at six hours notice. Rained nearly all day.	App. VII.

D. D. & L., London, E.C. (A8001) Wt. W1771/M2031 750,000 5/17 Sch. 52 Forms C2118/14

Instructions regarding War Diaries and Intelligence Summaries are contained in F. S. Regs., Part II. and the Staff Manual respectively. Title pages will be prepared in manuscript.

WAR DIARY
or
INTELLIGENCE SUMMARY.
(Erase heading not required.)

15th Infy Brigade

H. 6.

Army Form C. 2118.

Place	Date	Hour	Summary of Events and Information	Remarks and references to Appendices
AUCHEL AREA.	24/7		Training – Officers of all units reconnoitred the XIII. Corps back area. Heavy showers during the day.	
"	25/7		Training – Heavy showers during the morning – Reconnoitring of XIII Corps back area.	
"	26/7		Training – Heavy rain during the whole day.	
"	27/7		Training – Heavy showers during the morning	
"	28/7		Church parades. Weather much better.	
	29/7		Warning Order received that Divn will move into line in Arras Sector as part of XVIII Corps who relieve Canadian Corps on night 31st July/1st August. Brigade to move to BARLIN on 30th July by route march. Orders issued for the move (App VIII)	App VIII
	30/7		Brigade commences its move 8 a.m. and were all in BARLIN by 3 p.m. Orders received from Divn that Bde would move MADAGASCAR area tomorrow and Bde orders issued accordingly. Bgd and B.M. visited line held by [illegible] Canadian Bdes. All 3 Bdes of Divn to be in line. 15th Bde in centre. Orders for relief during 1st August issued	App IX App X

D. D. & L., London, E.C. (A8001) Wt. W1771/M2031 750,000 5/17 Sch. 52 Forms/C2118/14

Instructions regarding War Diaries and Intelligence Summaries are contained in F. S. Regs., Part II. and the Staff Manual respectively. Title pages will be prepared in manuscript.

Confidential

WAR DIARY
or
INTELLIGENCE SUMMARY.
(Erase heading not required.)

Army Form C. 2118.

157th Inf Bde
Vol III
(47)

Place	Date	Hour	Summary of Events and Information	Remarks and references to Appendices
Berlin	31/7		Brigade group moved to ~~Berlin~~ Madagascar Area commencing move at 12 midday and arriving about 7 p.m.	[illegible]
			[illegible] Capt	

D. D. & L., London, E.C.
(A8001) Wt. W1771/M2031 750,000 5/17 Sch. 52 Forms C2118/14

Instructions regarding War Diaries and Intelligence Summaries are contained in F. S. Regs., Part II. and the Staff Manual respectively. Title pages will be prepared in manuscript.

Confidential

WAR DIARY
or
INTELLIGENCE SUMMARY.
(Erase heading not required.)

157th Inf Bde

Vol III

(78)

Army Form C. 2118.

Place	Date	Hour	Summary of Events and Information	Remarks and references to Appendices
Boston	31/7		Casualties for the period during which the Brigade was in the line were as follows	

	Officers K	Officers W	Officers M	O.R's K	O.R's W	O.R's M
5th H.L.I	-	-	-	4	12	-
6th H.L.I	1	2	-	4	5	1
7th H.L.I	-	-	-	-	10	-
157 L.T.M.B	-	-	-	-	-	-
	1	2	-	8	27	1

[signature] Capt.

D. D. & L., London, E.C.
(A8004) Wt. W1771/M2031 750,000 5/17 Sch. 52 Forms/C2118/14

O. C.,   Appendix I

=====================

1.   Herewith tracing showing
          (a) Field Artillery Barrage.
          (b) Heavy Artillery S.O.S. Points.
        Also Instructions re the Field Artillery Barrage.
These should be meantime, attached to the defence scheme understood to be in your possession.

2.   It is hoped shortly to issue a new defence scheme when tracings and instructions mentioned above will be incorporated in same.

3.   Attached please find also list of 6" Newton Mortars with S.O.S. Points.

Major,
Brigade Major, 157th Infantry Brigade.

~~30th June~~, 1918.
1st July

NEWTON MORTARS.

No. of Bty.	No. of Emplacement.	Coordinate of Emplacement.	S.O.S. Line
Y/52	Y 5	T.20.c.20.10.	
	Y 6	T.20.c.15.30.	
	Y 7	T.13.b.48.35.	On line T.8.d.0.0. – T.14.central – T.15.c.0.0.
	Y 8	T.13.b.65.70.	
	Y 12 Y 13	T.19.b.20.50.	

= = = = = = = = = = = = = .

A P P E N D I X

Instructions Re. Field Artillery Barrage.

1. There will be 2 S.O.S. Barrages to be known as:-

(a) The OUTPOST BARRAGE.
(b) The BLACK BARRAGE.

The detail of these barrages are shown in the attached tracing " ".

2. There will be 2 different procedures in replying to an an S.O.S. Signal or message.

(a) <u>In Normal times</u>

The OUTPOST Barrage will be fired as follows:-

2 minutes INTENSE.
5 minutes RAPID.
8 minutes NORMAL.

After which fire will depend on the situation.

(b) <u>After the order "MAN BATTLE STATIONS" has been issued</u>

The OUTPOST Barrage will be fired as follows:-

10 minutes INTENSE.
10 minutes RAPID, during which barrage will roll forward 500 yards at the rate of 100 yards per 2 minutes and then jump back to original line for 2 minutes INTENSE followed by 8 minutes NORMAL.

After this fire will be controlled according to the situation.

On the Barrage coming back to the BLACKLINE, a similar 30 minutes burst will be fired.

3. The BLACK BARRAGE will not be fired till a definite S.O.S. call from the BLACK LINE is received. On this call being received the BLACK Barrage will be fired on the whole Divisional Front.

Pending the introduction of a distinctive signal, this call will be a message "S.O.S. BLACK".

4. In order to ensure continuity of fire along the whole front, the following procedure will be adopted until it is known that the fire of the flank Divisions has also been brought back.

2 of the guns superimposed on the right and left flanks will be used to connect the right and left points of the BLACK Barrage with the Right and left points of the OUTPOST Barrage.

5. The barrage will not be brought back from the BLACK Line to the BROWN LINE except by order of the G.O.C., Division.

Major,
Brigade Major, 157th Infantry Brigade.

30th June, 1918.

Appendix D

S E C R E T. Copy No....11......

157th Infantry Brigade Order No. 106.

2nd July, 1918.

1. 5th H. L. I. will relieve the 6th H. L . I. in the Left Sub-Section of the Brigade Section on 5th Julym 1918.
After relief 6th H. LL. I. will take over same dispositions as 5th H. L. I.

2. The relief will take place during daylight and in view of special operation should commence immediately after Breakfast and must be completed by 2 p.m.
Not more than 2 platoons of each Company of relieving Battn should be on the move in the open at the same time. Platoons will move in Sections at not less than 100 yards interval.

3. Details of relief will be arranged by Os.C. concerned. The usual observers, scouts, etc.. of reserve Battn should proceed to the line 24 hours in advance.

4. All trench maps, stores, log-booksetc., will be handed over.

5. Completion of relief will be wired "Priority" to Brigade Headquarters using the code word GLADYS.

6. Acknowledge.

Captain,
A/Brigade Major, 157th Infantry Brigade.

Issued at 10-30 PM

Copy No. 1 to 5th H. LL. I.
2 6th H. L. I.
3 7th H. L. I.
4 157th L. T. M. Bty.
5 Hqrs 52nd M.G. Battn.
6 Hqrs Artillery.
7 2nd Lowland Field Amb.
8 Hqrs 52nd Division.
9 Hqrs 155th Inf. Bde.
10 Hqrs. 60th Inf. Bde.
11)
12) War Diary.
13 File.

S E C R E T Copy No. 13

157th Infantry Brigade Order No. 110 ~~107~~.

Appendix III

Ref (Map 1/20,000 MAROEUIL.
(Attached Sketch.

3rd. July, 1918.

1. A Gas Beam attack will be carried out on the First Army Front on the night 5th/6th July, or on the first night after upon which the wind is favourable. 'O' Special Coy. R.E., will be in charge of the operation on the Divisional Front.

The cylinders can be discharged in any wind between W.N.W. and S.W. of velocity not less than 6 m.p.h.

2. On the Divisional Front Gas will be discharged from Nos.5 and 6 Railheads, (shown on attached Map) on the Mont Foret and Caribec Lines as follows -

Line.	Base	Power Heads	Discharge Points.	Trucks.	Cylinders
5.	TERRITORIAL. (N. of ECURIE).	T.21.a.3.9.	T.16.d.	50	1050
6.	TERRITORIAL.	T.14.b.1.9.	T.9.b.	50	1050

3. (a) The Infantry pushing parties will be furnished by 6th H.L.I. Four hundred men (exclusive of Officers and N.C.Os.) will be required.

(b) This personnel will be divided into 2 parties i.e., Detachment A and Detachment B, both Detachments to be employed in pushing trucks from the POWER HEADS to the DISCHARGE POINTS and in pulling them back again after the discharge.

(c) Both Detachment A and Detachment B will each be organized into 10 pushing parties numbered 1 to 10, each of 20 men exclusive of N.C.Os. with a senior ~~officer~~ N.C.O. in charge of each of the 10 parties One Officer will be in charge of every 2 parties and a Senior Officer in charge of Detachment A and of Detachment B.

Number of personnel required therefore will be:-

1 Senior Officer
5 Officers.
10 Senior N.C.Os.
200 Men.

Total, 6 Officers, 10 N.C.Os., 200 men for each Detachment.
Total for both Detachments,
12 Officers, 20 N.C.Os., 400 men.

(d) These parties must be very carefully organized, paraded beforehand, numbered and steps taken to ensure that every N.C.O. and man knows to which party he belongs and what his duties are.

Each man should have a label tied on to his Box Respirator bearing the number of the party to which he belongs or else the Box Respirator should have the number chalked on to it.

Strict discipline must be maintained, there must be no noise of any sort made by the men. All orders must be given in a low voice.

The trucks must be moved as silently as possible and their pace checked on declines

(e) One O.R. of "O" Special Coy R.E., will proceed and return with every truck.

4. Detachment A will work on line No.5, and Detachment B on line No.6.

From the two Power Heads trucks will be pushed up to the Discharge Points, each party of 30 men pushing a train of 5 trucks.

After pushing the trucks to the Discharge Points pushing parties will be withdrawn to a suitable trench system in the vicinity and there await the completion of the Discharge.

The O.C., 6th H.L.I. will have these places reconnoitred beforehand and made known to all officers in charge of parties.

After completion of Discharge the parties organized as before will pull (not push) the trucks containing the empty cylinders back to the Power Heads. They will wear their Box Respirators on the return journey.

The men of the Special Coy R.E., have been warned that they are not to give orders or advice to the Infantry pushing parties as to removing their Respirators.

5. Detachments A & B will report to Officers of "O" Special Coy., R.E. at their respective Power Heads (vide para 2), at 1045 p.m. on the night of the operation.

The trains will arrive at 11 p.m.

6. In the event of a cylinder being hit by hostile fire, all ranks will adjust Respirators but will not ring bells or sound Klaxon Horns. The danger will in any case be very local.

7. (a) Artillery action which might cause retaliation will be avoided otherwise artillery and M.G. fire will be normal.

(b) The O.C., 5th and 7th H.L.I., will each arrange for a Lewis Gun under an officer to be at the Discharge Point in each of the areas to cover the noise of the Discharge.

These guns should be in position at 11 p.m. and fire occasional short bursts. They will be withdrawn one hour after the trucks have left the Discharge Point.

If the officer hears any noise being made by the trucks moving he will order short bursts of fire to cover the noise.

Care must be taken not to draw the enemy's attention to the fact that anything unusual is going on.

(c) On the arrival of the first trucks at the Discharge Points the O.C. A and B Detachments will each arrange for a few sentry groups to be posted immediately on the enemy's side of the Discharge Point to afford local protection while the preparations for the discharge of the Gas are being made.

These sentry groups must be withdrawn to a place of safety just before ZERO Hour. They will be withdrawn under orders of the O.C. A & B Detachments respectively.

8. (a) The areas which must be clear of troops before Zero are marked RED on attached map. Those in which the Box Respirator must be worn are marked GREEN. Box Respirators should be worn from Zero - 2 minutes until orders for their removal are given by an Officer. This should not be given until Zero plus 30 minutes and then only if the trench system is reported clear of Gas.

(b) The Divisional Gas Officer assisted by the anti-gas personnel of Brigade and Battalions should make arrangements for;

(i) Clearing Dug-outs and cellars by means of fires etc., immediately after completion of Dischgrge.
(ii) Clearing trenches, saps etc., by means of Flappers etc immediately after completion of Discharge.
(iii) Troops should not reoccupy Trenches etc., until qualified anti-gas personnel have declared them to be safe.

These orders require most careful attention and C.Os. must satisfy themselves that the arrangements made by their Anti-Gas personnel/

personnel are satisfactory and issue orders that any instructions issued by the latter are to be carried out.

Special care must be taken to see that all Blankets of protected dugouts are let down prior to the discharge and that every dugout in the danger area is carefully cleared of gas after the discharge.

Company Commanders must work in cooperation with Anti-Gas personnel so that they may know when to give orders for the removal of Respirators and when to re-occupy trenches dugouts, etc

9. (a) A decision will be made by higher authority at 1 p.m. on 5th July (or succeeding days) as to whether the operation shall take place and all concerned will be notified as early as possible.

(b) The following code will be used:-

Operation will take place to-night.	JAPAN.
Operation postponed.	SPAIN.
Cancel operation previously ordered	RUSSIA.

10. Zero Hour will be at 1230 a.m. or as soon after as the trucks are reported to be in position.

The order for discharge will be given by O?C., Special Coys., R.E., First Army from Corps Heavy Artillery Exchange, NEUVILLE ST. VAAST, A.3.d.4.8. (51.B.N.W.)

He will be in telephonic communication with the Discharge Points

Battalions in the line in the Left Section will keep Left Section Hqrs., informed of the progress of the operation. These reports will be forwarded to Divisional Hqrs.

Frequent reports will be sent in by Battalions after 11 p.m. until the Discharge takes place.

11. The Brigade Signalling Officer will arrange to send out Signal time to O.C. Battalions at 7 p.m. on July 5th (and daily thereafter if required)

12. The O.C., 2nd L.F.A., will arrange for an officer with the necessary personnel and appliances for treating Gas cases to report to the O.C., A and B Parties at their respective Power Stations, and to accompany them until the completion of the operation, i.e. on returning to the Power Station again.

13. On the day fixed for the operation, the Light Railways will be closed to ammunition and supplies from 12 noon unless information is received that the operation is postponed. 2 days ammunition and supplies will therefore be taken up on 4th July. There will thus be 1 days supply in hand for use on the day following the night of the operation. Only normal transport will be employed on the night of the operation in distributing supplies.

14. ACKNOWLEDGE.

[signature]

Captain,
A/Brigade Major, 157th Infantry Brigade.

Issued at 3-30 P.m.

Copies No. 1 to 5th H. L. I.
2 6th H. L. I.
3 7th H. L. I.
4 157th L.T.M. Bty.
5. R. E.
6 155th Inf. Bde.
7 Hqrs. 60th Inf. Bde.

Copy No. 8 O.C., 2nd L.F.A.
9 Signalling Officer
10 Divnl. G. C.
11 Bde Gas Officer.
12 Staff Captain.
13)
14) War Diary.
15. File.
16. HQ 52nd Divn.

SECRET.   Copy No. 9

157th Infantry Brigade Administrative Instructions
No. 106.

3rd, July, 1918.

1. Reference 157th Brigade Order No. 110 dated 3rd. July.

Two days rations will be ~~issued~~ sent up to the Brigade on the night of 4/5th July, in preparation for the Gas beam Attack on the night 5/6th July.

2. The extra days rations thus sent up will accordingly be consumed during the 24 hours following the Gas Attack.

3. Should the attack be postponed, however, rations will be sent up nightly from transport lines as usual, until the night of attack, and the extra days rations will be kept for the day following the attack.

4. Rations will be issued daily as usual and taken to the Transport lines so that in the event of any postponment, rations will be available to be sent up at short notice.

5. Battalions and Transport Officers will be notified by Brigade each day if, owing to postponment rations are to be sent up as usual.

The code word "RATIONS" will be used.

6. ACKNOWLEDGE.

H M Hewison
Captain,
Staff Captain, 157th Infantry Brigade.

Issued at 1530 on 3/7/18.

Copies No. 1 to 5th H. L. I.
2 6th H. L. I.
3 7th H. L. I.
4 157th L. T. M. Bty.
5 52nd M.G. Battn.
6 2nd L. F. A.
7 B.G.C.
8)
9) War Diary.
10 File.

App IV

SECRET. Copy No. 11

Brigade Order No.111. 10/7/18.

1. The 6th H.L.I. will relieve the 7th H.L.I. in the RIGHT Sub-sector on 11th July, 1918. On relief, the 7th H.L.I. will take over the same dispositions as those at present held by the 6th H.L.I.

2. In view of the "Gas Beam Attack" which is ordered to take place, the Relief will commence immediately after breakfast and be completed by 2p.m.

3. All orders and instructions with reference to the "GAS BEAM ATTACK" will be handed over to O.C. 7th H.L.I. who will be prepared to furnish the "pushing parties" from the 11th July.

4. Details of Relief will be arranged between the C.O.s concerned.

5. Trench stores, log books, special maps and plans will be handed over.

6. Completion of Relief will be wired to Brigade H.Q. by the code word "PLANET".

7. ACKNOWLEDGE.

J.S. Stirling Cookson
Captain,
Brigade Major.

Issued at 10 am

Copy No. 1 to 5th H.L.I.		Copy No. 8 to Left Group H.G. Bn.	
2	6th H.L.I.	9	156th Inf. Bde.
3	7th H.L.I.	10	60th Brigade.
4	157th L.T.M.B.	11	War Diary.
5	2nd L.F.A.	12	War Diary.
6	Divn. H.Q.	13	File.
7	Left Group Arty.		

D E F E N C E   S C H E M E.

Left Section   52nd Division.

M E R I C O U R T   S E C T O R.

157th Infantry Brigade.

INDEX.

Appendices.

Maps.

157th Infantry Brigade Defence Scheme.

Left Section 52nd Divisional Sector.

Ref. Map MAROEUIL & ST. HAZAIRE RIVER, 1/20,000.

1. Boundaries.

On the SOUTH.

The ACHEVILLE Road (inclusive) - NEW BRUNSWICK Road (inclusive) as far as T.20.c.9.1. - thence to CEMETRY T.25.d.6.9. (exclusive) - Thence to BOIS DU GOULOT at T.25.c.0.0. and thence due WEST along the grid line.

On the NORTH.

The junction of BILLY BURKE and BETTY Trenches (inclusive) WESTWARD along the grid line to T.2.c.3.0. - T.1.d.7.3. - Junction RED Trench and LENS - ARRAS Road (inclusive) Thence RED Trench and CYRIL Trench (both exclusive) - S.11.c.0.4. - S.16.c.0.0. - S.19.b.0.0.

2. General Description of Area.

(a) The VIMY RIDGE from the SCARPE Valley to that of the SOUCHEZ River runs approximately N.N.W., and S.S.E., and is the dominating tactical feature of the area.
Its length from POINT du JOUR on the ST LAURENT - BLANGY - GRAVELLE Road is 6½ miles, its height throughout more than 100 metres above sea level and more than 40 above the level of the Plain to the Eastward.
The highest point of the RIDGE, HILL 145 (S.16.c.) falls just within the Northern Boundary of the Brigade Section, but the crest rises to about 140 metres at two other places also, i.e., the ECOLE COMMUNE (S.22.d.) and THELUS MILL (A.6.central). Those two latter are partially separated on the EAST by the BOIS DE BONVAL RE-ENTRANT (S.30.c.) which comes just within the SOUTHERN Boundary of the Section.

(b) The RIDGE commands a very extensive view both over the plain between and beyond ARRAS and LENS to the EAST and over the more undulating and higher ground to the WEST.

(c) The EASTERN slope of the RIDGE is very steep and from it two distinct Spurs run out into that part of the gently rolling plain stretching between ARRAS and LENS, which is in this Section.
These two Spurs are

(i) The VIMY SPUR. Over 60 metres in height, on which stands PETIT VIMY and VIMY Villages, runs first almost due EAST for 2,500 yards and then at CANADA & KURTON Trenches turns N.E. pointing to between MERICOURT & AVION. The knoll on which the ruins of VIMY stand covers the BOIS de BONVAL.

(ii) The CHAUDIERE SPUR. which has its highest ground at Hill 65 immediately WEST of the BOIS de la CHAUDIERE and the LENS - ARRAS Railway Embankment.

(d) Just outside the NORTHERN and SOUTHERN Boundaries of this Section there are two other Spurs i.e., the HIRONDELLE and the HUDSON SPURS respectively. The former runs from GIVENCHY to the N.W. corner of AVION and flanks the plain which lies between the VIMY RIDGE on the S.W. and the line AVION - ACHEVILLE on the N.E. The latter is the HUDSON SPUR

An advance along either of the SPURS mentioned in (i) & (ii) i.e., the VIMY or CHAUDIERE SPURS would afford the enemy support for an advance on similar spurs on either flank and so increase his chances of success in an operation against the VIMY RIDGE. Both SPURS have been strongly organized.

(e) Our Outpost Line of observation is situated EAST of the foot of the RIDGE and at a distance of about 3,000 to 4,000 yards from it; while the enemy's front line varies from about 800 yards on the RIGHT to 1,500 yards in the CENTRE, ~~from our Outpost Line~~, and about 1,000 yards on the LEFT from our Outpost Line of Observation.

(f) Two other important features must be noted, they are such marked lines as the enemy's customary tactics make it likely he will follow in an advance.

(i) The main LENS - ARRAS Road which crosses the VIMY Ridge immediately NORTH of the BONVAL re-entrant.

(ii) Approximately parallel with this road and about 1,000 Yards East of it is the Embankment of the LENS - ARRAS Railway.

3. Organization of Section.

The Brigade Section, called the CHAUDIERE Section is divided into three areas. These areas are as follows: the boundaries being shown in Appendix 1 and map "A".

(a) TOAST AREA	The Right Half of the Front Line; garrisoned by "A" Battalion.
(b) BETTY AREA.	The LEFT half of the Front Line; garrisoned by "B" Battalion.
(c) The VIMY - CHAUDIERE AREA.	The SECOND LINE; garrisoned by "C" Battalion.

4. Zones of Defence.

(a) The Section is divided into two Zones of Defence:-

(i) The OUTPOST ZONE. which includes the Outpost Line of Observation i.e., The MONTREAL - QUEBEC - LILY ELSIE - BILLIE BURKE Line and the Outpost Line of Supports which is the ~~NE~~ BRUNSWICK - TEDDIE GERRARD - KEANE Line.

(ii) The BATTLE ZONE. which comprises;- The MAIN LINE OF RESISTANCE (Black Line) which runs along the CANADA - GERTIE - JAMES - HAYTER - GLADYS - DARTMOUTH. Behind the Main Line of Resistance is the BROWN LINE (FARBUS - VIMY - LIEVIN LINE). In rear of the BROWN LINE is the strong point of VIMY Village.

(b) The garrisons of the MIAN LINE OF RESISTANCE (BLACK LINE); of the BROWN LINE and of VIMY BASTION will all fight to the last.
There will be no retirement from them, nor will they be reinforced from rear to front.

5. PRINCIPLES OF DEFENCE.

In order to provent local penetration developing into a break through, it is not only considered necessary to be distributed in depth but also to have rear lines and systems permanently garrisoned during the fight, so that the penetration may be localised and prevented from spreading.

The best method to affect this is to allot to each Battn. an area, which the Battalion Commander must be prepared to hold at all costs with his own Battalion without assiatance from outside. In other words he must fight it out to the last in that area and with his own resources. Each Battalion Commander will in turn sub-divide his area into Company and Platoon areas.

If one of these areas is overwhelmed, the enemy ought not to be ablo to make any headway so long as the localities in rear and on either flank hold out. The enemy will thus find himself in a pocket and can be dealt with later.

There must be no reinforcing fromthe rear locality to a a forward one, otherwise rear lines will be depleted of their garrisons and a further penetration may take place.

Every effort will be made to persuade the enemy that the OUTPOST LINE of OBSERVATION is the BATTLE LINE. To this end, at least 1 section per Coy., in Front Line will be sent to the LINE of OBSERVATION to repair any damage done to the trench, throw up a little bit of new earth and to fire their five rounds of S.A.A. from its vicinity in order to give the impression to the enemy that this trench is still occupied.

In order to secure maintenance of touch with the RIGHT BRIGADE of the 20th Division on the LEFT of this Section, combined Posts of 1 section from each Brigade under a Sergt., are established at the following points;-

(a) T.2.c.2.4. Trench junction in PARTRIDGE TRENCH
(b) S.12.b.9.4. Crossing of RED TRENCH and LENS - ARRAS ROAD.

Both these posts are under B.G.C. Right Brigade 20th Division and Commanded by a Sergeant in that Division.

Both Sections are furnished by the LEFT FRONT Battalion.

6. TROOPS.

The troops available for this Section are:-

1 Infantry Brigade (3 Battalions)
1 Light Trench Mortar Battery.

In addition but not under the immediate orders of the Brigade Commander, there are:-

6. TROOPS. (Contd).

6 six inch Newton Mortars.
24 Machine Guns under Divisional Machine Gun Officer
(Section in Brigade Reserve at S.23.b.7.5.)
1 Composite Brigade R.F.A. of 4, 18 Pdr Batteries and 2, 4.5" How. Batteries (H.Q. Left Group R.F.A. are situated at Infantry Brigade Hqrs).
% 2 Heavy Batteries (60 Pdrs).
% 4 Siege Batteries
Anti-Tank defence is provided by 3 15 Pdr Guns, situated at:-

T.19.b.77.75.
T.19.c.75.95.
T.26.a.58.15.

In addition all the Machine Guns in the Section are provided with at least 1 Belt of armour piercing bullets.

% These are not available exclusively for Defence of LEFT BRIGADE Section Front but for the whole Divisional Sector

There is a F.A. Liaison Officer attached to each Battn. in the Line.

7. DISPOSITION OF THE TROOPS.
Shown on Map "E".

(a) The two Battalions holding the TOAST and BETTY Areas are responsible for the Defence of the MAIN LINE of RESISTANCE (BLACK LINE).
Each Battalion has four Companies in the Line.
Each Company has 2 Platoons (less 2 Sections) forward in the OUTPOST LINE od SUPPORT.
Each Platoon in the OUTPOST LINE OF SUPPORT having 1 section in the OUTPOST LINE of OBSERVATION, except in the case of the 2 centre Companies of the LEFT Battalion, which have no men in the line of OBSERVATION, but 2 full platoons in the OUTPOST LINE of SUPPORTS.

The Sections in the LINE OF OBSERVATION are in this Line by day and by night, each Section posting a double sentry with S.O.S. Signal Rocket.
All withdraw to the OUTPOST LINE of SUPPORTS after the S.O.S. Rocket is sent up and responded to by the barrage fire in case of attack.

(b) The Battalion holding the second line of RESISTANCE (BROWN LINE) is, owing to the great depth of the section and owing to the fact of having only 3 Battalions to put into it, distributed differently from those in the BLACK LINE, it being on a wider front.

Two Companies are in the VIMY LOCALITY and BROWN LINE as far as its junction with the ARRAS - LENS Road (inclusive) Each Company has 3 Platoons in the line and 1 Platoon in Support.

One/-

One Company less 1 Platoon is in the Chaudiere locality (GLACE TRENCH) with 1 of its platoons in support.
The 4th Company is in the BROWN LINE with 3 Platoons in the line and one in support.
The 4th Platoon of the CHAUDIERE Company is in the BROWN LINE immediately EAST of the LENS - ARRAS Road.
No troops in this second Line of Resistance (BROWN LINE) are available to reinforce the MAIN LINE OF RESISTANCE (BLACK LINE) or forward of it, except as provided for in the event of a raid by the enemy.

8. POLICY AGAINST RAIDS.

(a) To deal with small raids of 50 men or less, Company Commanders of the two front Battalions will each detail one of their Platoons in the BLACK LINE as a counter-attach Platoon to restore the situation.
The O.C. of this platoon must make himself thoroughly acquainted with all the ground and trenches from which a counter-attack might likely have to be made and should prepare schemes and practice them with all ranks of his Platoon.

(b) Large Raids.-

To deal with a larger raid or minor attack, the Company of the Reserve Battalion which holds the NORTHERN Flank of the VIMY Locality and the BROWN LINE (to the ARRAS Road), together with the support platoon of the second Company in the VIMY Locality, will be available for counter-attack to restore the situation in the BLACK LINE and the OUTPOST ZONE forward of the BLACK LINE.
It will only be so used by the Reserve Battalion Commander on an Order from the G.O.C., Brigade.
When this Company is withdrawn from VIMY Locality its place will be at once taken by a support platoon in the CHAUDIERE Locality.

9. MACHINE GUNS.

There are 24 in the Section; of these 20 are under the orders of the Divisional M.G. Officer and 4 at the disposal of the G.O.C. Brigade.
The guns are distributed in depth and placed in pairs, situated generally in open emplacements.
For detailed positions and S.O.S. Line see Map "C".

10. LIGHT TRENCH MORTARS.

See map "C" for dispositions.

11. ARTILLERY.

For action of Artillery see Appendix 11.

12. THE S.O.S.

(a) The Signal at present is a Number 32 Rifle Grenade -"GREEN over GREEN over GREEN".

(b) The following are the arrangements for sending up or repeating the S.O.S. Signal;-

(i) By S.O.S. Rocket from Observation Line and Relay Posts in rear.
(ii) By S.O.S. Electric Alarm ~~Horn~~ GONG, located at T.22.d.9.4.
(iii) By Telephone from Coy. H.Q. to Battn H.Q.
(iv) By Power Buzzer.)
(v) By Cable.) From Battn. H.Q.
(vi) By Lamp or Helio.)
(vii) By Pigeon.
(viii) By Runners through Relay Posts.

(c) All Platoon and Section Commanders and sentries detailed for the purpose are authorised to send up the S.O.S. Rocket.

All "Look-out" men in and in advance of the MAIN LINE OF RESISTANCE are armed with Rifle Grenades S.O.S. Rockets.

Each Company and Battalion H.Q. furnishes a Relay Rocket Post.

There are Relay Rocket Posts in the BROWN LINE, at all Company and Battalion H.Q. and in addition special sentries to take up and repeat the signals, and one at Advanced Brigade H.Q. in the STAUBWASSER WEG.

Also Artillery S.O.S. Posts on VIMY RIDGE.

The S.O.S. Relay Posts will repeat the S.O.S. Signal when fired from the forward area or when the enemy's Infantry is seen advancing. When a rocket is fired, a runner is at once sent to the nearest Relay Post or Company H.Q. from where it is transmitted by telephone to Battalion, Brigade and Artillery H.Q.

Runners from Company H.Q. also take the messgge to Battalion H.Q. from where it is transmitted to Brigade H.Q. over the buried Cable or by Power Buzzer.

There is a possibility that the Observation Line might be surprised and overwhelmed and thus be unable to send up the S.O.S. Signal. It must therefore be made clear to all sentries in rear that should they see the hostile Infantry advancing in force, they must cause the S.O.S. Rocket to be fired without waiting to see it fired from the front.

(d) The S.O.S. electric gong is situated in a dug-out at T.22.d.9.4. and when the lever is pulled, sounds the gong at Brigade H.Q.

The personnel for operating it is found from the Battalion occupying the TOAST Area.

13. ACTION IN CASE OF ATTACK.

(a) When an attack is considered immenent "Prepare for Action" will be sent out to all concerned, when working parties will be cancelled and any troops not in their actual Battle positions will move to them.

(b) In case of surprise attack, working parties will report themselves to the nearest Infantry Commander who should inform Brigade H.Q. of the presence of these parties.

13. (contd.)

(c) Permanent garrisons of the two lines of resistance are to fight it out to the last.

The ground between the systems is to be fought for just as much as the systems themselves.

Every inch of the ground in the area is to be fought for.

(d) Localities are not to be given up because their flanks have been turned.

If local penetration takes place and garrisons of othe parts of the line hold out, the enemy will only find himself in a pocket and can then be dealt with later.

14. PROBABLE ENEMY ACTION.

(a) An attack may take any of the following forms:-

(i) A small raid by a Coy. or less.
(ii) A large raid by a Battalion or more.
(iii) A surprise general attack without any preliminary bombardment, tanks being used against the wire and infantry co-operating with them.
(iv) A general attack in mass on a large frontage, preceded by an intense but short (three to four hours) bombardment.

15. ACTION TO MEET ABOVE.

(a) To meet these two forms of raid, the S.O.S. barrage and the reserves in the hands of the Coy. Commanders, should be sufficient to deal with them. Should this not be sufficient in the case of the large raid, the troops occupying the BROWN LINE may be used under orders of the G.O.C. Section only.

A surprise attack could only be of limited application.

A general mass attack may be considered as coming:-

Frontally.
From the NORTH.
From the SOUTH.

(b) Action against FRONTAL ATTACK.

It is unlikely that the enemy will make a direct attack against the front of this position in the initial stages of an offensive: but should he obtain any success either NORTH or SOUTH of this area, he would probably try to confirm his success by pushing in against our front.

The front of the Section is too great to allow of the retention of an infantry reserve by the Brigade Commander or the C.O.s of Battalions.

It is, in any case, more important that Coys. should have platoons available for immediate counter attack.

15. (b) (contd.)

Troops must fight it out in their own areas; there are defended localities behind them, and if such localities are held, penetration between them by bodies of the enemy will not be able to make progress.

The Divisional Reserve (1 Infantry Bde. & 1 M.G. Coy.) in the event of a break-through by the enemy, id available for use by the G.O.C. Division, either for deliberate counter-attack ob to occupy the GREEN LINE, ECURIE, or PADDOCK SWITCHES.

(c) Action against FLANK ATTACKS.

To check a break-through by the enemy on the NORTH or an advance between the HIRONDELLE and CHAUDIERE SPURS, the line of PICTOU-GLASS - BLIGHTY Trenches should be held.

In the event of penetration SOUTH of the area, The defended localities of CANADA - KURTON - VIMY and part of GRAND TRUNK Trench will form a Defensive Flank.

16. ANTI-AIRCRAFT DEFENCE.

Lewis guns for defence, primarily for defence against low-flying enemy air-craft, are organised in three lines, each of four guns.

Line.	Co-ordinate.	Unit.
OUTPOST	T.16.c.85.25.	Right Battn.
"	T.15.b.60.55.	" "
"	T.15.a.8.8.	" "
"	T.8.a.8.5.	Left Battn.
BLACK	T.20.a.8.9.	Right Battn.
"	T.13.b.4.2.	Left Battn.
	T.13.b.8.7.	" "
	T.7.b.1.1.	" "
BROWN.	T.20.c.20.15.	Reserve Battn.
"	S.24.b.7.0.	" "
"	S.24.c.2.0.	" "
"	S.17.b.2.4.	" "

17. ADMINISTRATIVE ARRANGEMENTS.

SUPPLY SYSTEM.

(a) RATIONS.

Refilling Point, LEADLEY SIDING (A.2.c.5.9.)

Rations are drawn at 7.30 a.m. and delivered to the Transport Lines at ROSS & DALY CAMPS (F.11.b.9.2., by the Divisional Train.

METHOD OF FORWARDING TO UNITS.

RIGHT BATTN. IN FRONT LINE.

For 4 Companies	By Light Railway to CANADA DUMP (T.20.b.6.3.)
For Battn. Hqrs.	NEW BRUNSWICK (T.25.b.5.9.)

LEFT BATTN. IN FRONT LINE.

For Hqrs. and 4 Companies.	By Light Railway to VICTORIA DUMP (T.13.b.3.5.)

2nd LINE BATTALION.

Hqrs. and 2 Companies.	By Light Railway to CAYUGA DUMP (T.24.c.6.8.) or by Limber up the LENS ROAD.
1 Company.	By Light Railway to KEMP (T.25.a.4.8.)
1 Company.	By Light Railway to NEW BRUNSWICK (T.20.c.2.2.)

L.T.M. Battery.

By Light Railway to VICTORIA DUMP. (T.13.b.3.5.)

BRIGADE HQRS. By Limber.

Note. Rations forwarded by Light Railway must be loaded on Trucks at ZIVY Station by 7.30 p.m.

(b) WATER.

Water is supplied by Pipe Line in the trenches

MONT FORET SYSTEM. (RIGHT FRONT BATTN.)

T.15.b.7.6.	3	400 Gallon Tanks.
T.16.c.5.8.	3	" " "
T.16.c.8.2.	2	" " "
T.16.d.2.7.	3	" " "
T.16.b.7.0.	3	" " "

(b) WATER. (Contd).

GIVENCHY MAIN. (LEFT FRONT BATTN.)

S.12.c.1.6.	W.B.F. 12 Taps.
S.12.b.8.5.	2 400 Gallin Tanks.
T.8.a.0.0.	1 400 Gallon Tank.
T.8.a.7.8.	4 200 Gallin Tanks.
T.8.d.5.6.	4 200 Gallon Tanks.

VIMY.

S.18.c.9.3.	2 S. P.
S.24.c.2.0.	2 200 Gallon Tanks.
T.20.c.3.1.	2 400 Gallon Tanks.

(c) R SERVE RATIONS.

Reserve Rations are held at the following points.

For RIGHT LINE BATTN. TOAST AREA.

	Biscuits.	P.M.
One Dump (T.21.a.5.5.) containing	12 tins	288 tins

For LEFT LINE BATTN. BETTY AREA.

Two Dumps T.7.d.9.5. Containing	6 tins	144 tins
T.13.b.5.3.	6 "	144 "

BRIGADE RESERVE.

Three Dumps T.20.c.2.2. (1 Coy)	3 tins	72 tins
S.24.d.8.2. (1 Coy)	3 "	72 "
S.24.a.1.1. (2 Coys)	6 "	144 "
"	109 "	2736 "
Total Brigade Reserve.	145	3600

(d) S.A.A., GRENADE, FLARES ETC.

Brigade Ammunition Dumps are situated at the following Points:-

CAYUGA.	(S.24.c.5.7.)	Main Bde. Dump.
CULVERT.	(T.20.c.2.1.)	
PEGGY.	(T.19.b.7.8.)	Forward Dumps
NANAIMO.	(T.13.a.2.4.)	

Ammunition required to replace expenditure is obtained On Divisional Authority from HOOPER'S DUMP and forwarded by Light Railway.

(e) R.E. MATERIAL.

R.E. Material is sent up on application to the affiliated R.E. Coy., from ZIVY R.E. DUMP (A.10.a.4.7.)

(f) STRAGGLERS POSTS.

(f) STRAGGLERS POSTS.

Stragglers Posts are established at the following points, and are manned by personnel found by the A.P.M.

S.11.d.4.2.
S.18.c.9.2.
S.24.b.4.6.
T.19.c.2.5.

(g) BURIAL.

An Advanced Collecting Post is established at T.19.b.4.8.

The Divisional Burial Party collects bodies from this Post and convey them to Burial Ground.

(h) SALVAGE.

Salvage Dumps are situated at:-

VICTORIA	T.13.b.3.5.
CAYUGA.	S.24.c.6.8.
PEGGY.	T.19.b.7.8.

Salvage collected by Battalions is brought to these dumps and sent to Divisional Salvage Dump in returning empty ration wagons. These are arranged for by the Brigade Salvage Party.

th July, 1918.

Brigadier General,

Commanding, 157th Infantry Brigade.

SECRET. FOR INFORMATION OF UNIT COMMANDERS ONLY.

O.C. 5th H.L.I.
6th H.L.I.
7th H.L.I.
157th L.T.M.B.

The following instructions for action are additional to those given in the LEFT SECTION DEFENCE SCHEME issued herewith. They will be handed over with that Scheme personally to the C.O. of the unit which relieves you.

C.S. Stirling Cookson
Captain,
Brigade Major, 157th Infantry Brigade.

1. On receiving certain warning of an attack in force, the order "PREPARE FOR ACTION" is to be issued by the G.O.C., 52nd Division.

2. On receipt of this order the following action will be taken by platoons in, and forward of the OUTPOST LINE OF SUPPORTS i.e. the NEW BRUNSWICK - TEDDIE GERRARD - KEANE LINE.
   (a) One platoon per Company will be withdrawn to a position in support in BLACK LINE, where it will be available for counter-attack. This position may either be a trench, if one exists - or a series of shell holes which should be prepared.
   (b) In three Companies in each front line Battn. one platoon per Company will be withdrawn to strengthen the garrison of the BLACK LINE.

As regards (a) and (b) Company Commanders must not be told beforehand that this procedure is to be adopted, but they may be told that under certain circumstances any one company may have to bring it's two forward platoons back, one to the BLACK LINE and one behind it, as a counter attack platoon.
The Company Commander should therefore earmark one of the two platoons to go into the BLACK LINE and actually reserve fire bays for it, the platoon being frequently practised in taking up this position. The other platoon should similarly be earmarked to go behind the BLACK LINE, and places prepared for and made known to the platoon.

(c) In the remaining Company, one platoon will remain in the BLUE LINE (OUTPOST LINE OF SUPPORTS). It will furnish two observation posts which will push forward about 150 yards into "NO MAN'S LAND", in front of our own wire. Here they will be safe from our own and the enemy's barrage.
Their duty is to send up the S.O.S. Rocket or to warn our troops of the hostile advance, by any means available, and to engage the enemy scouts. They will not withdraw.
The S.O.S. Signal will be repeated from the BLUE and BLACK LINES. These observation posts have been fixed at the following places, and should be made known to the platoons furnishing the posts.

Square	T.10.a.20.60.
"	T.10.a.45.35.
"	T.16.b.15.35.
"	T.17.c.20.75.

The platoon on observation will be relieved every six hours after the "PREPARE FOR ACTION" has been notified.

2. Contd.

(d) In the RIGHT Battalion Sub-Section the Company supplying this Platoon will be the RIGHT CENTRE Company. When in the Observation Line as described above this Platoon will find personnel to man the S.O.S., Electric Alarm Gong in the Test dug-out, TN at T.22.d.9.4., which communicates with Brigade H. . LEFT Section.

In the LEFT Battalion Sub-Section the Company supplying the platoon will be the RIGHT Company.

3. On an S.O.S. message by telephone from BLACK LINE an S.O.S. barrage will be brought down in front of BLACK LINE instead of the Normal Barrage.

APPENDIX I.

Boundaries of Areas.

TOAST AREA.

On the SOUTH. ACHEVILLE - NEW BRUNSWICK Road as far as T.21.c.7.6. thence N.W. to T.20.a.8.6. thence to point 200 yards W. of junction of Embankment and PEGGIE. (incl.)

On the NORTH. By VESTA TILLEY (exclusive) to its junction with TEDDIE GERRARD thence S.W. to T.15.a.0.0. thence S.S.W. to junction of JULIA JAMES with GERTIE (exclusive) to junction of two railway embankments (exclusive) in square T.13.d.

On the WEST. From junction of two railway embankments (exclusive) in square T.13.d. S.E. parralel to, and 200 yards W. of the embankment, to junction of the embankment and PEGGIE. (inclusive).

BETTY AREA.

On the SOUTH. by TOAST AREA.

On the NORTH. From junction of BILLIE BURKE and BETTY Trenches (inclusive) WESTWARDS along grid line to T.2.c.3.0. to T.1.d.7.3. to junction of RED Trench and LENS - ARRAS Road.

On the WEST. From junction of RED Trench and LENS- ARRAS Road S.W. to junction of railway embankment in square T.13.d.

VIMY - LA CHAUDIERE AREA.

On the SOUTH. From T.21.c.7.6. to T.20.c.9. (inclusive) thence to CEMETRY - T.25.d.6.9. (exclusive) - thence to BOIS DU GOULOT at T.25.c.0.0. and thence due W. along grid line.

On the NORTH By junction of RED Trench and LENS- ARRAS Road (Inclusive) along RED Trench and CYRIL Trench (both exclusive) - S.11.c.0.4. - S.16.c.0.0. - S.19.b.0.0.

On the EAST. By TOAST and BETTY Areas.

APPENDIX II.

ACTION OF ARTILLERY. Vide MAP "D".

(a) On the S.O.S. being signalled the OUPOST BARRAGE is put down in front of the OUTPOST LINE of OBSERVATION as shown in Map "D".
Normally this barrage remains down for 15 minutes. If the order "MAN BATTLE STATIONS" has been given, the barrage will roll forward 500 yards, at the rate of 100 yards per 2 minutes and then jump back to the original barrage line, remaining down altogether 30 minutes.

(b) If the S.O.S. is signalled from the BLACK LINE, the OUTPOST BARRAGE ceases and the Barrage marked BLACK (vide Map "D") is put down.
This barrage will roll forward as the OUTPOST BARRAGE did and will also last for 30 minutes.
This barrage will only be put down on a telephone call for S.O.S. BLACK.

(c) Gaps have been purposely left in the artillery barrage for the double purpose of enabling the artillery barrage to be thicker (1 gun to 45 yards on the OUTPOST BARRAGE) than if it were spread over the whole front and also to create lanes which the enemy may try to make his way through These gaps are covered by a Machine Gun Barrage, but C.O.s should warn all ranks to expect the enemy to try to get through the gaps and to therefore train Lewis Guns on to them to thicken up the M.G. Barrage.

(d) Six Medium Trench Mortars (6" Newtons) are available for defence. They are located as shewn in Map "D".

The S.O.S. Lines are shewn on Map "D".

APPENDIX III.

COMMUNICATIONS.

1. Telegraph and telephone.

Battalion Hqrs are in touch with 2 of their Companies by Fuller-phone, the other 2 Companies have "D3" Joined up, but these are only used for S.O.S. work, their messages being delivered either by runner from Battalion H.Q., or from nearest signal office having a Fuller-phone.
All Company lines are in the Buried Route except Line to the LEFT Company of the RESERVE Battn.

2. The three Battalion Hqrs., are situated either in, or alongside the Test Boxes at which their Buried Line to Brigade terminate. Each Front Line Battalion having 2 Lines to Brigade, 1 for Fuller-phone and 1 for Telephone. The Reserve Battalion has 1 Line only to Brigade on which Fuller-phone is worked.

3. Lateral inter-battalion and inter-brigade lines are all on the buried system.

4. Buried Lines run direct to the following units from Brigade Headquarters:-

i.	Divisional Hqrs.	(2 lines)
ii.	Advanced Divisional Hqrs... ...	(1 line)
iii.	Brigade on Right.	(1 line)
iv.	Brigade on Left.	(1 Line)
v.	Right Line Battalion.	(2 Lines)
iv.	Left Line Battalion.	(2 Lines)
iiv.	Reserve Battalion.	(1 Line)
iiiv.	M. G. Company.	(2 Lines)
ix.	Brigade Visual Stn & O.P... ...	(1 Line)
x.	Artillery Brigade...	(1 Line)

5. Brigade is directly connected to its supporting Artillery Brigade.
Each Front Line Battalion has an Artillery Liaison Officer who is connected to his battery direct through them to Artillery Brigade.

6. Outposts are connected to Battalion Hqrs., by buried lines to which "D.3" are joined up for S.O.S. purposes.

VISUAL.

1. Brigade Visual Station is situated at S.23.c.6.6. and is manned by Battalion Signallers. The Station receives daily D.D. messages from all Battalion Hqrs., and Pipes are fixed up so that in an emergency this station can work forward without being noticed by the enemy.

2. Battalions are in touch with their Companies by visual wherever the configuration of the ground allows.

3. The Brigade Visual Station is connected to Brigade Hqrs. by/

3. (Contd).

by Fuller-phone line in the ~~xxxxx~~ buried system.

4. The Divisional Signal Station at MONT ST. ELOI can be picked up from Brigade Headquarters.

W/T and POWER BUZZER

1. Power Buzzers are installed at all Battalion and Brigade Headquarters. In addition the RIGHT LINE and RESERVE Battalions and BRIGADE have Amplifiers. The Reserve Battalion acting as a transmitting station when signals from Front are too weak to be read at Brigade.

2. The Trench Wireless set at Brigade Headquarters is in touch with Division and Lateral Brigades.

3. The W/T and Power Buzzer Stations are worked daily as far as possible to their full capacity.

4. All P.B., and Amplifier Stations are manned by Battalion Signallers.

PIGEONS.

Two Pigeons are sent up daily to Battalion Hqrs., in Front Line for use in emergency. If no such emergency arises, Birds are released with a practice message whenever a fresh pair arrives.

These birds "HOME" to Division and their message is forwarded by Priority telegram.

RUNNERS.

1. Brigade to Units. Four runs per day leave Brigade at fixed times for Battalions and other Units.

Owing to long distances Relay Posts for Runners have been established at fixed points and at Battalion Hqrs.

Each Post consists of 6 men.

No.1 Post at	S.23.c.6.6.	manned by 6 men from Reserve Battn.
No.2. " "	S.24.a.2.0.	" " 2 " from each Battn
No.3. " "	Left Battn H.Q.	" " Left Battn.
No.4. " "	Right Battn H.Q.	" " Right Battn.

1. (Contd).

The average time allowed for runs between Posts is:-

Brigade Hqrs to No. 1 Post	25 Mins.
No. 1 Post to No. 2.	17 "
No. 2. Post to No. 3 or 4.	25 "
Total to Front Battalions	67 Minutes.

2. Battalions to Companies and neighbouring Units. Owing to restrictions in use of "D.ßs", and shortage of Fuller-phones the runners are largely employed in Battalions and Relay Posts established at suitable points.

3. Brigade to Division. There are three ordinary runs daily from Division and 1 special run at 10.30 a.m. for Intelligence Repprt. These H.C., D.Rs., come right up to Brigade Hqrs.

MESSAGE CARRYING ROCKETS.

1. Each Battalion Headquarters has a number of these Rockets and a trough from which they are fired. The Front Battalion fire them into the Reserve Battn Hqrs., who relay them into Brigade Hqrs. This method of communication is somewhat unreliable.

S. O. S. GONG.

A Gong is fixed up in Brigade Signal Office connected to a switch in the Outpost Line at T.22.d.80.45. When the switch is pulled over the Gong Rings and the usual S. O. S. procedure is complied with.

---------- o O o -----------

APPENDIX IV.

MEDICAL.

Regimental Aid Posts are established at the following points:-

Right Line Battn.	T.20.b.1.5.
Left " "	T.13.b.5.4.
Support Battn.	T.19.c.2.5.

Evacuation is carried out as follows:-

Right Battalion. From R. A. P., T.20.b.1.5. by Light Railway to Advanced Dressing Station, S.18.c.9.3.

Left Battalion. From R.A.P., T.13.b.5.4., by R.A.M.C. Relay Post~~s~~ there via Relay Post at T.13.a.5.5. to A.D.S., at S.18.c.9.3.

Support Battalion. From R.A.P., T.19.c.2.5. direct to A.D.S., at S.18.c.9.3.

In Normal times the above applies to all cases.

During a general action stretcher cases only take these routes. All walking wounded go from R.A. Posts direct to Walking Wounded Collecting Station at AUX RIETZ, at A.8.c.5.5.

-------- o O o --------

APPENDIX V

LIST OF CO-ORDINATES.

Brigade Headquarters. S.27.b.0.5.

Area.	Battn. H.Q.		Company H.Q.
TOAST.	T.13.b.5.2.	Right	T.14.a.1.7.
		Right Centre	T.8.c.9.6.
		Left "	T.7.d.9.5.
		Left	T.8.a.0.0.
BETTY.	T.25.d.5.9.	Right	T.21.a.6.1.
		Right Centre	T.20.b.5.2.
		Left Centre	T.14.c.8.1.
		Left	T.14.c.8.1.
VIMY - CHAUDIERE	S.24.a.2.0	Right	T.26.a.3.9.
		Right Centre	T.19.c.1.5.
		Left Centre	S.24.a.5.1.
		Left	S.17.d.6.5.

Light Trench Mortar Battery.	T.13.b.5.1.
Left Group R.A. H.Q.	S.27.b.0.6.
M.G. Left Group H.Q.	S.27.b.0.5.
Y.52 Medium Trench Mortars (6" Newtons).	T.19.a.7.3.
2 Sections 413th Field Coy. R.E.	S.29.a.7.4.
Main Dressing Station.	S.18.c.9.3.

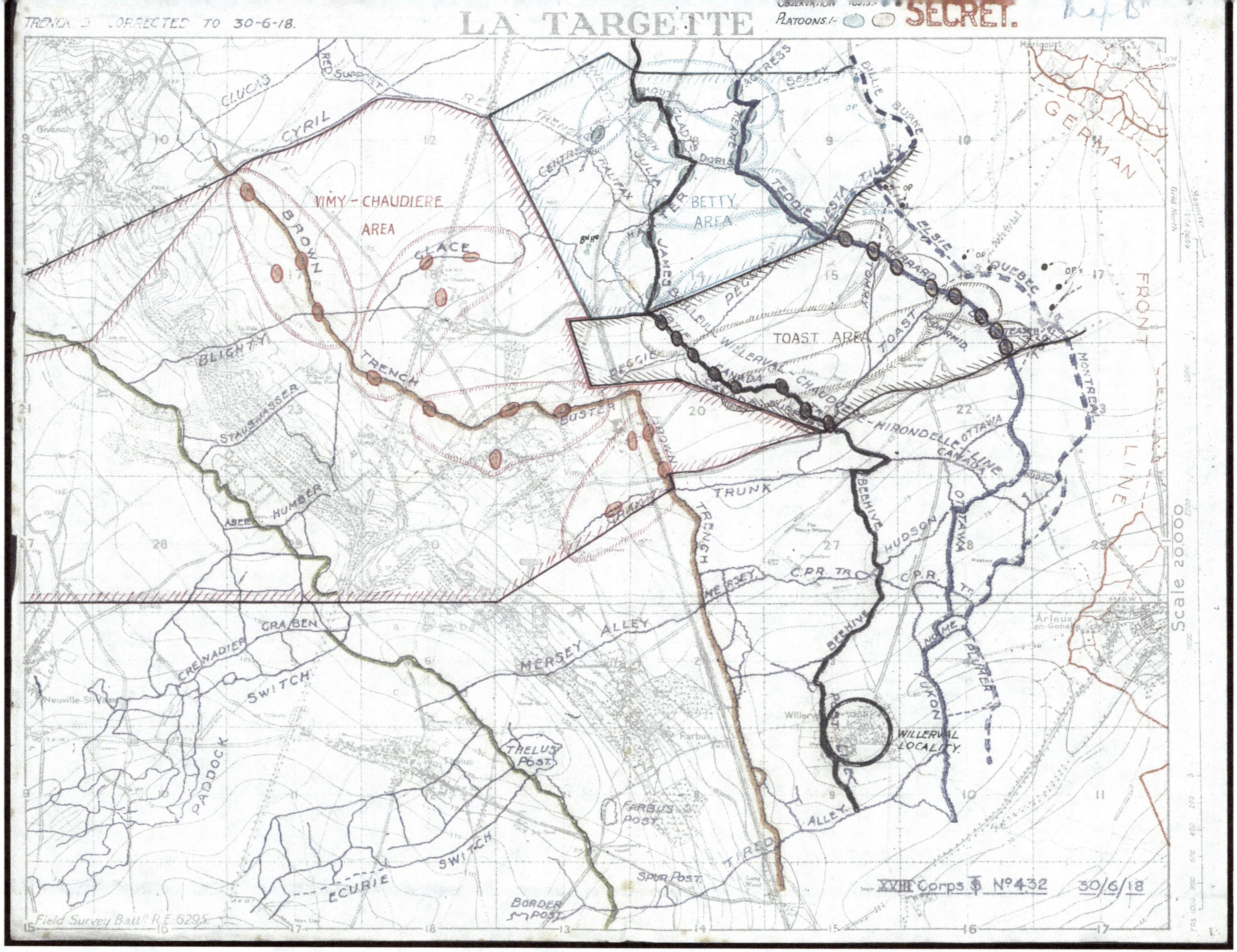
TRENCHES CORRECTED TO 30-6-18.
LA TARGETTE
PLATOONS:-
SECRET.
GERMAN FRONT LINE
VIMY-CHAUDIERE AREA
BETTY AREA
TOAST AREA
WILLERVAL LOCALITY
BROWN TRENCH
CYRIL
CLUCAS
RED SUPPORT
BLIGHTY
STAUSWASSER
HUMBER
BUSTER
TRUNK TRENCH
MERSEY ALLEY
GRABEN
GRENADIER
SWITCH
PADDOCK
ECURIE
THELUS POST
FARBUS POST
SPUR POST
BORDER POST
TIRED ALLEY
BEEHIVE
HUDSON
C.P.R. TR.
OTTAWA
HIRONDELLE LINE
CANADA
MONTREAL
QUEBEC
ELSIE
GERRARD
TOMMY
TEDDIE
VESTA TILLY
BILLIE BURKE
ACTRESS
KEANE
DORIS
GLADYS
JULIA
HALIFAX
JAMES
PEGGIE
WILLERVAL
YUKON
PLUMER
NOME
Arleux-en-Gohelle
Neuville-St-Vaast
Scale 20,000
XVIII Corps No 432
30/6/18
Field Survey Battn R.E. 6295

SECRET.

Copy No. 14.

App. V

Brigade Order No. 112.

14/7/18.

1. The Boundary between the 52nd Division and the 4th Canadian Divn. and the inter-Brigade boundary will be amended as shown on the attached tracing. This alteration will take place on the 15th and night of the 15/16th July. Relief to be completed by 6 a.m. 16th July.

2. The 6th H.L.I. will be relieved by the 4th Royal Scots. The former will proceed to NEUVILLE ST. VAAST on relief.

3. The 2 Companies of the 7th H.L.I., in the BROWN LINE, at present SOUTH of the new boundary, will be relieved by the 4 Companies of the 7th Scottish Rifles. On relief the 2 Coys. 7th H.L.I. will "side slip" to the NORTH of the new boundary, 1 Company holding the CHAUDIERE AREA, the other Companies the BROWN LINE.

4. The 5th H.L.I. will not move.

5. All details of relief will be arranged between C.O.s concerned.

6. O.C. 157th L.T.M.B. will arrange mutually with O.C. 156th L.T.M.B. as regards handing over gun positions and area stores. On relief O.C. 157th L.T.M.B. will withdraw his guns into Reserve in the BROWN LINE.

7. All details of work in hand and work projected will be handed over.

8. All trench stores, special maps and plans will be handed over. A copy of receipts for same will be forwarded to Brigade Headquarters as soon as possible after Relief.

9. (i) In the event of an Alarm or Enemy Attack during the relief, troops will halt and man the nearest trenches, reporting their dispositions at once to Brigade Headquarters.
(ii) O.C. Battalions will remain with their opposite numbers and await orders.

10. H.Q., 7th Scottish Rifles will be temporarily situated at LA FOLIE COPSE (S.17.c.) on relief.

11. Completion of Relief will be wired to Brigade Headquarters by the code word INTILT.

12. ACKNOWLEDGE.

C.B. Stirling Cookson

Captain,
Brigade Major, 157th Infantry Brigade.

Issued at 12 noon

Copy No. 1 to	5th H.L.I.	Copy No. 8 to	155th Inf. Brigade.
2	6th H.L.I.	9	60th Inf. Brigade.
3	7th H.L.I.	10	2nd L.F.A.
4	157th L.T.M.B.	11	413th Field Coy. R.E.
5	Left Group M.G. Bn.	12	52nd Division.
6	Left Group Artillery.	13	B.G.C.
7	156th Inf. Brigade.	14, 15	War Diary.
		16	File.

SECRET. Copy No. 11.....

157th Infantry Brigade Administrative Instructions
No. 107.

With Reference to 157th Brigade Warning Order dated 13th July.

14th July, 1918.

1. On relief 6th H.L.I. will occupy HANSON CAMP. Troops of 155th Brigade presently occupying this camp will be clear by 10 a.m. on 15th inst.

2. Rations will be drawn as at present from LEADLEY SIDING.

3. Water is laid on in the Camp. Strict supervision must be exercised to prevent wastage.

4. (a) 6th H.L.I. will hand over SOYERS Stoves, Food Containers Petrol Tins and all Trench Stores to relieving Unit and receipts obtained.
Ration Dump (NOVA SCOTIA) at T.21.a.5.5. will also be handed over and receipts obtained.

(b) 7th H.L.I. will retain Soyers Stoves, Food Containers, and Petrol Tins but will hand over Trench Stores in the area being evacuated, obtaining receipts for same.
Ration Dumps at VIMY (S.24.d.8.2.) and CULVERT (T.20.c.2.2.) will also be handed over and receipts obtained.

(c) The pro-forma issued with Q.198/5 will be used and instructions laid down carefully complied with. The duplicate will be sent to Brigade Hqrs by 1800 on 16th. This will be returned if required.

5. Any Area Stores taken over in HANSON CAMP should be carefully checked and a copy of the receipt sent to Brigade Hqrs by 1800 on 16th inst.

6. ACKNOWLEDGE.

Captain,
A/Staff Captain, 157th Infantry Brigade.

Copy No. 1 to 5th H.L.I.
2 6th H.L.I.
3 7th H.L.I.
4 157th L.T.M.Bty.
5 Hqrs. 52nd Division.
6 Hqrs. 155th Inf. Bde.
Copy No. 7 to Hqrs. 156th Bde.
8 2nd L.F.A.
9 Hqrs. 60th Inf Bde
10 B.G.C.
11 }
12 } War Diary.
13 File.

SECRET.

Copy No. 13

157th Infantry Brigade Order No. 113.

1. The 155th Infantry Brigade will relieve the 157th Infantry Brigade in the HERICOURT Sector on the 17th and night of the 17/18th July.

2. On relief, the 157th Infantry Brigade will move into Divisional Reserve in accordance with Table "A" on the reverse.

3. All details of relief will be arranged between C.O.s concerned.

4. All Defence Schemes, special maps, plans and trench stores will be handed over.
Special orders for units in Divisional Reserve will be taken over.
Copies of receipts for the latter will be forwarded to Brigade Headquarters on the morning after relief.

5. All details of work in hand and work projected will be handed over in writing.

6. (i) In the event of an alarm or attack during the relief, troops will halt and man the nearest defences, reporting their positions at once to Brigade Headquarters.
(ii) C.O.s will remain with their opposite numbers and await orders.

7. Brigade Headquarters will close at S.27.b.0.5. and open at ST. ELOI on completion of relief.

8. Completion of relief will be wired to Brigade Headquarters by the code word "HOGIA".

9. ACKNOWLEDGE.

C.S. Stirling Cookson

15/7/18.

Captain,
Brigade Major, 157th Infantry Brigade.

Issued at 6 am on 15/7/18.

Copy No. 1 to 5th H.L.I.
2 6th H.L.I.
3 7th H.L.I.
4 157th L.T.M.B.
5 Left Group M.G. Bn.
6 Left Group Artillery.
7 413th Field Coy. R.E.
8 2nd L.F.A.
9 155th Infantry Brigade.
10 52nd Division.
11 B.G.C.
12 A. & Q.
13)
14) War Diary.
15 File.

Table "A".

Serial No.	Date.	Unit.	From	To. Camp.	Relieved by
1	17	5th H.L.I.	Front Line	" FRASER and LANCASTER.	1/5th R.S.F.
2	17	6th H.L.I.	NEUVILLE ST. VAAST.	" OTTAWA and DURHAM.	-
3	17	7th H.L.I.	BROWN LINE.	" LE PENDE and SUBURBAN.	1/4th K.O.S.B.
4	18	157th L.T.M.B.	Line.	CUBBITT.	156th L.T.M.B.

Order of Relief on 17th July - Serials 1, 2.

" 2 Companies in each camp.

S E C R E T.   Copy No. 10....

157th Infantry Brigade Administrative Instructions
No. 108.

Issued with reference to Brigade Order No. 113.

15th July, 1918.

Ref. Sheet 51.c. N.E.

1. Relief of Duties.

Battalions will arrange to hand over to relieving Units the Water Point Duties furnished in this area.

2. Transport.

Transport will remain in its present site.

3. Supplies.

Rations for 18th will be drawn as at present from LEADLEY SIDING, and sent to the camps which units are to occupy. Rations for consumption from 19th will be drawn from BLACKPOOL SIDING with the exception of the L.T.M.Bty, who will continue to draw from LEADLEY SIDING and for whom the Brigade Transport Officer will provide Transport.

4. Water.

Water is laid on in the camps. Strict supervision must be exercised to prevent wastage.

5. Lorries.

The motor lorries which bring up the relieving Units will be available to convey the Battalions of this Brigade to ST. ELOI.
Embussing Officers :- Lieut. J.M. Stewart.
Lieut. .D. Nicholson.

6. Trench and Area Stores.

Soyers Stoves, Food Containers, Petrol Tins and all Trench Stores will be handed over and receipts obtained. Pro-forma issued with Q.198/5 will be used and the instructions laid down carefully complied with. The duplicate will be sent to Brigade Hqrs by 1800 on 19th. This will be returned if required.

7. Billet Improvements.

Units of 155th Brigade will hand over to relieving Units, their scheme of work for Billet ~~xxxxxxxxxx~~ Sanitation and minor improvements and a schedule of the work in progress.

8. Duties.

Battalion on Duty 18th .... 6th H. L. I.
Next for Duty .... 7th H. L. I.
Next for Duty .... 5th H. L. I.
and subsequently in this order.
The following Guards and Picquets will be furnished by Battalion on Duty.-

8. Duties (Contd.)

Duty.	Strength.	Location.	Time to report.
Bde. Hqrs. Guard.	1 N.C.O., 6 Men.	Bde. Hqr.	1700.
Police.	1 Regtl. Policeman at each Point.	F.15.a.0.7. F.14.a.7.5. F.13.b.8.6. F.13.a.2.7. F.1.a.4.2.	1500 - 2130.
Divnl. Canteen.	1 Sergeant.	OTTA A Camp.	1715 - 2030.

The Battalion on Duty will detail one Company to report to Transport Lines at 0900 for improvement work, 1 Platoon being detailed to each Battalion and 1 to Brigade Hqrs. These Platoons will work under orders of Os.C. Units to whom they report. Work will be from 0900 - 1200.

Battalion on Duty will also detail one platoon to report Area Commandant, ST. ELOI at 0800. This platoon will take its meals in Divnl Cookery School.

9. Duties to be Furnished by Battalion.

A. By 5th H. L. I.

Duty.	Strength.	Location.	Time to report.
(i) Prisoners of War Cage.	1 Officer 1 N.C.O., 12 men.	A.8.c.3.7.	When called on, see A.I. No. A.F.9 of 25/5/18 and amendment "A" Summary No. 4 of 11/7/18.

The names of Officer, N.C.O. and Men detailed for above will be sent direct to A.P.M.

Duty.	Strength.	Location.	
(ii) Water Picquet.	1 man	F.8.a.8.2. F.8.b.3.1.	Drinking. Horses.
	1 man	F.9.c.9.1. F.9.d.4.3.	Horses. Drinking.
	1 man	F.9.c.9.4. F.9.c.9.5.	Drinking. Horses.
	1 man	[redacted] F.11.b.1.2. F.11.b.6.3.	Horses. " "
	1 man	F.10.d.1.4. F.10.d.1.8.	Tank. Horses.

B. By 6th H. L. I.

Duty.	Strength.	Location.	Time to report.
~~Water Picquet.~~ Forward Battle Stragglers Station.	~~1 man~~ 1 N. C.O. & 5 men.	A.11.b.1.8.	When called on see A.I.No.A.F.9 of 25/5/18.
Water Picquet.	1 man	F.2.a.2.8.	Drinking.
	1 man	F.2.c.1.4.	"
	1 man	F.8.a.5.5.	"
	1 man		

12. Baths.

Baths are allotted to units as under.-

NEUVILLE ST. VAAST Baths.

60 men each half hour.

18th.	6th H. L. I.	0900 - 1200	360 men.
		1300 - 1600	360 "
			720
19th.	157th L.T.M.Bty.	0900 - 1000	120 men.

BERTHONVAL BATHS.

60 men each half hour.

18th.	5th H. L. I.	0800 - 1200	480 men.
		1300 - 1700	480 "
			960

ST. ELOI Baths.

40 men each half hour.

18th.	6th H. L. I.	0800 - 1100.	240 men.
	7th H. L. I.	1100 - 1200	80 "
		1300 - 1700	320 "
			640 "
19th.	Bde. Hqrs.	0900 - 1030.	120 men.

VILLERS AU BOIS Baths.

40 men each half hour.

18th.	7th H. L. I.	0800 - 1200	320 men.
		1300 - 1700	320 "
			640

13. Area Stores.

Area stores taken over should be carefully checked and a copy of the receipt sent to Bde. Hqrs by 1800 on 18th.

14. ACKNOWLEDGE.

W. Dear

Captain,
A/Staff Captain, 157th Infantry Brigade.

Issued at ....

Copy No. 1 to 5th H.L.I.
2 6th H.L.I.
3 7th H.L.I.
4 157th L.T.M.Bty
5 Bde. Transport Officer

Copy No. 7 to Hqrs 155 Bde
8 Hqrs 52 Divn
9 B.G.C.
10 (
11 (War Diary.
12 File.

9. Contd.
C. By 7th H. L. I.

Duty.	Strength.	Location.	
Water Picquet.	1 man	W.25.c.4.1.	Horses.
	1 man	(W.30.d.8.1. (E.6.b.8.8.	Horses. Horses.
	1 man	F.1.d.3.2.	Drinking.
	1 man	(F.3.c.5.9. (F.8.c.5.6.	Tank. Drinking.
	1 man	(F.4.d.1.2. (F.4.d.2.1.	Horses. Drinking.

Men in each Battalion detailed for Water Duty will report to 4th K.O.S.B. at 1800 on 16th inst at FRASER CAMP rationed for 17th. Written instructions xxx x stating for which post they are intended should be given them.

Water Picquets.

(a) Chloride of Lime is required for all water tanks and is provided by M.O. of unit finding water picquet.

(b) The duties of Water Picquets are detailed in 52nd Divnl Circular Administrative Instrucrions No.7 dated 24/5/18.

Orders in writing will be handed over by all Picquets being relieved.

Each Battalion will detail 10 men daily for Camp Improvement and Sanitation under Regtl. arrangements.

The Brigade Transport Officer will detail one Maltese Cart complete with team and driver to be attached to the Divnl Reception Camp during the period the Brigade is in Reserve.

10. Discipline.

N.C.Os. and Men are forbidden to leave the Divisional Area.

ECOIVRES and other villages in the 51st Divnl Area (i.e. South of an East and West Line through Cross Roads F.14.b.10.6.) are strictly out of bounds for all units of the Brigade.

11. Bounds.

The bounds for the Brigade are marked by 52nd Divnl Boards at the following points.-

F.15.a.1.7.
F.14.a.8.7.
F.13.b.8.6.
F.13.a.9.9.
F.1.d.5.2.

No. N.C.O. or man is allowed outside these points without a pass signed by his Commanding Officer and bearing the Office Stamp.

Battalion Bounds will be marked by Battalion Boards which have been issued.

No man will leave the area of the three camps at ST. ELOI without a belt.

It must be impressed on all men that they must be properly and tidely dressed when going out of Camp Area.

Steps will be taken to see that this is carried out.

SECRET. Copy No. 14

157th Infantry Brigade Order No.114

19th July, 1918.

Ref. Maps: LENS & HAZEBROUCK 1/100,000
44 B. 1/40,000

App VI

1. The 157th Infantry Brigade Group, less 413th Field Coy. R.E. will move by rail to the new area to-morrow, 20th July 1918, in accordance with Table "A" on the Reverse.

2. The following officers will act as entraining officers:- To 1st train Lieut. W.C.Gray. To 2nd Train Captain W.D. Macrae. They will travel on the 1st and 2nd trains respectively.
O.C. 7th H.L.I. will detail a detraining officer for the 1st train.
O.C. 5th H.L.I. " " " " " 2nd ".

3. Entraining statements shewing number of officers and O.R. will be handed to the R.T.O. by all units half an hour before time of departure of the train.

4. Transport will move by road, Brigaded and under orders of the O.C. 220th Coy. A.S.C.
Order of march will be as follows; Brigade Hqrs., 7th H.L.I., 6th H.L.I., 5th H.L.I., 157th L.T.M.Bty., 220th Coy. A.S.C., D Coy. 52nd Bn. M.G.C., 2nd Low. Field Ambulance.
The head of the column will pass WINNIPEG CAMP (F.7.b.9.9.) at 7.30 a.m.
Transport of the 2nd Low. Field. Ambulance will join the tail of the column at LES QUATRE VENTS (W.9.central).
Distance to be maintained between units, 100 yards.
Strict march discipline will be maintained, special attention to be paid to keeping to the RIGHT of the road.

5. Brigade Hqrs., will close at MONT ST. ELOY at 7 a.m. and open at AUCHEL at the same time.

6. ACKNOWLEDGE.

C. S. Stirling Cookson,
Captain,
Brigade Major, 157th Infantry Brigade.

Copy No.	1 to	5th H.L.I.
	2	6th H.L.I.
	3	7th H.L.I.
	4	157th L.T.M.B.
	5	G.O.C.
	6	220th Coy. A.S.C.
	7	2nd L.F.A.
	8	52nd Divn. G.
	9	52nd Divn. Q.
	10	Lt. W.C.Gray.
	11	Capt. W.D.Macrae.
	12	"D" Coy. 52nd Bn. M.G.C.
	13	Staff Capt.
	14)	War Diary.
	15)	
	16	File.

Issued at..11.30pm..

Table "A".

Serial No.	Unit.	Train	Entrain at.	Time of Departure.	Detrain at.	Billetted at.	
1	B.H.Q.	1st.	MONT ST. ELOY.	about 10. a.m.	CALONNE RICOUART.	AUCHEL	All units will
2	5th H.L.I.	2nd.	"	" 3 p.m.	"	LOZINGHEM	be at the
3	6th H.L.I.	1st.	"	" 10 a.m.	"	RAIMBERT	entraining station
4	7th H.L.I.	1st.	"	" 10 a.m.	"	AUCHEL	one hour before
5	157th L.T.M.B.	1st.	"	" 10 a.m.	"	RAIMBERT	time of departure of the train.
6	220th Coy. A.S.C.	2nd	"	" 3 p.m.	"	RAIMBERT	
7	2nd L.F.A.	2nd	"	" 3 p.m.	"	AUCHEL	
8	"D" Coy. 52nd Bn. M.G.C.	2nd	"	" 3 p.m.	"	LOZINGHEM	

Note. Transport of "D" Coy. 52nd Bn. M.G.C. will report to O.C. 220th Coy. A.S.C. at junction of roads in W.30.central, at 7.35 a.m.

Reference Brigade order No 114.

Sheet :- FRANCE 44 & 1/40,000.

1. MOTOR LORRIES. 1 Motor lorry will report each Battalion at 8 a.m. for extra baggage. As soon as loaded these lorries will proceed to destination. An officer should proceed with each. In addition 1 motor lorry will report 5th HLI at 1-30 P.m. to carry cooking utensils unable to be taken by horse transport on account of mid-day meal. This lorry will stop at LES QUATRE VENTS to pick up cooking utensils of 2nd L.F.A.

2 SUPPLIES. R.P. from 21st July inclusive will be on road C2 C4-8. Rations will be drawn daily from 21st inclusive at 10 a.m.

3. WATER POINTS. If water points are not relieved by relieving Brigade by 6 a.m. to-morrow 20th, they will be withdrawn by units concerned.

4. AMMUNITION. Full establishment of SAA will be taken in Horse Transport.

5. MEAT SAFES. Meat Safes will be taken and carried on Motor Lorry.

Capt,

19-7-1918. A/Staff Capt, 157th Inf Bde

To all recipients of 157th Inf Bde Order No 114.

SECRET.

App VII

Copy No. 11

157th Infantry Brigade Order No.115.

Ref. Maps: LENS 11)
HAZEBROUCK 5a.) 1/100000.

23rd July, 1918.

1. From 12 noon to-day the 52nd Division will be in G.H.Q. Reserve.

2. The 157th Brigade Group will be ready to move by bus or tactical train at 6 hours notice after 12 noon to-day.

3. Move by Tactical Trains.
(a) Entraining Station will be PERNES.
(b) All transport with the exception of certain wagons which will be ordered to move by rail, will proceed by road.

Move by Bus.
(a) Head of Embussing Point at Y in CHAUCY LA TOUR.
(b) Troops moving by bus will take with them all Lewis Guns, Stokes Mortars and Vickers Guns, and at least 24 filled Lewis Gun drums, 10 filled Vickers Gun belts, also one day's rations on the man.
(c) A Bus takes 1 Officer and 25 O.R.
A Lorry " 1 " " 20 O.R.
(d) Troops will rendezvous at the Embussing Point a quarter of an hour before the time ordered for embussing to start.
(e) Arrangements are being made to place Notice Boards at each end of the Embussing Point.

4. Should a strategical move be ordered and the complete Division be moved by rail, the Brigade Group and a portion of the Divisional Artillery will entrain.

5. In order to prevent delay, units will prepare skeleton orders for the move.
Companies will be told off in bus loads and in the order in which they will embus.

6. The Embussing and Entraining Points will be reconnoitred by day and night, also roads leading to them.

7. ACKNOWLEDGE.

C.S. Stirling-Cookson
Captain,
Brigade Major, 157th Infantry Brigade.

Issued at 6pm

Copy No. 1 to 5th H.L.I.
2 6th H.L.I.
3 7th H.L.I.
4 157th L.T.M.B.
5 "D" Coy. 52nd Bn. M.G.C.
6 413th Field Coy. R.E.
7 2nd Low. Field Ambulance.
8 B.G.C.
9 52nd Division.
10 A. & Q.
11) War Diary.
12)
13 File.

SECRET.

Copy No....15....

157th Infantry Brigade Order No. 116.

App VIII

Ref. Maps:- LENS 11 / HAZEBROUCK 5A. } 1/100,000.

29th July, 1918.

1. The XVII Corps will relieve the Canadian Corps in the ARRAS Sector. Infantry Relief will probably commence on night 31st July/1st August.

2. The 52nd Division will occupy the LEFT Sub-Sector of the Corps front, with all three Brigades in the line.

3. On 30th July, 1918, the 157th Infantry Brigade Group will move by road to billets in BARLIN as per Table "A" on the reverse.

4. When, and if necessary, the usual precautions against hostile aircraft will be taken.

5. ACKNOWLEDGE.

C. S. Stirling-Cookson

Captain,
Brigade Major, 157th Infantry Brigade.

Issued at 4pm........

Copy No.	1 to	5th H.L.I.
	2	6th H.L.I.
	3	7th H.L.I.
	4	157th L.T.M.B.
	5	2nd L.F.A.
	6	413th Field Coy. R.E.
	7	"D" Coy. 52nd Bn. M.G.C.
	8	220th Coy. A.S.C.
	9	B.G.C.
	10	52nd Division.
	11	Staff Captain.
	12	Bde. Sig. Officer.
	13 } 14 }	War Diary.
	15	File.
	16	Area Commandant.
	17	156th Infantry Brigade.

Table "A".

Serial No.	Unit.	Starting times Units' Parade Grounds.	From.	To.	Route.	Remarks.
1.	Bde. Hqrs.	8. a.m.	AUCHEL	BARLIN.	AUCHEL - CAMBLAIN CHATELAIN - HOUDAIN.	
2.	7th H.L.I.	8.10 a.m.	AUCHEL	"	-------- do -------	Transport will accompany units.
3.	2nd L.F.A.	10. a.m.	AUCHEL	"	-------- do ------- (To follow in rear of Bde. Group)	Dinners will be issued on arrival in Camp.
4.	5th H.L.I.	8.45 a.m.	LOZINGHEM	"	LOZINGHEM - HARLES-les-MINES - CAMBLAIN CHATELAIN - HOUDAIN.	10 minute halt will take place at 10 minutes to each clock hour. Times to be strictly adhered to.
5.	D. Coy. 52nd Bn. [illegible].G.C.	9.[illegible].a.m.	LOZINGHEM	"	-------- do -------	Distance to be maintained between units:- Between Battns. 500 yds. Between Coys. 100 " Between unit and) its Transport.) 100 "
6.	413th Fld. Coy. R.E.	9.10 a.m.	LOZINGHEM	"	-------- do -------	
7.	6th H.L.I.	8. a.m.	RAIMBERT	"	RAIMBERT - AUCHEL - CAMBLAIN CHATELAIN- HOUDAIN.	O.C. 2nd L.F.A. will detail 1 horse ambulance to follow in rear of:- 7th H.L.I. 6th H.L.I. 413th Fld. Coy, R.E.
8.	157th L.T.[illegible].B.	8.10 a.m.	RAIMBERT	"	-------- do -------	These ambulances will join the units concerned to-day.
9.	220th Coy. A.S.C.	8.20 a.m.	RAIMBERT	"	-------- do -------	

SECRET.

BM 7/34

O.C. 6th H.L.I.
157th L.T.M.B.
220th Coy. A.S.C.

Reference Table "A" of Brigade Order No.116 of to-day's date.

The above mentioned units will march by the following route.

RAIMBERT - Cross Roads. C.19.d. (sheet 44 B. 1/40,000)
CAUCHY-LA-TOUR - CAMBLAIN CHATELAIN - HOUDAIN - BARLIN. and not as stated in Table "A" mentioned above.

Captain,
Brigade Major, 157th Infantry Brigade.

29th July, 1918.

Copy to:- 5th H.L.I. "D" Coy. 52nd Bn. M.G.C. 413th Field Coy. R.E.
7th H.L.I. 2nd L.F.A.

Secret.

Copy No. 12

151st Infy Brigade Order No. 111.

App IX

30 July 1917

Ref. Maps. LENS 11. 1/40,000
French Map 36 B. N.W. 1/20,000

1. The 151st Brigade Group (less B Coy 50th Bn. M.G.C.) will proceed by route march tomorrow 31st July to camps in MADAGASCAR AREA. A.26.d. & A.21.c.

2. B Coy 50th Bn M.G.C. will proceed to take over the line (brigade sub-section) under orders issued by 50th Bn. M.G.C. Guides for this Coy will report at BARLIN at 2 p.m. on 31st inst.

3. Order of March.

Order of March.	Starting Point	Time head of unit to pass Starting point
9th A.L.I.	Road junction Road & Road of village of VERDREL	12-30 p.m.
5th A.L.I.	Do	12-50 p.m.
6th A.L.I.	Do	1-10 "
151st L.T.M.B.	Do	1-30
446th Fd. Coy R.E.	Do	1-40
228th Coy. A.S.C.	Do	[illegible]
2nd L.F.A.	Do	[illegible]

3. Units will [illegible] marching [illegible] to [illegible] Route to be followed:- Camp – VERMELLES – GRAND SERVINS – VILLERS AU BOIS – LE PENDU – MT. ST. ELOY – [illegible] – thence in an EASTERLY direction [illegible] [illegible] – ARRAS [illegible] ECURIE – ANZIN ST AUBIN R[illegible].

4. Transport will accompany units.

5. M.G. & L.T.M. will [illegible] [illegible] [illegible] [illegible] of Infantry Battalions.

6. At 5 mins past each hour units will halt for [illegible] During the halt the strictest discipline will be maintained. All Platoon Commanders will be with their Platoons. Men will not be allowed to [illegible] [illegible]. All wagons will be pulled well in to the side of the road.

7. Intervals to be maintained between Units:-

Between	Battns.	500 yards
"	Coys.	100 "
"	Units & Transport	100 "

8. Acknowledge.

Issued at 19.00.

[illegible]
Captain
Brigade Major [illegible] Inf. Brigade

Cop. ✕ 1 F 5th A. [illegible]
2 1st A. [illegible]
3 1st A. L. [illegible]
4 131st L. I. R. B.
5 [illegible]
6 [illegible] T.L.
7 D. by. [illegible] Mac.
8 [illegible] A. [illegible]
9 B. G. C.
10 52nd Division
11 } War Diary
12 }
13 File.

157th Infantry Brigade.

No 12

Administrative Instructions No 111

30th July 1918.

Reference Brigade Order No 117.

1 Billeting Parties

These have proceeded to MADAGASCAR AREA and will be responsible for meeting Units on arrival.

2 Lorries.

Baggage Lorries will report to units at 12 noon on 31st as follows:-

5th H.L.I. 2 Lorries. 6th H.L.I. 2 Lorries
7th H.L.I 2 Lorries. Brigade H.Q 1 Lorry.

One Lorry will accompany the march of the Transport of the Brigade Group.

This Lorry will deal with breakdowns, stragglers etc.

No man will be allowed on this Lorry without written permission from an officer.

3 Supplies.

Railhead on 31st inst will be MONT St. ELOY

Rations for 1st August will be carried in Train Wagons.

4 Ammunition

Full/

4 Continued

Full establishment of S.A.A. will be taken in Horse Transport.

5 Train Wagons

The Baggage wagons of the Brigade are already with the units.

The supply wagons will join units tonight

6 Tents & Area Stores

All Tents, Trench Shelters & Area Stores taken over will be handed over to O.C. 1st Division Reception Camp and a receipt obtained

7 Acknowledge

H.M. Hewison
Captain
Staff Captain, 151 Infantry Brigade

Copy No. 20

SECRET.

157th Infantry Brigade Order No. 118.

30th July, 1918.

App. II

Ref. Map, Sheet 51 B. N.W. 1/20,000.

1. On 1st August, 1918, the 157th Infantry Brigade will relieve portionsof the 10th Canadian Infantry Brigade, and 155th and 156th Infantry Brigades in the line.

2. The Brigade boundaries will be as follows:-
(i) On the North. TIRED ALLEY (inclusive to 155th Inf. Bde.)
(ii) On the South. B.23.a.9.7. - B.23.a.0.6. - B.22.b.5.0. - b.22.d.0.5. - B.22.c.0.0. - B.21.central - along North side of Sunken Road - B.20.d.6.3. - along North side of GAUL ALLEY (inclusive to 156th Inf. Bde.).
(iii) Inter Battalion Boundary. TOMMY ALLEY (inclusive to 7th H.L.I.)

3. (a) The 7th H.L.I. will take over the front line between (i) and (iii) from the 44th Canadian Infantry Battalion, and forward of the BROWN LINE, with Battalion H.Q., at B.15.c.6.2.

(b) The 6th H.L.I. will take over the front line between (ii) and (iii), with Battalion H.Q., at B.21.a.8.2.

(c) The 5th H.L.I. will take over the BROWN LINE between (i) and (ii), with Battalion H.Q. at B.15.a.25.30.
The 5th H.L.I. will take over portions of BROWN LINE occupied by 155th and 156th Infantry Brigades., troops of 155th and 156th Infantry Brigades side slipping to N. and S. of the Northern and Southern Brigade boundaries respectively.

(d) The 157th L.T.M.B. will take over from the 44th Canadian L.T.M.B. between (i) and (ii).

(e) The reliefs will be carried out by day, the 6th H.L.I. using the Concrete Road and OUSE ALLEY, the 7th H.L.I. using PLANK Road and Tired Alley.
The leading platoons of the 6th and 7th H.L.I. will move off from MADAGASCAR Camp immediately after breakfast, the 5th H.L.I. will arrange to follow immediately after the 6th H.L.I. and will make use of TIRED and TOMMY ALLEYS.
A distance of 200 yards will be maintained between platoons.

4. All details of relief including guides will be arranged between C.O.s concerned.

5. All trench stores, aeroplane photos, maps, work in hand and work projected will be taken over.

6. As far as possible similar dispositions to those of the outgoing unitswill be taken over.

7. In the event of alarm or enemy attack during the relief:-
(a) Troops will man the nearest defences, reporting their dispositions at once to the nearest Brigade Headquarters,
(b) C.O.s will remain with their opposite numbers and await Orders.
The 10th Canadian Infantry Brigade is situated at B.14.a.10.75.10.

8. O.s C. Battalions and L.T.M.B., will send officers on in advance to-morrow the 31st July, to visit the line and make necessary arrangements regarding the relief.

9. On 1st Aug 1918, The 157th Infantry Brigade H.Q., will open in ROCLINCOURT at 12 noon.

10. Completion of relief will be wired to Brigade H.Q. using the Code word "FOSS".

11. ACKNOWLEDGE.

C. S. Stirling Cookson
Captain,
Brigade Major, 157th Infantry Brigade.

Issued at..............

Copy No. 1 to 5th H.L.I.
2 6th H.L.I.
3 7th H.L.I.
4 157th L.T.M.B.
5 2nd L.F.A.
6 413th Field Coy. R.E.
7 "D" Coy. 52nd Bn. M.G.C.
8 52nd Battn. M.G.C.
9 52nd Division.
10 220th Coy. A.S.C.
11 10th Canadian Inf. Bde.
12 155th Inf. Bde.
13 156th Inf. Bde.
14 B.G.C.
15 Staff Captain.
16 Bde. Sig. Officer.
17 I.O.
18 Bde. S.A.A. Officer.
19) War Diary.
20)
21 File.

157TH I[illegible] BRIGADE
BM 2/36
31/7/18

SECRET.

O.C.

Ref. French Map [illegible]

Reference 157th Infantry Brigade Order No.113 of 30th July, 1918.

Brigade Headquarters will close at present site at 12. noon to-morrow, 1st August, and open at same hour at [illegible].

[signature]

31/7/18.

Captain,
for Brigade Major, 157th Infantry Brigade.

HQ 157 Infy Bde
Vol 5
Ags'18

Confidential

On His Majesty's Service.

The

D. A. G.

3rd Echelon

B. E. Force

ADVISER IN PATHOLOGY

No.

Date

Instructions regarding War Diaries and Intelligence Summaries are contained in F. S. Regs., Part II. and the Staff Manual respectively. Title pages will be prepared in manuscript.

Confidential

WAR DIARY
or
INTELLIGENCE SUMMARY.
(Erase heading not required.)

157th Inf Bde

Vol III

A1

Army Form C. 2118.

Place	Date	Hour	Summary of Events and Information — Reference Map MAROEUIL 1/20000.	Remarks and references to Appendices
Roclincourt	1/8		Brigade commenced relief at 8 a.m. of part of 10th C. I. B. and 156 Bde relief being completed about 6 p.m. Orders for Gas Beam attack to take place tonight or first suitable night issued (App I)	App I. [illegible]
	2/8		Nothing of interest to report. The usual patrolling took place during the night.	[illegible]
	3/8		Four patrols from each of the battalions in the front line Trenches at different hours during the night, patrolled "No man's Land" – No enemy parties observed.	Heavy rain during forenoon – misty. [illegible]
		3 p.m.	Between 3 pm. & 4 pm. the enemy carried out harassing fire on CONCRETE ROAD	
		6.40 pm	An air fight took place – height 5000 ft – LENS direction – one machine observed to crash, identity unknown.	
			From prisoner's statement enemy expect an attack on this front. Division orders special precautions to be taken to prevent enemy obtaining identification.	
			CASUALTIES. 1 OR. wounded (7 H.L.I.)	
	4/8		"No man's Land" patrolled throughout the night – no enemy observed.	
		10.30 am	4 Hostile planes patrolled the front line, flying at 2500 feet. They were engaged by M.G. & L.G. fire.	
		6.3 pm	A daylight patrol of 1 NCO & 2 OR (6 H.L.I.) entered Enemy Trench near OUSE ALLEY. One enemy O.R. observed, but patrol was unable to fire without giving away its position. Enemy Trench mortar fire was opened on patrol on withdrawal.	
			Orders issued re new dispositions of Battalions (see Appendix II)	APPENDIX II G.B.
			CASUALTIES. 1 O.R. wounded (7 H.L.I.)	
	5/8		Usual patrolling throughout night – nothing of interest to report.	Wet & cloudy G.B.
			CASUALTIES. 1 OR. wounded accidentally (1/5 H.L.I.)	

W. D. Macrae(?) Capt

D. D. & L., London, E.C.
(A8001) Wt. W1771/M2031 750,000 5/17 Sch. 52 Forms/C2118/14

Army Form C. 2118.

WAR DIARY
or
INTELLIGENCE SUMMARY.
(Erase heading not required.)

Instructions regarding War Diaries and Intelligence Summaries are contained in F. S. Regs., Part II. and the Staff Manual respectively. Title pages will be prepared in manuscript.

CONFIDENTIAL

157th Infy Bde
VOL. 3 (A2)

Place	Date	Hour	Summary of Events and Information	Remarks and references to Appendices
ROCLINCOURT (A28 b 7.3)	6/8		Front patrolled as usual - no enemy observed. New dispositions as detailed in APPENDIX II taken up by 4 p.m. Code word 'GOAT' received & forwarded to units (See APPENDIX I). Owing to wind falling operations for night were cancelled at 12.45 a.m. CASUALTIES NIL	GPS
REFERENCE MAP MAROEUIL 1/20000	7/8		Nothing of interest to report. Each Battalion sent a team to 1st Army Rifle meeting MATRINGHEM. CASUALTIES 1 OR killed (1/7 H.L.I)	GPS
	8/8	8.30 pm	Patrols in "no man's land" encountered no enemy. 300 Gas drums successfully projected on ARLEUX. CASUALTIES 1/6 H.L.I. 1 killed & 4 O.R. wounded. 1/7 H.L.I. 1 OR wounded.	GPS
	9/8		Brig. Gen. HAMILTON-MOORE took over command temporarily of 52nd Division vice Div General on leave - Lt Col ANDERSON 1/6 HLI assumed command temporarily of 157th Bde. Lieut IAN CARMICHAEL 1/5 H.L.I D.S.O. awarded military Cross for good work on patrol. CASUALTIES Nil	GPS
	10/8		Front patrolled as usual - The S.O.S Barrage was put down about 3.30 am along our front on account of an enemy raid on the Division on our right. CASUALTIES 1 OR wounded (1/7 HLI)	GPS
	11/8		Nothing of interest to report. CASUALTIES Nil (Orders issued midday for new dispositions of Battalions APPENDIX III)	GPS
	12/8		Usual patrols during night. No enemy patrols encountered. Bde area shelled intermittently throughout the day & BAILLEUL heavily shelled between 5 & 5.30 pm. Enemy planes active during night in rear area bombing & machine gunning. CASUALTIES - - - 1 OR wounded (7th HLI). Further orders received re Gas Beam attack (APPENDIX IV)	APPENDIX III. APPENDIX IV. (Not available - handed over on relief)
	13/8		Front patrolled as usual - no enemy seen - New dispositions taken up as detailed in APPENDIX III by 11.35. Enemy artillery fairly quiet - Orders received at 5 pm for relief of Div. by night 14/15th + 15/16th (See APPENDIX V). CASUALTIES - - - - 2 O.R's wounded (1 accidentally) 5th HLI	APPENDIX V

[signature] Capt

D. D. & L., London, E.C. (A8001) Wt. W1771/M2031 750,000 5/17 Sch. 52 Forms C2118/14

Instructions regarding War Diaries and Intelligence Summaries are contained in F. S. Regs., Part II. and the Staff Manual respectively. Title pages will be prepared in manuscript.

CONFIDENTIAL.

WAR DIARY
or
INTELLIGENCE SUMMARY.
(Erase heading not required.)

157th Inf. Bde.

VOLUME III (A3)

Army Form C. 2118.

Place	Date	Hour	Summary of Events and Information	Remarks and references to Appendices
ROCLINCOURT (A28b7.3)	14/8/18		Usual patrols in "No Man Land" during night. One daylight patrol went forward towards DUKE STREET. Enemy post seen at B17c 80.55. ~~Orders~~ ~~received~~ Orders cancelling appendix V received ~~[illegible]~~ for Bde relief on night of 16/17th (APPENDIX VI) - Bde on left relieved (155th) - ~~[illegible]~~ Warning order issued to units (APPENDIX VI). CASUALTIES — NIL	[initials] APPENDIX VI. ~~[illegible]~~
REFERENCE MAP MAREUIL 1/20,000	15/8		Yellow X (& mustard) gas on BAILLEUL & POST TRENCH in early morning (1am till 2.30am). Front patrolled as usual - 2 ADDENDUMS received to APPENDIX VI - Nothing of interest to report during day - Bde on right relieved (156th) - Move orders issued to units at 4 pm (APPENDIX VII).	APPENDIX VII. [initials]
			CASUALTIES — 5th HLI 1 officer (wounded) *(2/Lt PARK) 7 OR (wounded) 2 OR injured. 6th HLI 3 OR (wounded) 1 OR (Self inflicted wound). Total: Officers 1, O.R. 13	
	16/8		Patrols were carried out as usual - advance parties of relieving units reported at BHQ between 8 & 10 am & proceeded up to the line to take over - Relief commenced at 6pm and was reported complete at 10.30 pm. Bde HQ closed at ROCLINCOURT & opened at ST ELOI at that hour. At midnight 16/17th orders were issued to units for move on 17th to CHATEAU DE LA HAIE (APPENDIX VIII) - Enemy aircraft active during hours of darkness bombing & machine gunning - ST ELOI shelled with H.V. gun -	APPENDIX VIII [initials]
			CASUALTIES: 5th HLI wounded 13 OR (including 11 suffering from effects of Yellow X). 6th HLI wounded 1 officer (Lt M.C.F. REID) & 3 O.R. 7th HLI wounded 2 O.R. Total: Officers 1, O.R. 18	
MONT ST ELOI	17/8		During morning units prepared to move to new area - the 6th & 7th HLI from MONT ST ELOI and 5th HLI from ROCLINCOURT. -	
BOIS DE LA HAIE X13a9.9			2pm - Bde commenced to move - Units arrived in their new areas between 4pm & 7pm respectively. (For locations etc see APPENDIX IX)	[initials]
REF MAP SHEET 36B 1/40,000	18/8		Information received that Division would be prepared to carry out small attack on enemy salient South of the R. Scarpe. Reconnaissance carried out by G.O.C. B.M. S.C. and all unit commanders. Church parade at all units	[initials]

[signature] Capt

D. D. & L., London, E.C. (A8003) Wt. W1771/M2031 750,000 5/17 Sch. 52 Forms C2118/14

Army Form C. 2118.

WAR DIARY
or
INTELLIGENCE SUMMARY.
(*Erase heading not required.*)

Instructions regarding War Diaries and Intelligence Summaries are contained in F. S. Regs., Part II. and the Staff Manual respectively. Title pages will be prepared in manuscript.

CONFIDENTIAL. 157th Infy Bde VOL: 3 (A 4)

Place	Date	Hour	Summary of Events and Information	Remarks and references to Appendices
Chateau de la Haie (REF MAP SHEET 36A 1/40,000)	19/8		Training carried on with during day.	
	20/8		Training as usual.	
		1700	Orders received for Bde to move at 10 p.m. to Agnez-les-Duisans and "Y" Huts.	App IX
			Orders issued to units accordingly (App IX)	
	21/8		Brigade arrived in new area during night last unit being in camp at 4.30 a.m.	
			Bde Hqrs situated at Agnez-les-Duisans and all other units of Bde at "Y" Huts.	
			Warning order received that Brigade must be prepared to move tonight to a new area. No order of confirmation arrived however and Brigade remained for the night in present site	
"	21/8	2200	~~The Brigade marched off to AGNEZ-LES-DUISANS last unit reaching that place at 4 a.m.~~	
HANEZ-les-Duisans	22/8		Brig. General C.D. Hamilton Moore assumed command of the Bde on return of G.O.C. to Division & Col Anderson left Bde Hq & took over command of 6th HLI	
			The Bde Group moved today to BELLACOURT, last unit reaching that place at 4 a.m. 23/8/18 -	App. X
	23/8	11.40am	G.O.C. & B.M. proceeded to 176th Bde H.Q. to arrange to take over MERCATEL SECTOR	
		1.40pm	While reconnoitring 176th Bde's Area Division phoned to stop taking over & that 157th Bde was to be ready to move at a half hours notice.	
		4pm	Bde started leaving BELLACOURT & proceeded to positions in vicinity of FICHEUX & brick works and squares M32 & M33 preparatory to attack next day. Bde commenced to arrive in these positions at 10 pm.	
Ficheux (Ref. MAP Sheet 51C SW)	24/8	12.30am	Orders for this operation received and attacking troops to pass through 156 Bde at 7a.m. ~~In Bde Line~~ Conference of C.O's was held at Bde Hqrs about 2 a.m. and orders then issued for the attack.	App XI

D. D. & L., London, E.C. (A5004) Wt. W1771/M2031 750,000 5/17 Sch. 52 Forms C2118/14

W. D. Whalen(?) Capt

Instructions regarding War Diaries and Intelligence Summaries are contained in F. S. Regs., Part II. and the Staff Manual respectively. Title pages will be prepared in manuscript.

CONFIDENTIAL

WAR DIARY or INTELLIGENCE SUMMARY.

(Erase heading not required.)

Army Form C. 2118.

157th Infy Bde VOL 3 (A5)

Place	Date	Hour	Summary of Events and Information	Remarks and references to Appendices
Fichuise [illegible] REF MAP SHEET 51B 1/20,000	24	5am	Owing to orders being issued late Btts did not have their forming up position behind railway till 5 a.m. instead of 4.15 a.m. In spite of this they passed through 156 Bde almost on time. They pushed forward quickly and took their first objective without trouble. The second objective was reached but owing to our heavies putting down a heavy barrage in this area they could not enter the Hindenburg Line and owing to communications being cut the heavies could not be turned off sufficiently quickly with the result that the enemy was able to reinforce his line with M.G's and no further progress could be made meantime.	[initials]
		3.45pm	Assisted by a light barrage a determined attempt was made to reach second objective but owing to depth of wire uncut this attempt did not succeed. Nothing happened during night. Orders re dispositions, Defence, etc issued	Appendix XII
HENIN REF MAP SHEET 51C S.W. 1/20,000	25/8	4am	Orders recd from Divn that no troops were to be within 250x of HINDENBURG LINE (Bde Order 132 issued accordingly)	APPENDIX XIII
		12.45pm	Above orders cancelled by Division & troops ordered not to be nearer to HINDENBURG LINE than 500x. (Bde Order 133 issued accordingly.)	
		11.30pm	Troops in new positions by this hour	
			Memo issued regarding patrolling –	Appendix XIV
	26/8	3.20pm	5th HLI ordered to establish liason at T4d 6.0 with 167th Bde on right	[initials]
		3.40pm	Division report British patrols in HINDENBURG LINE at T6c. 5th HLI ordered to send patrol to HENIN HILL immediately to investigate	
		4.45pm	155 Bde seen from Bde HQ advancing up Southern slopes of COJEUL VALLEY along HINDENBURG LINE.	
		7.35pm	Bde ordered to take over HENIN HILL from a battalion of 155th Bde who were to be left there.	[signature] Capt

D. D. & L., London, E.C. (A8051) Wt. W2771/M2031 750,000 5/17 Sch. 52 Forms C2118/14

Army Form C. 2118.

Instructions regarding War Diaries and Intelligence Summaries are contained in F. S. Regs., Part II. and the Staff Manual respectively. Title pages will be prepared in manuscript.

WAR DIARY
or
INTELLIGENCE SUMMARY.
(Erase heading not required.)

CONFIDENTIAL. 157th Infy Bde VOLUME 3 (A6)

Place	Date	Hour	Summary of Events and Information	Remarks and references to Appendices
Henin		contd.	the Bde then to be in Divisional Reserve.	
	26/8	7.35pm	5th HLI patrol reported enemy holding summit trench & HENIN HILL.	
		8.14pm	Division report Batts 155 Bde passed over HENIN HILL at 5.30 pm. - this contradicted by our Batts as patrols reported enemy to be still in occupation of HENIN HILL. Apparently mistake made by 155 Bde as to location of HENIN HILL as 4 K.O.S.B. located in T1 34 d where they said they were remaining. Division asked whether this Bde was to relieve 4th K.O.S.B. in T 34 d (APPENDIX XV)	Appendix XV
		9pm	Verbal message received from Div in the negative.	
	27/8	4.0am	Orders for attack received from Div. Brigade Order 135 issued accordingly. 1st objective FONTAINE CROISILLES and final objective RIENCOURT. 6th HLI on right 7 HLI on left & 5 HLI in reserve. Units ordered to be in position by 9 a.m.	App XVI
		9.30am	Brigade moved off under barrage up to time.	
		9.45am	Slight check to advance to cut wire at SUMMIT TRENCH	
		11.0am	Report from Div that enemy were reported attacking in mass along line T5c 5.5 to T5d 5.5	
		11.50am	After reconnaissance Div notified that there were no signs of enemy counterattack - our progress good.	
		12.15pm	Our troops reported to have reached FONTAINE CROISILLES	
		1.30pm	Line reported in same position as at 12.15 p.m. and FONTAINE CROISILLES reported to be clear of the enemy.	
		3.30pm	Brigade again ordered to advance under cover of barrage. Barrage however postponed till 4 pm then till 4.30pm eventually advance did not take place owing to Bdes on flanks being unable to assist	
		9pm	Brigade ordered to get in touch with G.O.C. 155 Bde who was to lend 2 Batts to assist in taking high ground in U14 A & B	

REFERENCE MAP - SHEET 51 B. S.W. 1/20000

[signature] Capt.

D. D. & L., London, E.C. (A2005) Wt. W1771/M2031 750,000 5/17 Sch. 52 Forms C2118/14

Instructions regarding War Diaries and Intelligence Summaries are contained in F. S. Regs., Part II. and the Staff Manual respectively. Title pages will be prepared in manuscript.

WAR DIARY
or
INTELLIGENCE SUMMARY.
(*Erase heading not required.*)

Army Form C. 2118.

CONFIDENTIAL. 157th Infy Bde VOLUME 3 (A7)

Place	Date	Hour	Summary of Events and Information	Remarks and references to Appendices
HENIN	27/8	5.5 pm	Div. issued that above assistance will not be given by G.O.C. 155 Bde. Verbal instructions from Divn that Bde would be relieved during night	
		10 pm	G.O.C. 172 Bde and relieving Batts arrived to take over	[illegible]
	28/8	7 am	Relief completed and reported to Divn. Brigade moved to MERCATEL AREA	[illegible]
	29/8		Reorganization being carried out. Corps Commander visited B.G.C.	[illegible]
	30/8		Reorganization continued	[illegible]
	31/8	7 am	Orders received from Div that Bde would be ready to move tonight at 1 hrs notice and pending further orders would concentrate in HENIN HILL [illegible] 1st prox	[illegible] APP: XVII
			For (a) casualties 23rd/27th see Appendix XVIII	
			(b) prisoners & captured material see appendix XIX	
			(c) objectives trenches etc see Appendix XX (Sheet 51b S.W.)	

REFERENCE MAP SHEET 51b 1/20000

31/8/18. Wm D. Wallace Capt.

D. D. & L., London, E.C. (A8093) Wt. W1771/M2031 750,000 5/17 Sch. 52 Forms C2118/14

Appendix I

Copy No. 7.

SECRET.

52nd Division Order No. 137.

24th August, 1918.

1. The Army will advance and allow the enemy no respite in this retreat. The VI Corps has been directed on Line QUEANT - VIS-EN-ARTOIS. Accordingly 56th Division will move on CROISILLES so as to take the defences of HENIN HILL within their Area from S.W. 52nd Division will conform to the movement of 56th Division. 157th Brigade will take over line now held by 156th Brigade from about T.2.c.5.0. to T.1.a.8.8. by 6.45. a.m. and attack due East at 7. a.m. conforming to and keeping touch with advance of 56th Division on right. The final line of 157th Brigade before moving to this assault on HENIN HILL will be approximately from N.33.c.6.5. to T.9.b.9.0., the final objective being the HINDENBURG LINE in N.34.d. and T.5.a.

2. 156th Brigade will advance on left of 157th Brigade at 7. a.m. to the general line of the road N.32.b.7.8. and to N.26.central. conforming to movement of 157th Brigade and being echeloned in left rear.

3. 155th Brigade will move to intermediate line starting from BRETENCOURT at 5. a.m.

4. The Canadian Corps will conform to movements of 156th Brigade.

5. Field Companies and Pioneers will move to Brickstack area and thence under orders of C.R.E.

6. 1 Coy. Machine Guns will be under orders of each 156th and 157th Brigades.

7. 1st Line Transport of 156th and 157th Brigades will close up to general line immediately West of BLAIREVILLE and there get well clear of road.

8. A.D.M.S. will push forward 2 sections Field Ambulance to open A.D.S.

9. S.A.A. Section will move under orders of "Q".

10. Divisional Headquarters will close at BRETENCOURT 8. a.m. and re-open BLAIREVILLE same hour.

11 Acknowledge. by telephone immediately.

(sgd) H.V. Curtis, Major,
for Lieut. Colonel,
General Staff,
52nd Division.

Issued at 1.40 a.m.

APPENDIX II

SECRET. Copy No. 11

157th Infantry Brigade Order No. 120.

5th August, 1918.

1. The 5th H.L.I. will relieve the 6th H.L.I. in the RIGHT Sub-Sector on the 7th August, 1918.
   On relief, the 6th H.L.I. will take over the same dispositions as those at present held by the 5th H.L.I.

2. The relief will commence immediately after breakfast, and be completed by 2. p.m.

3. If the Gas Beam Attack which is ordered to take place, has not been carried out before the 7th inst., all orders and instructions regarding this will be handed over to O.C. 5th H.L.I. by O.C. 6th H.L.I.
   O.C. 5th H.L.I. will place his gas personnel at the disposal of the Brigade Gas Officer, in accordance with this office B.M.4/38, para. 4, (d), of 1st inst.

4. Details of relief will be arranged between the C.O.s concerned.

5. Trench Stores, Log Books, Special Maps and Plans will be handed over and receipts taken. Lists of Stores etc. handed over will be forwarded to Brigade Headquarters by 8th inst.

6. O.C. 6th H.L.I. will hand over to O.C. 5th H.L.I. all details regarding the new dispositions.

7. All work in hand and projected will be handed over in writing.

8. Completion of relief will be notified to Brigade Headquarters by code word "ZEBRA".

9. A C K N O W L E D G E.

[illegible signature]

Captain,
for Brigade Major, 157th Infantry Brigade.

Issued at 10.30 a.m.

Copy No. 1 to 5th H.L.I.
2 ✓ 6th H.L.I.
3 7th H.L.I.
4 ✓ 157th L.T.M.B.
5 2nd L.F.A.
6 ✓ 52nd Division.
7 ✓ 277th Brigade R.F.A.
8 ✓ "D" Coy. 52nd Bn. M.G.C.
9 155th Inf. Bde.
10 156th Inf. Bde.
11) War Diary.
12)
13 File.

H.Q.
157TH INFANTRY
BRIGADE.
No. B.M.7/171
4/8/18.
Date ...

SECRET.

O.C. 5th Bn. H.L.I.
6th Bn. H.L.I.
7th Bn. H.L.I.
157th L.T.M.B.
"D" Coy. 52nd Bn. M.G.C.
277th Bde. R.F.A.

G.O.C. 155th Inf. Bde.
156th Inf. Bde.
D.T.M.O. 52nd Divn.
I.O. 157th Inf. Bde.

Reference 157th Infantry Brigade Order No.119 of 4th August, 1918.

The following instructions will be complied with by C.O.s when deciding on the new dispositions required.

(a) One Company per Battalion in front line will hold BOW Trench and BOW SUPPORT Trench System.

(b) Company or ½ Company localities will be selected in and around BOW Trench for this Company. The positions of localities selected must not be obvious to the enemy.

(c) Under ordinary circumstances, BOW Trench and BOW SUPPORT Trench will be occupied by this one Company only. 2 Platoons being in BOW Trench and 2 Platoons in BOW SUPPORT Trench.

(d) On the order "MAN BATTLE STATIONS", this one Company per Battalion, with its Platoons, will close up into the localities. The Battalion front being observed by patrols pushed out in front from this Company, in, or in front of BOW Trench.

(e) As soon as these localities have been decided upon, and the above orders come into force, it will be part of the daily routine of Platoons in the OUTPOST LINE (BOW Trench) and the OUTPOST LINE of SUPPORTS (BOW SUPPORT Trench) to be taken into their respective positions in their Company, or ½ Company localities, as the case may be, in order to become acquainted with their fire-bays, etc. The platoons will be taken to their respective positions at irregular hours each day, to prevent the enemy surmising that such localities exist.

(f) All officers will be informed of these orders, but the men will only be told that the various positions their platoons take up are to be occupied in case of necessity.

J.S. Stirling-Cookson
Captain,
Brigade Major, 157th Infantry Brigade.

4th August, 1918.

SECRET.

Copy No....13....

157th Infantry Brigade Order No.119.

4th August, 1918.

Ref. Map. Trench Map. 51 B. N.W.

1. The 52nd Division Southern Boundary will be altered to run as follows:- B.30.a.2.3. - H.3.b.8.2. - H.3.a.0.0. - H.2.c.0.8. - G.6.c.0.9. - G.3.b.7.3.
Simultaneously with the above, the Inter-Brigade Boundaries will be altered as follows:-

(a) Between RIGHT (156th) and CENTRE (157th) Brigades - A line from B.23.b.5.5. due WEST to point of Junction of BACK TRENCH with POST LINE (inclusive)to 156th Brigade) - down road through BAILLEUL - B.21.d.5.8. (inclusive to 156th Brigade) - B.21.c.6.6. - due WEST.

(b) Between CENTRE Brigade (157th) and LEFT Brigade (155th) - from B.10.b.6.9. along TIRED ALLEY to its Junction with BROWN LINE (inclusive to 157th Brigade) - TIRED ALLEY (inclusive to 155th Brigade) as far as its Junstion with GREEN LINE - Thence due WESTWARDS.

(c) The Inter-Battalion Boundary - TOMMY ALLEY (inclusive to RIGHT Battalion).

2. The above alterations will take place on August 6th. Moves to be completed by 6. p.m.

3. Completion of moves will be reported to Brigade Headquarters, by wire, using the code word "GOAL".

4. A rough sketch shewing new dispositions will reach Brigade Headquarters, by 6. p.m. on 6th August.

5. ACKNOWLEDGE.

C. S. Stirling Cookson.
Captain,
Brigade Major, 157th Infantry Brigade.

~~4th~~

Issued at 11. p.m.

Copy No,	1 to	5th Bn. H.L.I.
	2	6th Bn. H.L.I.
	3	7th Bn. H.L.I.
	4	157th L.T.M.B.
	5	"D" Coy. 52nd Bn. M.G.C.
	6	277th Brigade R.F.A.
	~~155th~~	
	7	155th Infantry Brigade.
	8	156th Infantry Brigade.
	9	D.T.M.O.
	10	52nd Division.
	11	G.O.C.
	12	I.O.
	13)	War Diary.
	14)	
	15	File.

Appendix II.
4th & 5th/8/18.

APPENDIX III

SECRET.

Copy No. 12

157th Infantry Brigade Order No. 121.

11th August, 1918.

1. The 6th H.L.I. will relieve the 7th H.L.I. in the LEFT Sub-sector on the 13th August, 1918.
   On relief, the 7th H.L.I. will take over the same dispositions as those at present held by the 6th H.L.I.

2. The relief will commence immediately after breakfast and be completed by 2. p.m.

3. If the gas Beam Attack which is ordered to take place, has not been carried out before the 13th inst., all orders and instructions regarding this will be handed over to O.C. 6th H.L.I. by O.C. 7th H.L.I.
   O.C. 6th H.L.I. will place his gas personnel at the Disposal of the Brigade Gas Officer, in accordance with this office B.M.4/38. para. 4, (d), of 1st inst.

4. Details of relief will be arranged between the C.O.s concerned.

5. Trench Stores, Log Books, Special Maps and Plans will be handed over and receipts taken. Lists of Stores etc., handed over, will be ~~handed over~~ forwarded to Brigade Headquarters by the 14th inst.

6. O.C. 7th H.L.I. will hand over to O.C. 6th H.L.I. all details regarding the new dispositions.

7. All work in hand and projected will be handed over in writing.

8. Completion of relief will be notified to Brigade Headquarters by the code word " RINGU ".

9. A C K N O W L E D G E .

[signature]
Captain,
for Brigade Major, 157th Infantry Brigade.

Issued at 10.30 a.m. on 11th August, 1918.

Copy No. 1 to 5th H.L.I.
2 6th H.L.I.
3 7th H.L.I.
4 157th L.T.M.B.
5 2nd L.F.A.
6 413th Field Coy. R.E.
7 52nd Division.
8 Centre Group R.A.
9 "B" Coy. 52nd Bn. M.G.C.
10 155th Inf. Bde.
11 156th Inf. Bde.
12 } War Diary.
13 }
14 File.

Appendix III

11/8/18.

Conf.

APPENDIX VI

VERY SECRET

WARNING ORDER.

O.C.

5th H.L.I.
6th H.L.I.
7th H.L.I.
157th L.T.M.B.

52nd Division will be relieved by 51st Division. Relief to commence night 14/15th inst, and to be completed night 16th/17th inst.

On relief 52nd Division will be withdrawn into G.H.Q. Reserve.

Wm D. Maclean Capt

13th August 1918. Brigade Major, 157th Infantry Brigade

SECRET. WARNING ORDER.

O.C.
5th H.L.I.
6th H.L.I.
7th H.L.I.
157th L.T.M.B.

Further to Warning Order of to-day date.

152nd Infantry Brigade will relieve 157th Infantry Brigade on night of 15th/16th inst as follows:-

5th Seaforths will relieve 5th H.L.I.

6th Seaforths will relieve 6th H.L.I.

6th Gordons will relieve 7th H.L.I.

152nd L.T.M.B. will relieve 157th L.T.M.B.

No troops will be East of POINT du JOUR, THELUS RIDGE Line before 6 P.M. 15th inst.

Relief to be completed by 5 A.M., 16th inst.

On relief, 157th Infantry Brigade will probably be located in SAVY-AUBIGNY area.

One Coy, 51st Battn, M. G. Corps, will relieve CENTRE Coy, 52nd Battn, M. G. Corps.

13th August 1918.

[illegible]
Captain,
Brigade Major, 157th Infantry Brigade

Appendix VII.

13 8/18

[illegible]

APPENDIX VII

SECRET.

Copy No. 15

157th Infantry Brigade Order No.122.

Ref. Map. 1/40,000 36 B.&.C.
1/40,000 51 B.&.C.
1/100,000 LENS 11.

15th August, 1918.

---

1. The 52nd Division will be relieved in the line by the 8th and 51st Divisions in accordance with Table "A" on the reverse.

2. The 24th Infantry Brigade will relieve the 157th Infantry Brigade in the OPPY Section.

3. All details of relief, including guides, will be arranged between C.O.s concerned.

4. Defence Schemes, Log books, Maps, 1/10,000 and 1/20,000, Photographs, and all trench stores will be handed over and receipts taken. Details of pending gas operations will be carefully handed over.

5. During the relief there will be no movement EAST of the PONT du JOUR - THELUS Ridge line before 6 p.m.

6. (i) In the event of an alarm or enemy attack during the relief, troops will halt and man the nearest defences, reporting their dispositions at once to Brigade Headquarters.
(ii) C.O.s will remain with their opposite numbers and await orders.

7. Brigade Headquarters will close at A.28.b.30.35 on completion of relief.

8. Completion of relief will be wire "Priority" to Brigade Headquarters, using the code word "ACHA".

9. A C K N O W L E D G E.

C.S. Stirling-Cookson.
Captain,
Brigade Major, 157th Infantry Brigade.

Issued at 4 pm on 15/8/18.

Copy No.	1 to	5th H.L.I.
	2	6th H.L.I.
	3	7th H.L.I.
	4	157th L.T.M.B.
	5	2nd L.F.A.
	6	413th Fld. Coy. R.E.
	7	220th Coy. A.S.C.
	8	52nd Division.
	9	24th Infantry Bde.
	10	8th Division.
	11	155th Inf. Bde.
	12	156th Inf. Bde.
	13	"A" & "Q".
	14	Bde. Sig. Officer.
	15)	War Diary.
	16)	
	17	File.

Appendix VII
15/8/18

TABLE "A".

Serial No.	Date of Relief.	~~From.~~ Unit.	From.	~~Relieved.~~ To.	Relieved by.
1	16/17th August.	157th Bde. Hqrs.	A.28.b.30.35.	WHITE HOUSE, Mt. St. ELOY.	24th Bde. Hqrs.
2	" "	5th H.L.I.	Front Line (Right).	ROCLINCOURT West Camp.	2nd Northampton. Regt.
3.	" "	6th H.L.I.	Front Line (Left).	DURHAM and LANCASTER Camps.	1st Worcestershire Regt.
4.	" "	7th H.L.I.	BROWN LINE (Support).	FRASER Camp.	1 Sherwood Foresters.
5.	" "	157th L.T.M.B.	Line.	FRASER Camp.	24th L.T.M.B.

Reliefs will take place in following order :- Serials 2, 3. Simultaneously No, 2 using CONCRETE Road and OUSE ALLEY, No. 3 using Plank Road and TIRED ALLEY. No. 4 using OUSE and TIRED ALLEYS, No.5 under their own arrangements.

A distance of 200 yards between platoons will be maintained when crossing the Ridge before dark.

SECRET.   Copy No......

157th Infantry Brigade Administrative Instructions
No. 113.
Issued with reference to Brigade Order No. 122.

15th August, 1918.

On relief by the 24th Infantry Brigade Battalions will move to Camps as under :-

5th H.L.I.	ROCLINCOURT WEST.
6th H.L.I.	Durham & Lancaster Camps, Mt.St. ELOI
7th H.L.I.	Fraser Camp, MONT ST. ELOI.
157th L.T.M.Bty.	" " " " "
Brigade Hqrs.	WHITE HOUSE, " " "

Move.

5th H.L.I. will move by March route the remainder of the Brigade by Busses which bring up releiving Battalions.

Transport & Q.M. Parties.

These will remain at their present positions, in ECOIVRES.

Supplies.

Rations will be drawn as at present from Supply Dump at ECOIVRES. Rations for 5th H.L.I. will be sent up by Battalion Transport.

AREA STORES.

All Trench and Area Stores will be handed over and receipts taken.

Duplicate lists of stores handed over will be forwarded to Brigade Hqrs., by 1800 on 17th inst.

Duplicate lists of Area Stores taken over will also be forwarded to Brigade Hqrs.

DUTIES.

Battalion on Duty 17th August,	7th H. L. I.
" " " 18th "	6th H. L. I.

DISCIPLINE.

Battalion Bounds will be marked by Battalion Boards. No man will leave his Battalion area without a pass and without being properly dressed.

NECLEUS & BRIGADE PIONEER COY.

All personnel of the Brigade Pioneer Coy and Necleus will rejoin their Units at MONT ST. ELOI on 17th inst. They will be rationed up to and including the 18th.

ADVANCED PARTIES.

1 Officer and 6 O.R. per Battalion (Less 5th H.L.I.) and 1 Officer from L.T.M.Bty., will report to Bde. Hqrs., Representative at WHITE HOUSE, MONT ST. ELOI, at 3 p.m. on 16th inst to take over Camps.

An Officer and Billetting party from 5th H.L.I. will report at present Brigade Hqrs at 3 p.m. on 16th inst to take over Camp.

ACKNOWLEDGE

H M Hewison

Captain,
Staff Captain, 157th Infantry Brigade.

Appendix VII
15/8/18

SECRET. Copy. No. 1.....

157th Infantry Brigade Order No. 123.

APPENDIX VIII

Ref. Map. LENS 36 B. 1/40,000. 16th August, 1918

1. The 157th Infantry Brigade will move to the CHATEAU-de-la-HAIE Area on 17th August, 1918, in accordance with Table "A" on reverse.

2. Transport will accompany units with the exception of 5th H.L.I. The usual distances will be maintained between units on the march.

3. One lorry will report to 5th H.L.I. at ROCLINCOURT West Camp, at 11. a.m. and one at transport lines ECOIVRES at same time. 3 lorries will report at Brigade Headquarters ST. ELOI, at 12. noon for Brigade Headquarters, 6th & 7th H.L.I. for conveyance of baggage.

4. Brigade Headquarters will close at ST. ELOI at 2 p.m. and open at CHATEAU de la HAIE at the same time.

5. O.C. 5th H.L.I. will detail an entraining and detraining officer.

6. Advance parties will be sent on in advance to-morrow morning, 17th. They should report to the Area Commandent CHATEAU de la HAIE at 10. a.m. where they will be met by the Staff Captain.

7. Acknowledge.

W.Wallace Captain,
for Brigade Major, 157th Infantry Brigade.

Issued at 12. midnight.

Copy No. 1 to 5th H.L.I.
2 6th H.L.I.
3 7th H.L.I.
4 157th L.T.M.B.
5 Hqrs. 52nd Division.
6 Staff Captain.
7) War Diary.
8)
9 File.

Table. "A".

Serial No.	Unit.	From.	To.	Remarks.
1	Brigade Hqrs.	St. ELOI.	CHATEAU de la HAIE. X.13.a.9.9.	Route March. Starting 2. p.m. from ST. ELOI.
2	5th H.L.I.	ROCLINCOURT W. CAMP.	St. LAWRENCE CAMP. X.7.a.	Route March. Starting from present Camp 2. p.m.
3	6th H.L.I.	DURHAM and LANCASTER CAMPS.	CANADA CAMP. X.7.a.	Route March. Starting 2.30 p.m. from Camp.
4	7th H.L.I.	FRASER CAMP.	MARQUEFFLES HUTS. R.26.b.	Route March. Starting 2. p.m. from Camp.
5	157th L.T.M.B.	FRASER CAMP.	St. LAWERENCE CAMP. X.7.a.	Route March. Starting 3. p.m.

No restrictions as regards routes.

O.C. 5th Bn. H.L.I.
6th Bn. H.L.I.
7th Bn. H.L.I.
157th L.T.M.B.

Bm 7/45
17/8/18

Reference Brigade Order No. 13[illegible] of 16th inst.

Map Reference should read 36 [illegible]/20,000 and not [illegible] 36 [illegible]/40,000

When on the march, units will march in threes and not in fours.

[illegible] Captain,

17th August, 1918. for Brigade Major, 157th Infantry Brigade.

BM3/44

[illegible]

Warning Order

1. The 10th [illegible] Bn. will move to the CHATEAU-de-la-HAIE area [illegible] [illegible]

2. [illegible] will move by road [illegible] [illegible] and [illegible] [illegible] by route march.
[illegible] of starting and destination will be [illegible] later.

3. [illegible] [illegible] [illegible] [illegible] [illegible] [illegible] [illegible] [illegible] [illegible] [illegible] [illegible] [illegible] [illegible] [illegible] [illegible] [illegible] [illegible] [illegible] [illegible]

C. S. [illegible]

[illegible] [illegible] [illegible]

Copies to [illegible]
[illegible]
[illegible]
[illegible]
[illegible]

APPENDIX IX

SECRET. Copy No. 9

157th Infantry Brigade Order No. 124.

20th August 1918.

Ref: map LENS 11, 1/100,000.

1. The 52nd Division will concentrate, starting to-night 20th/21st August.

2. The 157th Infantry Brigade Group will move by route march to AGNEZ LES DUISANS including "Y" Huts to-night, 20th August.

Route:- via VILLERS-AU-BOIS - ACQ - HAUTE AVESNES.

3. Units will move off from their present billets as follows:-

Brigade Headquarters	10 P.m.
5th H.L.I.	10.15 P.m
6th H.L.I.	10.45 P.m.
7th H.L.I.	10.15 P.m.
157th L.T.M.B.	11 P.m
413th Field Coy, R.E.	10.45 P.m
2nd Low. Field ambulance	11-30 P.m.

4. The usual interval between Companies will be maintained on the march.

5. Brigade Headquarters will close at CHATEAU de la HAIE at 9.45 P.m. and open at AGNEZ LES DUISANS at the same hour.

6. ACKNOWLEDGE.

W. D. Wallace Captain,

for Brigade Major, 157th Infantry Brigade.

Issued at 8-30 P.m on the 20th inst.

Copy No. 1 to 5th H.L.I.
2 6th H.L.I.
3 7th H.L.I.
4 157th L.T.M.B.
5 2nd L.F.A.

Copy No. 6 to 413th Field Coy, R.E.
7 52nd Division.
8 Staff Captain.
9, 10 War Diary.

Copy No. 11 to File.

SECRET. APPENDIX X Copy No. 12

157th Infantry Brigade Order No. 136.

Ref. Map LENS 11. 1/100,000. 22nd August, 1918.

---

1. The 157th Infantry Brigade Group will move by route march to-night, to BELLACOURT and BRETENCOURT, via WARLUS - BERNEVILLE - BEAUMETZ LES LOGES.

2. Order of march will be as follows :-

7th H.L.I.	start from present camp at ZERO.	
6th H.L.I.	" " " " " "	plus 30 minutes.
5th H.L.I.	" " " " " "	" 60 "
157th L.T.M.B.	" " " " " "	" 75 "
413th Field Coy. R.E.	" " " " "	" 90 "
220th Coy. A.S.C.	" " " " "	" 120 "
2nd L.F.A.	" " " " "	" 130 "

Transport will accompany units.

3. ZERO Hour, i.e time to march off, will be notified later.

4. The usual intervals will be maintained between all units on the march.

5. ACKNOWLEDGE.

B Stirling Cookson
Captain,
Brigade Major, 157th Infantry Brigade.

Issued at.........

Copy No. 1 to 5th H.L.I.	5 to 413th Field Coy, R.E.	9 Staff Captain.	
2 6th H.L.I.	6 2nd L.F.A.	10) War Diary.	
3 7th H.L.I.	7 220 th Coy A.S.C.	11)	
4 157th L.T.M.B.	8 52nd Division.	12 File.	

SECRET.

O.C. 9th Bn. H.L.I.
     6th Bn. H.L.I.
     7th Bn. H.L.I.
     157th L.T.M.B.

220th Coy. A.S.C.
413th Field Coy. R.E.
2nd L.F.A.

An officer from Brigade Headquarters has been sent ~~on~~ forward to arrange billets and will, if possible and if the cross country road from BERNEVILLE S.W. to BRETENCOURT is practicable, send guides to BERNEVILLE to meet units which will be billetted in BRETENCOURT.

Captain,
Brigade Major, 157th Infantry Brigade.

22nd August, 1918.

Appendix X

22 8/18

[illegible]

Secret Copy No

157th Infantry Brigade

APPENDIX XI

Administrative Instructions

Ref map 1/20,000 25th Aug 1918

Sheet 51 C SE

Sheet 51 B SW.

1. SAA Grenades etc Stores

(a) Main Divisional Dump BLAIREVILLE (R.34.c.4.4)

x (b) Main Brigade Dump - BLAIREVILLE QUARRY (R.34.d.4.4)

x (c) Forward Brigade Dump M.34.d.8.3.

(d) 157th Brigade Dump M.27.a.5.0

(e) " " " M.27.a.5.8

(f) " " " S.3.b.2.3

(g) " " " M.35.d.7.3.

(h) Battalions will notify Brigade before sending to Main Divisional Dump the number of rounds required to complete to mobile Establishment

x. These dumps belong to 156th Brigade but 157th Brigade has a call on them.

2. Reserve Rations

One days reserve rations will be ~~held~~ dumped at Brigade Refilling Point tonight. Position will be notified later.

3. Water

(a) Two 500 gallon and five 100 gallon mobile water tanks will be in reserve at Divisional Headquarters. Application for water from this source should be made to Brigade Headquarters.

(b). 1,000 petrol tins (2 gallon tins) will be dumped in the Main and Forward Bde Ammunition Dumps (see 1. (b) & (c) above). These belong to 156th Brigade but 157th Brigade has a call on them.

(c) 1,200 filled water bottles are also in (b) & (c) Brigade dumps.

(d) Water points in the Back and Forward Areas are as under.

	Horse Troughs.	Water Cart R.P.	Pumping Station	Hand Pumps	Reservoirs	Remarks
BRETONCOURT						
GROSVILLER						
RIVIERE						
R.27.a.3.4.			1			
R.26.d.8.9			1			
FICHEUX R.36.a.5.2					1	
BELLACOURT R.31.a.2.8	1					
R.31.a.3.9.				1		
R.31.b.3.9.	1					
R.31.b.5.9				1		
R.33.a.9.5	1					

(e)/

(e) Battalions will arrange to fill their Mobile Petrol tins from their water carts and establish Battalion forward Water Dumps. Carts should immediately be sent back to be refilled.

(f) All men must be in possession of a filled water bottle at dawn on morning of 24th inst.

4 RE. Dumps.

Main Divisional RE. Dump. GROSVILLE R.26.a.6.0

Advanced RE Dumps. S.5.d.8.4 and M.35.d.6.7

5. Medical Arrangements.

Regimental Aid Posts.	S.4.c.9.0
	M.35.a.7.9.
	S.2.b.5.0
	M.29.c.1.9.
Advanced Dressing Station	M.31.d.1.6.
Corps Main Dressing Station	Q.31.d.5.6

6 Prisoners of War.

(a) Advanced Prisoners of War Collecting Station.

Boiryville Quarry. R.34.d.5.4.

(b) Divisional Prisoners of War Cage. R.27.c.1.1.

Prisoners will be brought back to (a) under Battn arrangements. From (a) to (b) by an escort supplied by Division.

7. Veterinary
Collecting Post at Divisional Headquarters BRETON COURT.

8. Burial Bodies will be sent under Brigade arrangements to BLAIREVILLE CEMETERY. X.4.d.2.9. Units will collect bodies and notify location to Brigade.

9. A.P.M. arrangements. Battle Straggler Posts.
(a) No 1. R.33.a.9.4. No 2. R.27.d.2.2. No 3. R.22.c.2.0.
(b) Prisoners of War Camp. This is located at R.27.d.2.3. The corps cage is at GOUY-EN-ARTOIS. Q.19.a.

10. Transport lines & Ration Refilling Point.
Transport lines and Ration Refilling Point will remain in their present position at Bellacourt.

11 Acknowledge H.M. Hewison
Capt.
24/8/18 Staff Capt. 157th Inf Bde

Issued at

Copy No 1	to 5 H.L.I.	7	2nd L.F.A.
2	6 H.L.I.	8	B.M.
3	7 H.L.I.	9	War Diary
4	157 L.T.M.B.	10	
5	413th Field Coy R.E.	11	File.
6	220th Coy A.S.C.		

SECRET.

APPENDIX XI

157th Infantry Brigade Order No 130.

Reference Sheet 51 B. S.W.

24th August 1918.

1. The Army will advance to allow the enemy no respite in this retreat. Accordingly the 52nd Division will conform to the movements of troops on ~~its~~ flanks.

2. The 157th Brigade will pass through the line at present held by the 156th Brigade and which runs approximately from T2c 5.0 to T1a 8.8. The 157th Brigade will attack eastwards maintaining touch with the 56th Division which will be attacking on our right. The 157th Brigade will finally assault and consolidate that portion of the HINDENBURG LINE between T5a and N34d. Both Front and Support systems to be captured.

3. The 156th Brigade will advance on the left of the 157th Brigade at 7 a.m to the road N32b7.6 and to N26 Cent conforming to movement of 157th Inf Brigade and being echeloned in LEFT Rear.

4. The 6th H.L.I. will attack on the RIGHT. The 5th H.L.I. will attack on the LEFT. The 7th H.L.I. and 157th L.T.M.B. (less 2 Sections), C Company, 52nd Battalion, M.G. Corps (less 1 section) will be in Brigade Reserve.

5. The approach march will be timed to bring the two assaulting Battalions into line held by the 156th Brigade by 6-45 a.m. The attack will be carried forward from this line punctually at 7 a.m in conjunction with the 56th Division on our RIGHT and our troops on our LEFT, the 156th Brigade following echeloned behind our LEFT FLANK. For the approach march, the 6th & 5th H.L.I. will start in Artillery formation from the W side of the Railway running NORTH and SOUTH from S3a & c. The 6th H.L.I on the RIGHT with its RIGHT at the junction of the Road with the Railway at S3c 7.2 and a frontage of approximately 800 Yards. The 5th H.L.I forming up on the LEFT. Advance from here to commence at 4-15 a.m. The Advance to be regulated so that the leading lines do not pass through the 156th Brigade lines until 6-45 a.m.

2.

6. The 7th H.L.I. and other troops in Brigade Reserve will move to a position of assembly so as to follow about 1½ miles in rear of 6th H.L.I. when the latter Unit moves forward at 4.15 a.m. During the advance the 6th H.L.I. will direct.

7. O.C., 157th L.T.M.B. will detail 2 Guns to 6th H.L.I. & 2 Guns to 5th H.L.I. to report on the Railway Line at 4 a.m. O.C. 157th L.T.M.B. will be prepared to reconnoitre and place the remainder of the Guns in position to cover consolidation.

8. O.C. M.G. Coy will detail 1 Section of Guns for an independent mission as a Battery of opportunity. He will, with the remainder of his guns take every advantage of covering the advance, 1 Section to be always in Brigade Reserve following in rear of 7th H.L.I. After the capture of the final objective he will dispose his guns in depth, to cover the consolidation and repel counter attacks.

9. On arrival in the 156th Brigade Lines the 6th H.L.I. will at once gain close contact with LEFT, 51st Division maintaining it throughout the attack.

10. During the attack the 6th H.L.I. will direct. All Company Officers will work on Compass bearings.

11. Rations for 24th, plus 1 days Iron Rations will be carried on the man.

12. Frequent information and situation reports will be sent to Brigade Headquarters.

13. Prisoners will be sent back under a small escort to behind the Railway at starting point.

14. Brigade Headquarters will be at S.5.c.9.3.

15. ACKNOWLEDGE.

A.S. Stirling Cookson

Captain,

Brigade Major, 157th Infantry Brigade.

Appendix XI
23rd + 24th/8/18

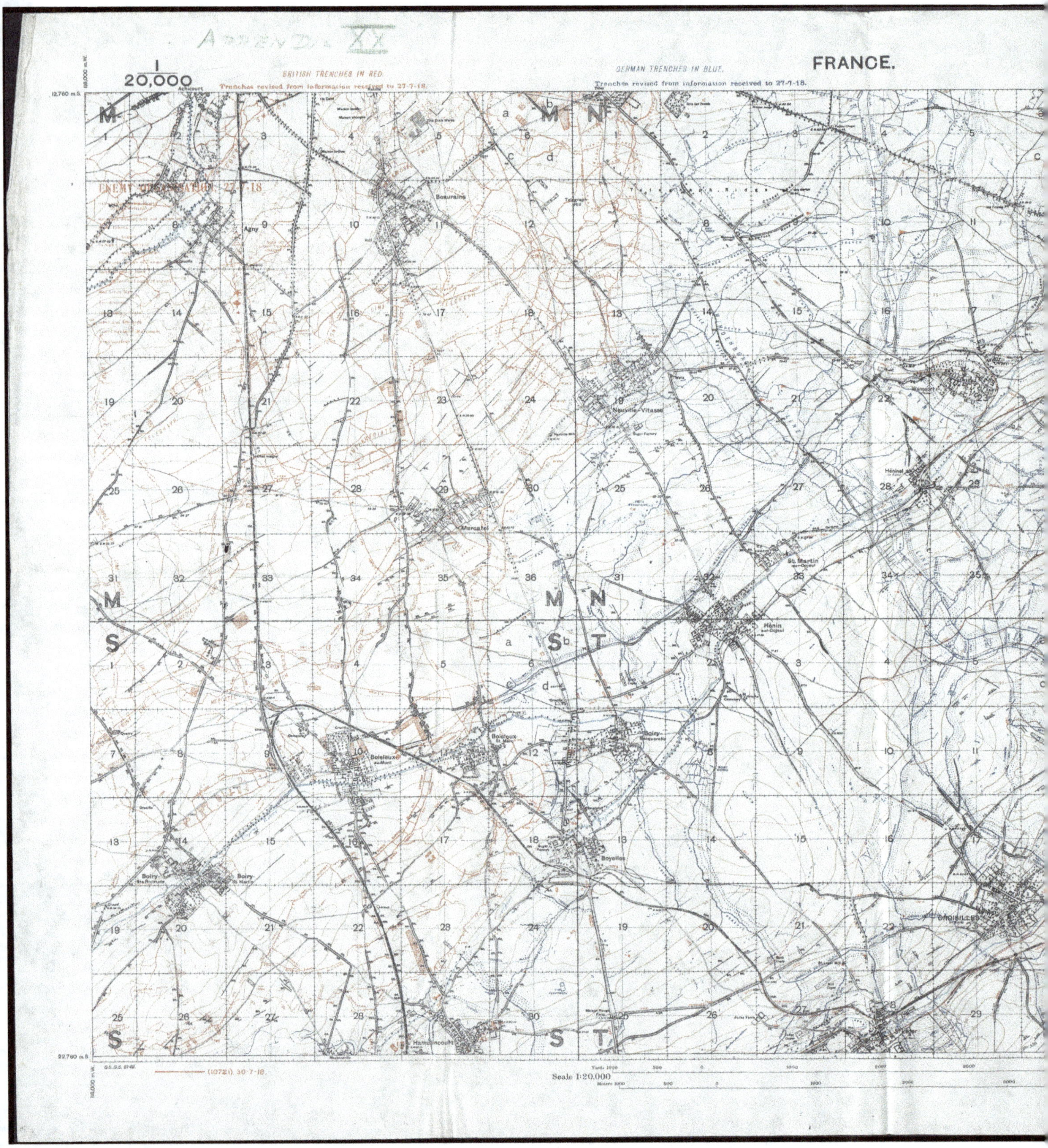

Appendix XX
1
20,000
BRITISH TRENCHES IN RED.
Trenches revised from information received to 27-7-18.
GERMAN TRENCHES IN BLUE.
Trenches revised from information received to 27-7-18.
FRANCE.
Agny
Beaurains
Neuville-Vitasse
Mercatel
Héninel
St. Martin
Hénin
Boisleux-au-Mont
Boisleux-St. Marc
Boyelles
Boiry
Hamelincourt
CROISILLES
(10721). 30-7-18.
Scale 1:20,000

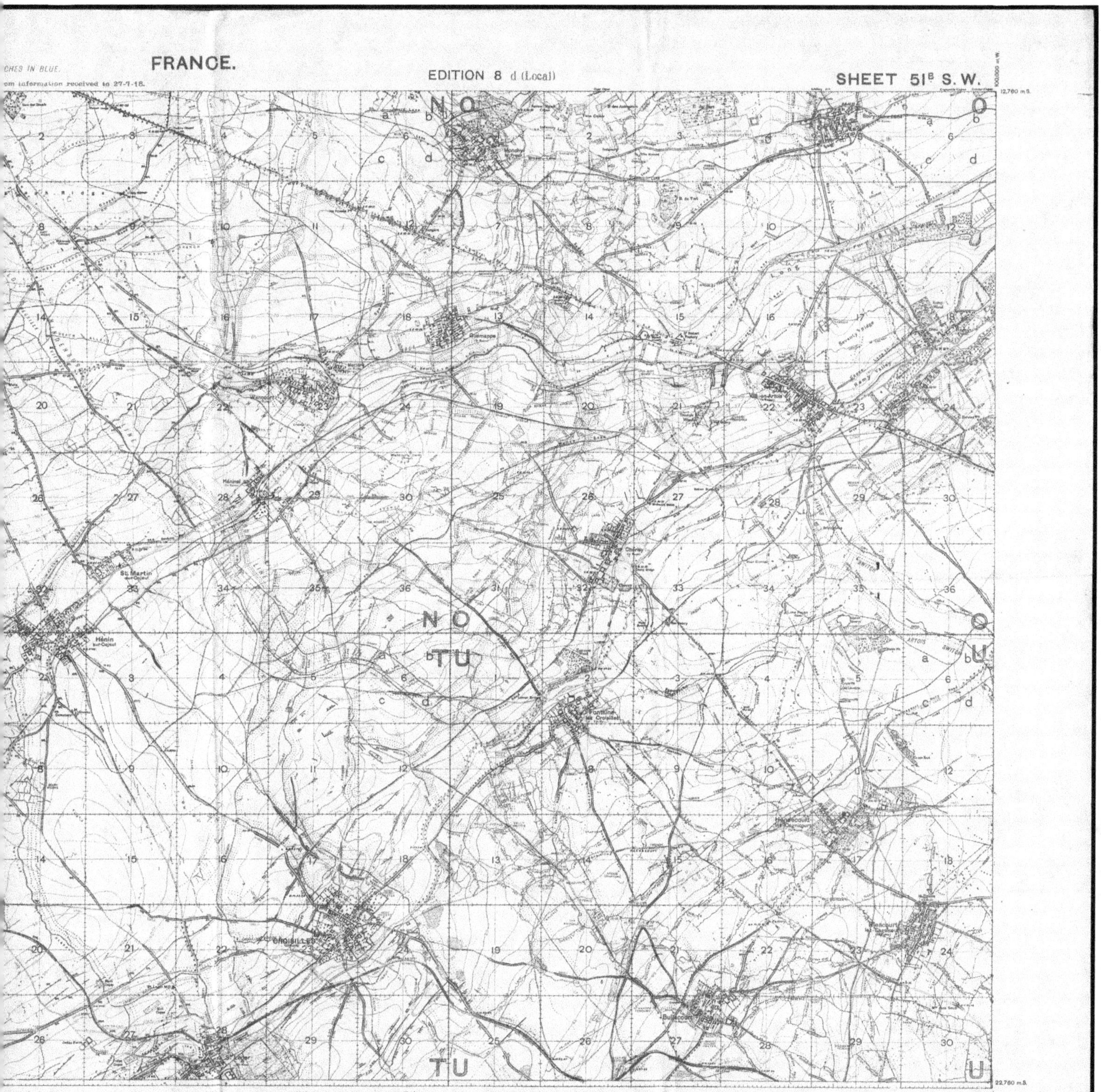

FRANCE.
EDITION 8 d (Local)
SHEET 51B S.W.
...CHES IN BLUE.
...om information received to 27-1-18.
NO
TU
O
U
Monchy
Guémappe
Héninel
St. Martin
Hénin sur-Cojeul
Chérisy
Fontaine les Croisilles
Hendecourt
Croisilles
Bullecourt
Riencourt
Ordnance Survey, May, 1916.
12,760 m.S.
22,760 m.S.
Yards
Metres

H.Q.,
157TH INFANTRY
BRIGADE.
No. ....
Date ....

APPENDIX XII

SECRET

154th Infantry Brigade Order No. 131.

24th August 1918

1. Units will maintain their present line and watch the outer flanks, both of which are exposed.

2. Positions will be strengthened against counter-attacks. Present front line will be Main Line of Resistance.

3. 12 MG's are disposed in depth on the Brigade Front.

4. Defensive Patrols will be sent out to cover the front. 7th HLI will send a patrol to be in touch with 156th Brigade on the LEFT.

5. 9 Brigades of Field Artillery are presently covering the Brigade Front and will put down an S.O.S. on HINDENBURG LINE when called for.

6. Brigade Headquarters will remain at T2c 2.8.

7. 154th Brigade will be prepared to attack early to-morrow morning.

Order of Battle:-

5th HLI in RESERVE.
6th HLI on RIGHT.
7th HLI. on LEFT.
MG's & LTMB as for to-day.

8. ACKNOWLEDGE

C.S. Stirling Cookson
Captain,
Brigade Major, 154th Infantry Brigade

Appendix XII

24 8/18

[illegible]

SECRET. APPENDIX XIII

157th Infantry Brigade Order No 132.

25th August 1918.

1. The 157th Brigade will alter & establish its dispositions, as follows, to-day with the intention of carrying out a prepared attack on the HINDENBURG LINE (not to-day) in conjunction with the troops on our RIGHT.

2. Dispositions:-

(a) Observation line to be about 250 yards from HINDENBURG LINE

(b) Main Line of Resistance T3b & T4c.

(c) Reserve Line (Road through T3 a, c & d).

The 6th & 7th H.L.I will be in (a) & (b) & suitably placed between (a) & (c). The 5th H.L.I. in (c).

3. The adjustment will be carried out gradually to-day without attracting attention. The 7th H.L.I. taking over from 5th H.L.I., the latter going into the RESERVE Line.

The adjustment will be arranged between all 3 C.O.s.

4. Strong Patrols must be sent out by day and night to reconnoitre and bring in information regarding the HINDENBURG LINE which is to be systematically attacked.

5. 6th H.L.I. will occupy SUMMIT TRENCH and if possible FAT SWITCH in T4d & T5c respectively and without serious fighting.

6. 6th H.L.I. will be in close touch with the troops of the Division on our RIGHT Flank.

[signature] Captain,

Brigade Major, 157th Infantry Brigade

Appendix XIII

25 8/18

hwe

SECRET. APPENDIX XIV BMX/1304

5th, 6th & 7th HLI & (157th LTMB for information).

I. O.C. Battns will send out one Officer patrol at once to work in the direction of the HENIN HILL & HINDENBURG LINE to see if the Enemy will shew his hand

As the heavies are still firing on HINDENBURG LINE, the patrols must not go too close up to that line.

This patrolling will be constantly kept up, the patrols however must not get involved but are to obtain information, this information to be wired to Brigade H.Qrs as soon as received.

II The 155th Bde have captured the HINDENBURG line and are working down the line to cross our Front, clearing the HINDENBURG Line as they go.

As soon as the 155th Brigade are seen approaching our Front, each Battn will send out 2 or 3 patrols, these patrols will not however get mixed up with the 155th Bde, but are merely to make the enemy think we are about to launch an attack.

III MONCHY has been captured by the Canadians and our troops are on the E outskirts of GUEMAPPE.

IV ACKNOWLEDGE.

A.S. Stirling Cookson
Captain
Brigade Major, 157th Infantry Brigade

26th August 1918.

Appendix XIV

SECRET APPENDIX XV

Addendum to 154th Infantry Brigade Order No. 134.

1. O.C, C Coy, 52nd Battn, M.G. Corps will detail 4 Machine Guns to be placed at the disposal of O.C, 4th H.L.I.

The remainder of C Coy, 52nd Battn, M.G. Corps will concentrate in the area alloted to 5th H.L.I.

2. The L.T.M.B will concentrate also in the area alloted to 5th H.L.I.

J. Stirling Cookson

Captain,

26th August, 1918. Brigade Major, 154th Infantry Brigade

SECRET.

I

157th Infantry Brigade Order No 134.

26th August 1918.

1. The 155th Brigade is clearing the HINDENBURG LINE as far as SENSEE RIVER and will cross the river and establish itself about FONTAINE-CROISILLES.

The 156th Brigade, with objective the Road in U1 d 8-9 to O32 Central, will be echeloned to the left rear of the 155th Brigade.

2. The 155th Brigade is dropping one Battalion at HENIN HILL.

3. The 7th HLI will take over HENIN HILL from this Battalion of 155th Brigade. 7th HLI to face N & E.

4. The 6th HLI will concentrate in the area T4a - T3 b & d (exclusive of SUNKEN ROAD in T3d) and T4c.

5. The 5th HLI will be located in the vicinity of the SUNKEN Road T3d - T3c and, if necessary, in T9b.

6. The 157th Brigade is in Divisional Reserve.

7. ACKNOWLEDGE.

[signature]

Captain,

Brigade Major, 157th Infantry Brigade

Appendix XV
(~~Duplicate~~)
26/8/15
mon

SECRET. APPENDIX XVI

157th Infantry Brigade Order No. 135.

27th August 1918.

1. The 157th Brigade will attack at 9-20 a.m. to-day under barrage and will capture FONTAINE CROISILLES and continue advance S.E. and take RIENCOURT U24.

2. 6th & 7th H.L.I. will be assaulting Battalions, 6th H.L.I. on RIGHT, 7th H.L.I. on LEFT and 5th H.L.I. in RESERVE.

3. Assault Battns will assemble along the line of SUMMIT TRENCH from T4 d 6 0 to junction with HINDENBURG SUPPORT Line at N35 c 3-4. Approach to this line to be concealed from FOOLEY TRENCH.

4. Frontage for 6th H.L.I. will be from the RIGHT of this line to where the track crosses it in T5 c 3.9. Frontage for 7th H.L.I. from there to LEFT.

5. Battalions will be ready to advance at 9-20 a.m. Barrage will come down on FOOLEY TRENCH from T11 a 3.7 to T5 b 1-9 and remain down till 9-36 a.m., by which time the assaulting Battalions will have moved forward close up under the barrage. At 9-36 a.m. barrage and assaulting troops will move forward at 100 yds per 4 minutes direct on FONTAINE CROISILLES. 7th H.L.I. will direct.

6. The 155th Brigade will mop up HINDENBURG LINE behind our attack as far as FOP LANE. The Left of the 7th H.L.I. will be directed on S end of FONTAINE CROISILLES.

7. The 156th Brigade will be attacking under a separate barrage on our LEFT. The Right of this Brigade is being directed on N end of FONTAINE CROISILLES.

8. The barrage for 52nd Division will remain on general line of UNA TRENCH EAST of FONTAINE CROISILLES for 30 minutes after when it will lift and 157th Brigade will push on to RIENCOURT and 156th Brigade to HENDECOURT.

9. On assaulting Battns approaching FONTAINE CROISILLES, 5th H.L.I., in reserve, will close up 1 Coy close behind 7th H.L.I. to mop up FONTAINE CROISILLES. This Coy will follow the Brigade when its mission is finished.

10. While barrage is on general line UNA Tr for 30

154th Inf Bde. Order No 135
Para 10 Contd.

minutes, the Assault Battalions will re-organise and get their direction for REINCOURT, the advance to which should be continued, without further order, the moment the barrage lifts.

11. The 5th H.L.I in reserve will form up behind the junction of 6th HLI & 7th HLI, WEST of SUMMIT TRENCH & follow the advance, one mile behind.

12. The L.T.M. Bty will follow as soon as transport can be provided. 4 MG's will follow close behind the leading wave. The remainder of the Guns will support the advance under separate order from their C.O.

13. Advanced Brigade HQrs will be established in FAT SWITCH where track crosses it in T5c3-9. Frequent reports showing location of Front Lines and progress must be sent in.

14. The 56th Division will be attacking on our RIGHT, forming up on SUMMIT TRENCH just S of 6th HLI.

15. ACKNOWLEDGE.

[signature]
Captain,
Brigade Major, 154th Infantry Brigade.

Appendix XVI

8

27/18

[illegible]

SECRET. APPENDIX XVII Copy No ....

157th Infantry Brigade Order No 136.

31st August 1918.

1. The 52nd Division will take over the battle line at BULLECOURT from 56th Division, starting on the night 31st August/1st September.

2. The 157th Infantry Brigade will move to HENIN HILL area on 1st September in the following order:-

Brigade HQ	leaving present camp	7-30 a.m
5th HLI	" " "	6.45 a.m
7th HLI	" " "	7.00 a.m
6th HLI	" " "	7.15 a.m.
157th L.T.M.B.	" " "	7-30 a.m.

A distance of 500 yards between Battalions on the march and 100 yards between Companies will be maintained.

3. One Officer per Battalion and L.T.M.B. will proceed in advance to HENIN HILL to-day to be alloted their respective bivouac areas by Capt Speirs.

4. From 7 O'Clock on the night 31st August/1st September the 157th Infantry Brigade will be ready to move at one hour's notice.

5. Brigade Headquarters will close at its present site at 7-30 a.m on 1st prox, and open at T.4.b.8-6 at same time.

6. ACKNOWLEDGE.

[signature]

Captain,

Brigade Major, 157th Infantry Brigade

Copy No 1 to 5th HLI	Copy No 7 to 52nd Division	Issued at 11-30 a.m on 31/8/18
2 6th HLI	8 220th Coy. A.S.C	
3 7th HLI	9 Staff Capt.	
4 157th L.T.M.B.	10, 11 War Diary	
5 413th Field Co R.E.		
6 2nd L.F. Amb.	12 File	

~~Appendix XVII~~

~~C 9~~

~~31 / 14~~

~~[illegible]~~

APPENDIX XVIII

KILLED

DATE	5 H.L.I. OFF	5 H.L.I. O.R	6 H.L.I. OFF	6 H.L.I. O.R	7 H.L.I. OFF	7 H.L.I. O.R	L.T.M.B OF	L.T.M.B O.R
24/8/18	1	14	1	16	1	3		
25/8/18	·	1	·	1	·	·		
26/8/18	·	·	·	1	·	·		
27/8/18	1	3	2	14	3	28		
28/8/18	·	·	·	·	·	·		
TOTAL	2	18	3	32	4	31		

WOUNDED

DATE	5 H.L.I. OF	5 H.L.I. O.R	6 H.L.I. OF	6 H.L.I. O.R	7 H.L.I. OF	7 H.L.I. O.R	L.T.M.B OF	L.T.M.B O.R
24/8/18	6	134	9	138	4	84	2	1
25/8/18		2	1	20		12		
26/8/18		1		11	1	1		
27/8/18	3	44	1	141	3	122		1
28/8/18		2		1				
TOTAL	9	233	11	311	8	222	2	2

WOUNDED (GAS)

DATE	5 H.L.I. OF	5 H.L.I. O.R	6 H.L.I. OF	6 H.L.I. O.R	7 H.L.I. OF	7 H.L.I. O.R	L.T.M.B OF	L.T.M.B O.R
24/8/18	·	1	·	·	·	1	1	1
25/8/18					1	4		1
26/8/18								4
27/8/18		13			1	3		
28/8/18								
TOTAL		14			2	8	1	6

DIED OF WOUNDS

DATE	5 H.L.I. OF	5 H.L.I. O.R	6 H.L.I. OF	6 H.L.I. O.R	7 H.L.I. OF	7 H.L.I. O.R	L.T.M.B OF	L.T.M.B O.R
24/8/18	1	·	·	4	·	·	·	·
25/8/18				2				
26/8/18				2				
27/8/18		1						
28/8/18								
TOTAL	1	1		8				

MISSING

DATE	5 H.L.I. OF	5 H.L.I. O.R	6 H.L.I. OF	6 H.L.I. O.R	7 H.L.I. OF	7 H.L.I. O.R	L.T.M.B OF	L.T.M.B O.R
24/8/18	3	50	·	9	·	14	·	·
25/8/18		2						
26/8/18		1		1				
27/8/18		6				15		
28/8/18								
TOTAL	3	59		10		29		

WOUNDED & MISSING

DATE	5 H.L.I. OF	5 H.L.I. O.R	6 H.L.I. OF	6 H.L.I. O.R	7 H.L.I. OF	7 H.L.I. O.R	L.T.M.B OF	L.T.M.B O.R
24/8/18	·	9	·	·	·	·	·	·
25/8/18								
26/8/18								
27/8/18								
28/8/18								
TOTAL		9						

Totals.

	Officers	Other Ranks
Killed	9	87
Wounded	30	468
Wounded (Gas)	3	28
Died of Wounds	1	9
Missing	3	98
Wounded & Missing	·	9
	46	993

Appendix XIX

Estimated captured personnel & materiel 23rd to 27th inst both inclusive.

	Approx No.
Prisoners	200
Guns	6
Machine Guns	48
Trench Mortars	20.

31/8/18

W. D. Macrae
Capt.
for Bde Major 157th Inf Bde

Vol 6

H Qrs, 157th Inf Bde

War Diary

Volume III

September 1918.

CONFIDENTIAL.

Instructions regarding War Diaries and Intelligence Summaries are contained in F. S. Regs., Part II. and the Staff Manual respectively. Title pages will be prepared in manuscript.

WAR DIARY
or
INTELLIGENCE SUMMARY.
(Erase heading not required.) — SEPTEMBER 1918 —

157th INFY BDE. S1

Army Form C. 2118.

VOLUME III.

REFERENCE MAP 51b SW 1/20000

Place	Date	Hour	Summary of Events and Information	Remarks and references to Appendices
S4a 2.4 (near BOISLEUX AU MONT)	1/9/18	7 am	Bde left S4a & moved to HEMIN HILL T4a & b in accordance with Bde Order No 136. Units arrived in their bivouac areas by 10 am & remained there for the rest of the day and the following night.	See APPENDIX XVII for August
		7 pm	Bde Order 137 issued (Appendix I)	Appendix I.
			CASUALTIES:- Nil	
T4a & b HEMIN HILL	2/9/18	5 am to 5.30 am	Bde moved from HEMIN HILL to U13a & b & U7c & d in accordance with Bde Order 137	
		7 am	Arrived in this area but immediately received orders to push on to new area in U21 - just N. of BULLECOURT.	
		11 am	Arrived at U21.	
		7 pm	Bde received orders to attack at 11 am on 3rd inst	
			CASUALTIES.- 2 OR wounded - 7th HLI.	
U21 (N. of BULLECOURT)	3/9/18	2.30 am	Bde order 138 issued to units (Appendix II)	Appendix II.
		7.30 am	Bde HQ moved to U27d 4.4	
		8 am	Bde learned that the towns of QUEANT & PRONVILLE through which we had been ordered to attack were now in possession of our troops.	
		10 am	BM1000 (Appendix III) issued giving further instructions re the attack timed for 11 am	Appendix III
		11.45 am	Bde moved off according to Bde Order 138 & took their objectives without opposition taking 1 off. & 14 prisoners. On the objective being reached the 4th RSF of 155th Bde relieved the 7th HLI (Appendix IV) 2 pm B.G.C found a German in a shell hole & took him prisoner.	
		3.10 pm	B.M. 1510 issued & all dispositions as laid down therein taken up by 7 pm	Appendix IV
		—	Bde placed in "Corps Support" having been "pinched out" of front line by Guards Division on right and 63rd Division on left the two last named Divisions gaining touch with each other. - Nothing special occurred during the night	
			CASUALTIES:- 1 OR 5th HLI wounded - 2 OR 7th HLI (wounded) (gassed)	

Wm D. Maclae Capt.

D. D. & L., London, E.C. (A6001) Wt. W1771/M1031 750,000 5/17 Sch. 52 Forms C2118/14

Instructions regarding War Diaries and Intelligence Summaries are contained in F. S. Regs., Part II. and the Staff Manual respectively. Title pages will be prepared in manuscript.

CONFIDENTIAL

Army Form C. 2118.

WAR DIARY
or
INTELLIGENCE SUMMARY.
(Erase heading not required.)

157th INFY BDE — SEPTEMBER 1918 — A 2 — VOLUME III

Place	Date	Hour	Summary of Events and Information	Remarks and references to Appendices
Near QUEANT German Hutments C12 b 95.85 57c N.E. 20000	4/9/18		Still in "Corps Support". Uneventful day on our immediate front. Warning Order issued to units of probable move tomorrow into reserve.	[initials]
			CASUALTIES – 1 OR 5th H.L.I. wounded.	
"	5/9/18	10.30am	Bde Order No 139 issued (Move Orders – Appendix V) – cancelled by OR 52 (Appendix VI)	Appendix V. Appendix VI.
			Shelling during afternoon in neighbourhood of Bde H.Q. and Transport lines.	
		9.30pm	Bde H.Q. & Transport lines shelled by High Velocity Gun. QUEANT & neighbourhood bombed. Night passed quietly.	[initials]
			CASUALTIES – 1 OR 6th H.L.I. wounded 1 OR 7 H.L.I. wounded (gassed)	
"	6/9/18		Up till midday probability of move into reserve in the evening.	
		12.00	Bde notified that this would not take place today. Transport lines & neighbourhood of Bde H.Q. again shelled with H.E. intermittently during the day & also at night. QUEANT bombed. Orders issued by Divn to move into reserve 7th inst.	Appendix VII
		10.30pm	Bde Order 140 issued by which units were ordered to move into reserve commencing at dawn 7th inst.	[initials]
			CASUALTIES – 1 Officer 7th H.L.I. wounded	
CORPS RESERVE near CROISILLES Sq. T30 (Sheet 51b S.W.)	7/9/18	06.00	Leading Battn (6th H.L.I.) passed D16 a 2.9 (Sheet 57c N.E.) & proceeded via QUEANT – MOREUIL – LONGATTE – thence LONGATTE–CROISILLES Rd to T30. The remainder following – L.T.M.B., 5th H.L.I., 7th H.L.I. The last unit arrived in new area shortly before midday. Remainder of day spent in erecting bivouacs, washing etc.	[initials]
		4pm	G.O.C. visited Bde H.Q. & Battns with B.G.C.	
			CASUALTIES. 45 OR 5th H.L.I. wounded gassed 2 OR 5th H.L.I. wounded	

[illegible] Capt.

D. D. & L., London, E.C. (A8001) Wt. W1771/M2031 750,000 5/17 Sch. 52 Forms C2118/14

Army Form C. 2118.

Instructions regarding War Diaries and Intelligence Summaries are contained in F. S. Regs., Part II. and the Staff Manual respectively. Title pages will be prepared in manuscript. CONFIDENTIAL.

WAR DIARY
or
INTELLIGENCE SUMMARY.
(Erase heading not required.)

157th Infy Bde A 3
VOLUME III. SEPTEMBER 1918

Place	Date	Hour	Summary of Events and Information	Remarks and references to Appendices
NEAR CROISILLES T.30 (Sheet 51B S.W.)	8 9/18.		Battns training & salving materiel in their respective areas. CASUALTIES. NIL	W.D.M.
— do —	9 9/18		Heavy showers all day - Units were conducted in G.S. wagons to Divisional Baths - Salvage and burying our own and enemy dead was carried out during the day. CASUALTIES NIL	W.D.M.
— do —	10 9/18		Rain interfered with training in morning.	
		2.45pm	A platoon demonstration took place on a suitable site near Bde H.Q. This demonstration was given by a representative from the Inspector General of Training handling a platoon of the 7th H.L.I. & was attended by all available officers and NCOs of the Bde. The B.G.C was present. Salvage & burying dead was carried out throughout the day. CASUALTIES NIL	W.D.M.
— do —	11 9/18		Heavy showers fell during the day - Training carried on - Salvage collected - B.G.C left for CALAIS for three days rest - Lt Col. Gibbons 7th H.L.I. assumed command of the Bde temporarily. CASUALTIES NIL	W.D.M.
— do —	12 9/18		Rained intermittently during the day - Training carried on - Salvage Collected CASUALTIES - NIL	W.D.M.

D. D. & L., London, E.C. (A8001) Wt. W1771/M2031 750,000 5/17 Sch. 52 Forms C2118/14

Instructions regarding War Diaries and Intelligence Summaries are contained in F. S. Regs., Part II. and the Staff Manual respectively. Title pages will be prepared in manuscript. - CONFIDENTIAL -

WAR DIARY
or
INTELLIGENCE SUMMARY.
(Erase heading not required.)

157th INF^Y B^de — SEPTEMBER 1918 — VOLUME III (54)

Army Form C. 2118.

Place	Date	Hour	Summary of Events and Information	Remarks and references to Appendices
NEAR CROISILLES T 30 (Sheet 51b S.W.)	13/9/18		Battns carried out training during the day Rained intermittently all day —	Moay
			CASUALTIES - NIL	
— do —	14/9/18		Battalions carried out training —	
			During morning Orders recd from Division that this B^de would relieve 172nd B^de in the line night 15/16th (Divnl Orders 131 & 132)	
		10.30	B^de H.Q. respirators tested in Lachrymatory Gas Chamber under supervision of Gas N.C.O.	
		3.30	B.G.C. returned from Calais and resumed command	Moay
			CASUALTIES — NIL	
— do —	15/9/18	9 am	B.G.C. B^de Major and Staff Captain visited new H.Q. (V28 d 0.0) - Sheet 57c SE. returning at midday.	
		1.30 pm	Battns Advance Parties left for new section of the line.	Moay
		3 pm	B^de paraded near B^de H.Q.	
		3.30 pm	G.O.C. visited B^de on parade & presented Military Medal ribbons to N.C.O.s & men of the 3 Battns & the L.T.M.B.	
		6 pm	Move orders issued to Units (B^de Order 141)	Appendix VIII.
			CASUALTIES - NIL	
T 30 till 2 pm — from 2 pm V28 d 0.0 (57c SE) (VICHY EN ARTOIS SECTOR)	16/9/18		B^de Nucleus left for BOISLEUX AU MONT (Reception Camp) during morning.	
		2.15 pm	The 5th H.L.I. left camp followed by 6th H.L.I. - 7th H.L.I. - L.T.M.B. - the last named unit leaving at 4 pm.	
			Units halted 1 mile W. of QUEANT for evening meal.	
		4 am (17/9/18)	Relief completed reported by the last unit in	Moay
			No infantry action on our front during the night. Our L. Trench Mortars fired intermittently between 10.30 pm and 1.30 am (17th inst) covering Post at E14c during relief.	
			CASUALTIES	

M. D. Wallace Capt.

D. D. & L., London, E.C. (A8001) Wt. W1771/M2031 750,000 5/17 Sch. 52 Forms/C2118/14

Instructions regarding War Diaries and Intelligence Summaries are contained in F. S. Regs., Part II. and the Staff Manual respectively. Title pages will be prepared in manuscript.

Army Form C. 2118.

WAR DIARY
or
INTELLIGENCE SUMMARY.
(Erase heading not required.)

Confidential — 157th Inf Bde (15) — September 1918 — Vol III —

Place	Date	Hour	Summary of Events and Information	Remarks and references to Appendices
V28d.0.0 (Sheet on Artois [illegible])	17/9	10.30pm	Enemy put down barrage on right of Bde front and reported to be attacking MOEUVRES from N. S.O.S. went up from Right Bde. and our barrage put down. Enemy attack evidently did not mature and all quiet again by 11.30 p.m.	
		0.30am	Enemy put down barrage in front of MOEUVRES moving eastwards to INCHY and increasing in intensity. Enemy under cover of barrage attacked and drove out right Brigade from MOEUVRES. Righthand part of our right company (5th HLI) reported missing. Our right flank was during the night slightly refused to conform to new dispositions of Brigade on right. Left Battalions report all clear during night	AHB
	18/9	1pm	Verbal information received that 5th Canadian Bde would relieve the Brigade on night 19th/20th. Warning order issued to Batts	App IX
		5pm	Orders received from Div confirming above and issued to Batts accordingly	
			All quiet on front during day	AHB
	19/9	5am	Heavy shelling in forward areas during greater part of night. Enemy made several bombing attacks during night on our right post but all were repulsed.	
		1pm	Orders received from Div that right Bde (53 Bde) assisted by 2 coys 157 Bde would today retake MOEUVRES. Zero hour to be 7pm and at same time this Bde would push forward its right flank and reestablish the two posts previously withdrawn. Orders issued to units. The 2 Coys mentioned to be taken from 7th HLI	App X
		8pm	Attack successful and MOEUVRES retaken and our posts reestablished. On arrival missing post found having hung on for two days without water or rations.	AHB

D. D. & L., London, E.C. (A8001) Wt. W1771/M2031 750,000 5/17 Sch. 52 Forms/C2118/14

Instructions regarding War Diaries and Intelligence Summaries are contained in F. S. Regs., Part II. and the Staff Manual respectively. Title pages will be prepared in manuscript.

Army Form C. 2118.

WAR DIARY
or
INTELLIGENCE SUMMARY.
(Erase heading not required.)

Confidential — 157th Inf Bde — September 1918 — Vol III

Place	Date	Hour	Summary of Events and Information	Remarks and references to Appendices
V 26d 0.0 (Inchy-en-Artois Sector)	19/9	10 p.m.	Lt. Col. E. L. Gibbons D.S.O. Cmdg 7th H.L.I. reported killed in action.	[illegible]
	20/9	12.30 a.m.	Relief complete. Casualties during period in line	
		4.30 a.m.	Units arrived in new area. 10 officers 108 ORs.	[illegible]
			Day employed in cleaning up etc.	
	21/9	6.30 a.m.	2 Coys of 7th HLI attached 155 Bde rejoined their Batt.	[illegible]
			Nothing of interest to report.	
	22/9	7 a.m.	Orders received for 6th HLI to relieve portion of 1st Guards Brigade on right of 156 Bde. in MOEUVRES sector and to come under orders of 156 Bde. Brigade orders issued accordingly. 6th HLI commenced to move out of camp at 6 p.m.	App XI [illegible]
	23/9		Training carried out by units in vicinity camp. Major General Marshall assumed command of the Division vice Major General Hull.	[illegible]
	24/9		Orders issued for 5th HLI to relieve 6th HLI in line on night 24th. Remainder units carried out training in camp.	App XII [illegible]
	25/9		Orders for forthcoming operations received from Div and Bde orders issued accordingly.	App XIII
			Bde less 5th HLI (already in line) and Bde Hqrs moved up to area S. of Pronville after dark without incident.	[illegible]

H.W. Dearbarn

D. D. & L., London, E.C. (A8004) Wt. W1771/M2031 750,000 5/17 Sch. 52 Forms C2118/14

Army Form C. 2118.

Instructions regarding War Diaries and Intelligence Summaries are contained in F. S. Regs., Part II. and the Staff Manual respectively. Title pages will be prepared in manuscript.

WAR DIARY or INTELLIGENCE SUMMARY.

(Erase heading not required.)

Confidential. 157th Inf Bde (S7) September 1918 Vol III

Place	Date	Hour	Summary of Events and Information	Remarks and references to Appendices
Near MOEUVRES	26/9		Bde. H.Qrs moved to Old British front line S. of Pronville	
		7 p.m.	7th H L I commenced their move to assembly positions for attack.	MD
	27/9	12.30 am	6th H L I — " — " — " — " — " — " — " —	
		5 a.m	Both battalions in assembly positions	
		6 a.m	Brigade less 5th H L I attacked as per orders (zero + 40) and gained all objectives by 11 a.m. Casualties officers other ranks	MD
		3 p.m	Brigade reorganised and faced E with 2 batts in line. 7th H L I on left 6th H L I on right and 5th H L I in reserve. Our front now however completely covered by 63rd & Guards Divs.	
	28/9.		Orders received from Div that all troops of 52 Div would make themselves as comfortable as possible as we would be in present position for a day or two. Salving of own area carried out.	MD
	29/9.		Whole Brigade out all day salving corps area. Orders received from Div. that Brigade would be at 12 hours notice from now	MD
	30/9.		Brigade continued salvage work. Orders received from Div & issued to units that on 1st Oct Div would relieve 63rd Div in line & that 157 Bde would be in support	MD Appx XIV

[signature] Dearbarn

D. D. & L., London, E.C. (A8001) Wt. W1771/M2031 750,000 5/17 Sch. 52 Forms/C2118/14

SUMMARY OF OPERATIONS

157th INFANTRY BRIGADE.

From August 20th, 1918, to September 7th, 1918.

Date. Time.

August.

20th The Brigade Group moved from CHATEAU DE LA HAIE to AGNEZ-LES-DUISANS by night. Here the Brigade remained until the night of 22nd August.

22nd The Brigade Group moved by route march to BELLACOURT.

23rd 4. a.m. The Brigade Group arrived in billets in the BELLACOURT Area.

11.40 a.m. The G.O.C. and the Brigade Major proceeded to 176th Inf. Brigade Headquarters to arrange to take over MERCATEL AREA.

1.40 p.m. While reconnoitring this area, Division phoned to stop taking over the area and return at once as 157th Infantry Brigade was to be ready to move at half an hour's notice.

On arriving back at BELLACOURT, I received orders to march at once and concentrate my Brigade about FICHEUX. I at once requested that I might be allowed to take it further forward in thettrench system, then held by the 59th Division, as there appeared every likelihood of the Brigade being employed in active operations the following day, and by taking up a forward position would considerably reduce the length of the approach march if we went into action. The request could not be allowed as the Corps Commander did not wish any forward concentration to take place.

4. p.m. The Brigade started leaving BELLACOURT and marched to positions in the BRICKWORKS in squares 32 and 33, and also in FICHEUX (Ref. Sheet 51 b. S.W.) The Brigade commenced to arrive in these positions about 10. p.m.

24th 12.30 a.m.

52nd Division Orders for the operation received. (Appendix I) By those Orders the 157th Infantry Brigade had to pass through the line then held by the 156th Infantry Brigade, which ran approximately from square T.2.c.5.0. to T.1.a.8.8. (sheet 51 b. S.W.) and then to attack EASTWARD, maintaining touch with the 56th Division on the Right; the Brigade to finally assault and consolidate that portion of the HINDENBURG LINE between squares T.5.a. and N.34.d., both front and support lines of this system to be captured.

This meant an approach march of 4 miles across un-reconnoitred country, which was very much broken up by trenches and lines of barbed wire, before the Brigade could pass through the 156th Infantry Brigade. From here it had to attack across a further 1½ miles of unknown and un-reconnoitred country.

Brigade Order No. 130 (APPENDIX II) was issued at 2.30 a.m. By these orders 6th H.L.I. attacked on the Right, 5th H.L.I. on the Left, 7th H.L.I., 157th L.T.M.B. (less 2 Sections) and "C" Company, 52nd Bn. M.G.C. (less 1 Section) in Brigade Reserve.

Immediately the Divisional Orders had been received, a Warning Order was sent to units to be prepared to rendesvous about 4. a.m.

The Rendesvous was fixed immediately W. of Railway Cutting in squares N.3.a. and c.

Owing to the short time given, the writing and issueing of orders, and to the difficulties of moving in the dark over unknown country covered with barbed wire, units were three quarters of an hour late in forming up at the rendesvous and it appeared almost impossible to pass through the line held by the 156th Infantry Brigade, and so connect up with the Left of the 56th Division, in time to start the attack conjointly with the 56th Division. I therefore warned the 52nd Division that the Brigade might be late and asked them to notify the 56th Division. I personally saw the Commanding Officers and told them that they must appeal to their men to make a special effort, Otherwise we might let the 56th Division down by exposing their left flank.

All ranks responded wonderfully to the call, and/

Date. Time.

24th

and in spite of the darkness and obstacles and slippery ground, for it was now raining, they covered the last 2 miles almost at the double, arriving in the line held by the 156th Infantry Brigade, and connecting up with the Left of the 56th Division, 4 minutes before the attack was to start and the barrage due to come down. Great credit is due to all ranks of the units for this effort.

7. a.m.

The Brigade pushed forward with the attack under the artillery barrage. The enemy was shelling fairly heavily with Heavy Artillery but appeared to have very few light field guns. His defence seemed to consist chiefly of Machine Gun and Light Trench Mortar fire.

The attack proceeded well, and in due course HENIN was captured and the assaulting Battalions arrived close up under the wire of that portion of the HINDENBURG LINE which was our objective. Here the attack was held up for two reasons;-

Firstly:- The troops on our Right had been unable to keep in line, with the result that our Right Flank was enfiladed by fire from Machine Gun Nests, coming from the spur on HENIN HILL which runs due S. between Squares T.4. and 5.

Secondly:- Owing to the fact that our Heavy Artillery was for some unknown reason still bombarding the Front Line of the HINDENBURG System opposite my front, my 2 assaulting Battalions were now about 300 to 400 yards from the Front Trench of the HINDENBURG LINE, approximately on the line T.4.b.7.0. to N.34.c.8.5. Frequent messages were sent asking for the Heavy Artillery fire to be lifted forward some 500 to 800 yards to allow us to assault the HINDENBURG LINE, but, owing to communications failing, the bombardment still continued.

Had this fire been lifted at once, there is little doubt that we could have entered the HINDENBURG LINE, as we were at that time only opposed by hostile rearguards consisting of Machine Gun nests and Light Trench Mortars.

My battalions were now losing a fair number of casualties by our own Heavy Artillery, shells from which were frequently falling short, and the enemy seeing my Right Flank exposed, brought more Machine Guns down on to HENIN HILL. I therefore decided to withdraw the Main Line a few hundred yards. As a matter of fact this was done automatically by the Battalions themselves before they received the order.

While we were held up in this position. I notified the Brigade of the 56th Division on my Right of the situation, and asked it to push forward to connec up with my Right, and at the same time the Commanding Officer of the 6th H.L.I. (my Right hand assaulting Battalion), personally went across to interview the Battalion on his Right. He there learned that this Battalion had not been given an objective in the HINDENBURG LINE. He informed me of this.

As it was now getting dark, and the enemy bringing up more Machine Guns, both to my front on the HINDENBURG LINE and on my Right on HENIN HILL, I notified the Division of the situation and suggested that as the Brigade on my Right was not going into the HINDENBURG LINE, it was inadvisable for me to make another attempt to push in and occupy it without any other Troops on my Right or Left. I suggested digging in on my present line, this was approved of by the Divisional Commander.

During the course of the afternoon I went up to the front line to see what the situation was, and found that the leading line was close up under the enemy's wire, and patrols were actually walking and crawling about inside the wire. The enemy seemed to take very little notice of

Date. Time.

24th 7. a.m. notice of this, but when any considerable movement was made by us, heavy machine gun and trench mortar fire was opened from nests which appeared to be located in depth.

There is no doubt that on this day the HINDENBURG LINE was very lightly held by the enemy and had our Heavy Artillery barrage not stopped us, and the troops on our right been able to come on, we should have had little difficulty in capturing it.

Owing to this long advance, just on 5 miles, communications were difficult to arrange, consequently the obtaining of information on this day was not good. No time had been available for making arrangements for telephone communications, and owing to distances, Brigade Headquarters had to make three bounds forward, runners finding it very difficult to locate the new Headquarters.

The Light Trench Mortars were practically useless; They were brought up as far as possible on limbers and then the guns and ammunition had to be manhandled by carrying parties. None of the guns got into action as the carrying parties were quite exhausted and unable to complete their journey. It is suggested that pack animals be provided both for guns and ammunition.

Casualties.

Killed.		Wounded.		Missing.		
Officers.	O.R.	Officers.	O.R.	Officers	O.R.	
3	33	23	417	3	82	

25th 4. a.m. Orders received that no troops were to be within 250 yards of the HINDENBURG LINE, as the Heavy Artillery were again to bombard it.

Brigade Order No.132 (Appendix III) was issued, ordering a slight retirement, with the main line of resistance on the line T.4.c. and T.3.b., and for the 7th H.L.I. to relieve the 5th H.L.I. on the Left and the 5th H.L.I. to come into Brigade Reserve.

Shortly afterwards, I and my staff, went up to see what the situation was. I there found that during the night the enemy had been very considerable reinforced and that our troops were pinned to the ground. As far back as Battalion Headquarters, one could only move about in the open by crawling. As soon as a head was shewn a shower of M.G. bullets came down. Consequently I went to all Commanding Officers and told them that it was impossible to carry out Brigade Order No.132 - they were to delay the retirement and relief until after dark, and commence to do it the moment dusk fell.

12.45 p.m. At 12.45 p.m. this day, orders were received that our troops were not to be nearer than 500 yards from the HINDENBURG LINE, in consequence of which, Brigade Order No.133 (Appendix IV) was issued.

These orders were carried out after dusk, but before they were completed, Divisional Orders were received that our leading troops were not to be nearer than the HENIN - CROISILLES Road. This order was carried out.

Casualties

26th

Killed		Wounded		Missing		
Officers.	O.R.	Officers	O.R.	Officers	O.R.	
~	2	2	41	~	2	

Date. Time.

26th Troops remained in their present positions during the day, while the 155th Infantry Brigade attacked the trench system within the PENTAGON in order to prevent the enemy escaping into the HINDENBURG LINE Tunnels.

7.35 p.m. At 7.35 p.m. the Brigade was ordered to take over HENIN HILL from a Battalion which the 155th Infantry Brigade was to drop there after its attack, after which the 157th Infantry Brigade was to come into Divisional Reserve.

Patrols were at once sent out to HENIN HILL to get touch with the Battalion of the 155th Infantry Brigade, but they came back and reported that the enemy was holding HENIN HILL and had many Machine Guns in SUMMIT TRENCH running along its top.

8.14 p.m. The Division was notified of the situation, but at 8.14 p.m. reported that the 155th Infantry Brigade had passed over HENIN HILL at 5.30 p.m.

8.30 p.m. Further patrols from each Battalion were consequently sent out to HENIN HILL from different directions in order to clear the situation up and make sure who was holding the HILL. All patrols reported that the enemy was in occupation of the HILL, and one patrol that they had got in touch with the Battalion of the 155th Infantry Brigade (4th K.O.S.B.) who were supposed to be on HENIN HILL. This Battalion was then located in square N.34.d. where, it was stated, they were staying. There had evidently been some misunderstanding as to where HENIN began and ended.

9. p.m. The Division cancelled the Order for the Battalion of the 155th Infantry Brigade on HENIN HILL to be relieved.

Casualties.

Killed		Wounded		Missing		
Officers.	O.R.	Officers.	O.R.	Officers.	O.R.	
—	1	1	19	—	2	

27th 4.20 a.m. Divisional Orders (Appendix V)✓ received 4.20 a.m. for the capture of FONTAINE CROISILLES and a subsequent advance to RIENCOURT by the 157th Infantry Brigade. The 156th Infantry Brigade attacking on the Left with its Right on FONTAINE CROISILLES (exclusive) thence on to HENDECOURT. Both attacks to go forward under an Artillery barrage moving at the rate of 100 yards every 4 minutes.

9.20 a.m. 10.3 a.m. The 157th Infantry Brigade to start the attack at 9.20 a.m. and the 156th Infantry Brigade at 10.3 a.m.

Brigade Order No.135 (Appendix VI)✓ was issued.

For this attack the 6th H.L.I. formed the Right Assaulting Battalion, the 7th H.L.I. the Left. The 7th H.L.I. was to direct with its left just clear of the Southern end of CROISILLE. The 5th H.L.I. to be in Brigade Reserve, but, as the Assaulting Battalions approached FONTAINE CROISILLE, 2 Companies 5th H.L.I. were to gradually close up and enter and mop up FONTAINE CROISILLE.

The Brigade moved off under the barrage, punctually to time/

Date. Time.

27th punctually to time. The barrage, however, was very ragged, owing to the artillery not having had sufficient warning to take up their new positions and in consequence coming into action piecemeal.

Very heavy Trench Mortar and Machine Gun fire was experienced at the outset, and the Brigade had some difficulty in getting a start, owing not only to the hostile fire, but to having to cut its way through meshes of barbed wire. The barbed wire at this place was a very serious obstacle, for it was not only very thick, but laid in great depth. The fact that the men were able to cut their way through it under close and accurate M.G. and Trench Mortar fire, shews a fine performance on the part of the men and good leading by the Regimental Officers. A good many casualties were caused there.

However, once SUMMIT Trench and TOOLEY Trench had been cleared, a rapid advance was made and the enemy was got on the run.

Further lines of barbed wire were encountered which considerably broke up the attack and so delayed it, that the Infantry dropped well behind the Artillery barrage. Still, the enemy was on the run and very little opposition, other than ~~Infantry~~ M.G. fire was encountered, until after the Brigade had got down into the bottom of the valley, across the SENSEE River and half way up the further slope, where they found that they were being very badly enfiladed from the Right Flank, besides getting heavy M.G. and Trench Mortar fire from the slopes of the ridge just across the SENSEE River.

It was then discovered, that the 169th Inf. Brigade of the 56th Division on our Right, had been unable to advance and in consequence, the Right Flank of the Brigade was not only in the air and being enfiladed from the Right, but was even being fired into from behind. Without some protection on the Right it was not possible to continue the advance. The 2 Companies of the 5th H.L.I., in Brigade Reserve, were behind the Left Flank, as this was, at the start, considered the dangerous Flank owing to the possibility of resistance from FONTAINE CROISILLE.

After the line was held up in the bottom of the valley it was impossible to move the Brigade Reserve across to the Right Flank to afford protection there to a further advance, owing to the heavy Machine Gun fire now encountered. A message was therefore sent to the 169th Infantry Brigade, giving them the situation, and asking them if they could close up and maintain touch with my Right Flank. Owing to opposition they were apparently unable to do this.

Further advance was planned to take place at 3. p.m. under a fresh barrage, but just before 3. p.m. this had to be postponed as I had not given the Artillery sufficient time to work out the Artillery Barrages.

The Germans had now very considerable reinforced their front line, and their reinforcements could be seen dribbling over the slopes via communication trenches and sunken roads. The enemy was now occupying TUNNEL Trench in strength with Infantry, Trench Mortars and Machine Guns. He completely encircled my Right Flank by coming round the trench system in U.13.b., and was firing into my Right rear.

The two assaulting Battalions were now down to about 150 to 160 men and they were holding approximately the line HUMBER SUPPORT - Square U.7.d. - BURG SUPPORT and U.13.b., with 2 Companies occupying the Southernnand the Eastern edge of FONTAINE CROISILLE, which had been mopped up by these Companies.

Date. Time.

27th The situation was put before the Division who ordered an attack to be made at once on the high ground running from U.14.b. through U.15.a. up to CRUX Trench, the 155th Infantry Brigade co-operating in the attack.

The 169th Infantry Brigade on the Right was at once informed and asked if they could co-operate as well, but owing to the situation on their Right they stated they would be unable to render any assistance by the time required.

Endeavours were made to get in touch with the G.O.C. 155th Infantry Brigade, but owing to communications having failed, due to shell fire, no message could be got through, subsequently however, just as it was getting dark, information was received that all three Battalions were engaged on special missions and would be unable to co-operate. The Division accordingly cancelled the operation.

The Brigade was relieved in the Line at FONTAINE CROISILLES by the 172nd Brigade and withdrew and Bivouacked in N.34.d.

The relief was completed at 7. a.m. on the 28th August, all units being in the new area by 11. a.m.

Killed 6 off 45 ORs. Wnd. 8 off. 326 OR. Miss 21 OR

28th to 30th. The Brigade rested, cleaned up and reorganised.

3 OR wnd

31st. At 7. a.m. the Brigade received orders to be ready to move to the HENIN HILL Area at half an hour's notice after 7.p.m.

Sept.

1st. The Brigade started marching off from N.34.d. at 6.45 a.m. reaching the HENIN HILL AREA by 10. a.m.

2nd. The Brigade remained in this area in Divisional Reserve until next morning, when it moved forward to the Area U.13. a and b. starting at 5. a.m. On reaching this area, orders were received that the Brigade was to move forward again into Area in U.21. just W. of BULLECOURT.

7. p.m. At 7. p.m. instructions were received over the phone that the Brigade was to attack the HINDENBURG LINE through QUEANT and PRONVILLE, jumping off at 11. p.m. It was, however, pointed out to the Division, that owing to the long approach march entailed and the difficult country over which the troops would have to pass, the Brigade could not reach the jumping off point in time or during the dark. The matter was referred to Corps, with the result that the operation was ordered to take place at 11. a.m. on 3rd., orders being received at 11.30 p.m.

2 ORs wnd

3rd. At 5. a.m. according to orders, the Brigade moved forward and took up the following position shortly after 11. a.m. U.26.c. - U.25.d., preparatory to attacking and capturing the HINDENBURG LINE on a line D.14. a. and b. to D.15.a. and b. thence along RIENCOURT STREET.

This attack was to start at 11. a.m. under a barrage, attacking through QUEANT and PRONVILLE in a S. and S.E. direction. The 5th H.L.I. being on the Left. 7th H.L.I. on the Right and 6th H.L.I. and 157th L.T.M.B. in Reserve.

Date.	Time.	
3rd		The Brigade took up its position, advanced at 11.48 a.m. and captured all its objectives without opposition, troops of 63rd Division having occupied the objectives during the night 2nd/3rd, when the enemy withdrew.
	3.10 p.m.	According to orders the Brigade concentrated in the HINDENBURG LINE and MELBOURNE STREET between D.18.a.3.3. and D.17.central, thus becoming Corps Support, the Guards and 63rd Division joining up the line in front.
		3 OR. wnd
4th, 5th, 6th. & 7th.		The Brigade remained in this position until 7th Sept. when it withdrew by route march to the Area in T.30. and became Corps Reserve. Units started marching back at 8. a.m. the last Battalion, the 5th H.L.I. reaching the new area at 11. a.m. The 5th H.L.I. were delayed in moving off owing to heavy hostile gas shelling.
		1 off 3 OR. wnd

A P P E N D I X   VII.

CAPTURED PERSONNEL AND MATERIAL.

1. Operations from 23rd to 29th August, 1918, both dates inclusive.

Prisoners.	5 Officers.	195 Other Ranks.
Field Guns.	6	
Machine Guns.	48	
Trench Mortars.	20	

2. Operations from 1st to 7th September, 1918, both dates inclusive.

Prisoners.	1 Officer.	52 Other Ranks.
Field Guns.	5	
Machine Guns.	11	
Trench Mortars.	1	

Total for both Operations.

Prisoners.		Guns.	Machine Guns.	Trench Mortars.
Officers.	O.R.			
6	247	11	59	21
6886				

APPENDIX - I

Secret 157 INF BRIGADE Copy No. ....

Order No. 137 1/9/18

1.

(a) The Canadian Corps of the First Army on our left, will attack the DROCOURT QUEANT line, S. of the SCARPE Tomorrow

(b) The third Divn of the VI Corps on our right will capture LAGNICOURT and push on towards BEAUMETZ-le-CAMBRAI.

(c) The XVII corps will co-operate with the attack of the Canadian Corps on right of 1st Army, and by pushing its left forward, endeavour to gain position to attack QUEANT from the N.

(d) The 57th Divn on left of XVII Corps will not make a frontal attack on QUEANT - DROCOURT line, but will pass through the gap made by the Canadian Corps in V.13 and then turn S.E.

2 The 52nd Divn will conform to movement of 57th Divn & move forward to assault when it is known that 57th Divn is advancing.

3 The 155th Inf. Bde. is attacking this evening, objective being roughly C.5.d central to U.29.d.7.7. MIN: SANS SOUCI inclusive. 57th Divn will maintain touch with their line running roughly Northwards.

4 (a) The 156th Inf. Bde. will attack tomorrow through 155th Inf. Bde and clear area MIN: SANS SOUCI to the road in V.25.c.6.2. - D.1.a.5.1.

– D.1.a.5.1 – C.6.b.9.0. Zero hour for attack will be notified later.

(b) The 155th Inf. Bde. will move its right to keep touch between 3rd Divn on its extreme right and the right of the attack of the 156th Inf. Bde.

(c) The 155th Inf Bde. will attack through 156th Inf. Bde as far S. as QUEANT – LAGNICOURT Road

5. The 157th Inf. Bde. will stand by, prepared to move up to push through 156th Inf. Bde. to attack HINDENBURG SUPPORT LINE as far as the communication trench from V.26.d.1.9. to V.26.d.1.4

6. Consequent on the above, the 157th Inf. Bde will move as under tomorrow 2nd September.

Bde Hd. q/rs to V.7.c.95.80. at 5 a.m.

5th H.L.I. to trenches in U.13.b.&.d. leaving present site at 5 a.m.

6th H.L.I. " " " U.13.a. – do – 5-20 a.m.

7th H.L.I. " " " V.7.d. – do – 5-10 a.m.

157th L.T.M.Bty " " U.13.a. – do – 5-30 a.m.

7. On arrival in the new area the 157th Inf Bde will be prepared to move at half an hours notice

8 Acknowledge

(Sgd) C.S. Stirling-Cookson Capt.
Bde. Maj. 157th Inf. Bde.

Issued at 7.15 p.m. on 1/9/18.

over

3.

Issued at 7.15 pm on 1/9/18.

Copy No 1 to 5th H.L.I.
2 6th H.L.I.
3 7th H.L.I.
4 157th L.T.M.Bty.
5 2nd L.F.A.
6 413 Field Coy.
7 155th Bde.
8 156th Bde.
9 } War diary.
10 }
11 File.

APPENDIX II.

[illegible] No. 13[illegible]

[illegible] September 19[illegible]

1\. [illegible]

2\. [illegible]

3\. [illegible]

RIENCOURT (& other buildings SUPPORT)
which will then E. [illegible] of RIENCOURT
[illegible] [illegible] [illegible] etc.
[illegible] [illegible] [illegible] to the two
[illegible] to HINDENBURG SUPPORT LINE in
V.25.b. and V.26.a. [illegible] 7th Bde [illegible]
will move down HINDENBURG SUPPORT
LINE to where it turns the [illegible] Road
[illegible] [illegible] of 7th Bde.
will [illegible] [illegible] [illegible] W. of
this.
4th Bde [illegible] [illegible] and will
[illegible] S. [illegible] [illegible] 7th Bde [illegible]
the right along [illegible] the road [illegible]
[illegible] in V.26.a. 6.3.
[illegible] [illegible] [illegible] [illegible]
[illegible] [illegible] as follows. 5th Bde on
right [illegible] E. [illegible] of QUEANT
to the HINDENBURG LINE in D.[illegible]
D.[illegible] 6th Bde [illegible] [illegible] S.E.
[illegible] PRONVILLE. The latter [illegible]
[illegible] HINDENBURG SUPPORT LINE
[illegible] [illegible] [illegible] [illegible]
[illegible] [illegible] Road [illegible] D.3.a.
6th Bde in [illegible] [illegible] [illegible]
from RIENCOURT about 1 mile [illegible] the
[illegible] [illegible] [illegible] [illegible]
HINDENBURG SUPPORT LINE.

3

[illegible] 2.30 a.m. on 6.
During the night [illegible] forward
2 Coys of 6th [illegible] will be [illegible]
[illegible] the Right [illegible]
to help in [illegible] the OUTPOST. [illegible]
[illegible]
[illegible]
[illegible]

(b) Artillery. The assault will be made in the [illegible] barrage [illegible] from D.2. [illegible] D.3 [illegible] at [illegible] for 8 minutes then moving forward at 100 yards every 3 minutes.

5. [illegible] [illegible] [illegible] [illegible] [illegible] [illegible] [illegible] [illegible] [illegible] [illegible] [illegible] HINDENBURG SUPPORT LINE [illegible] [illegible] [illegible] [illegible] [illegible])

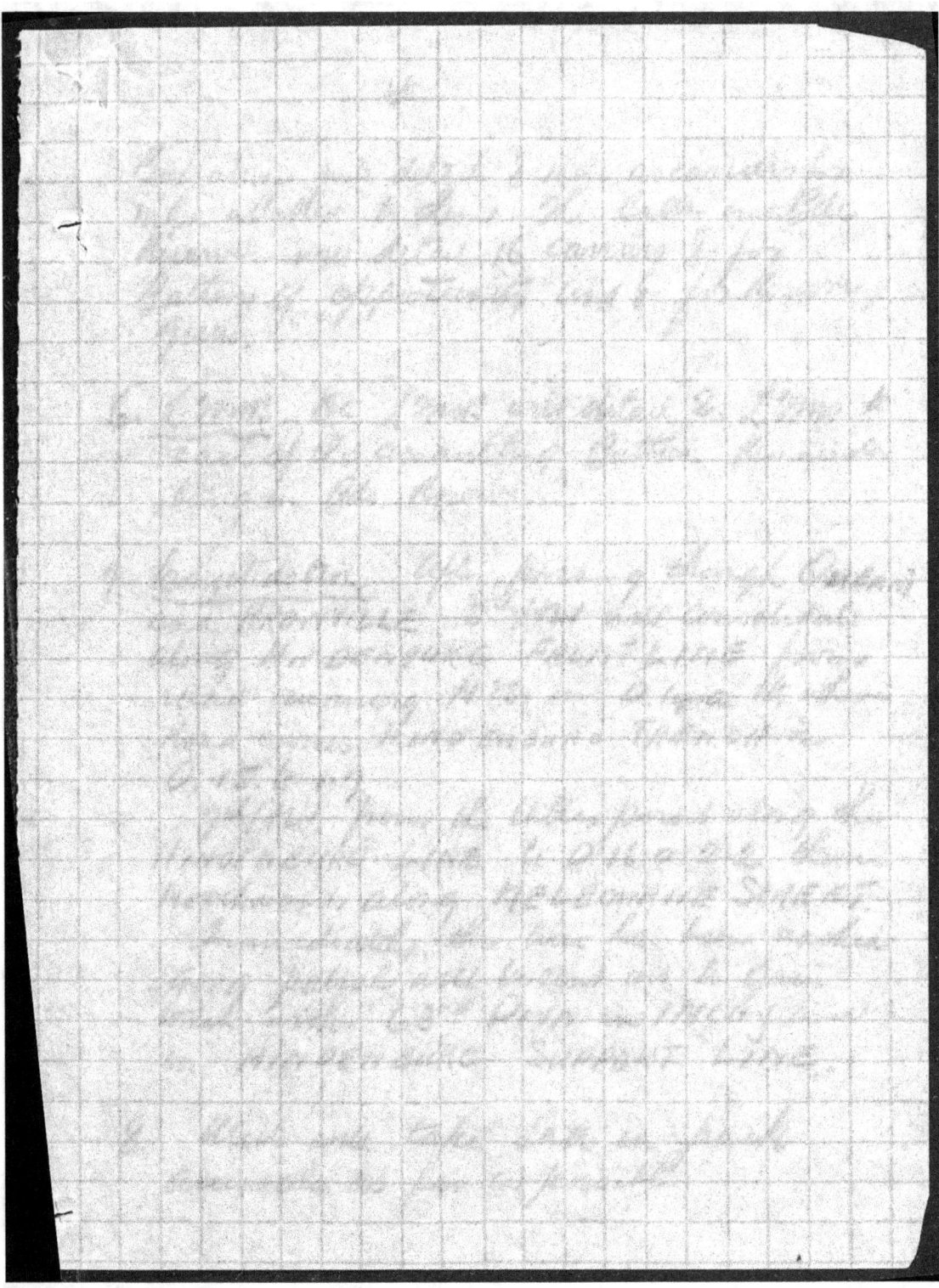

[illegible]

6. [illegible]

7. [illegible]

[illegible]

8. [illegible]

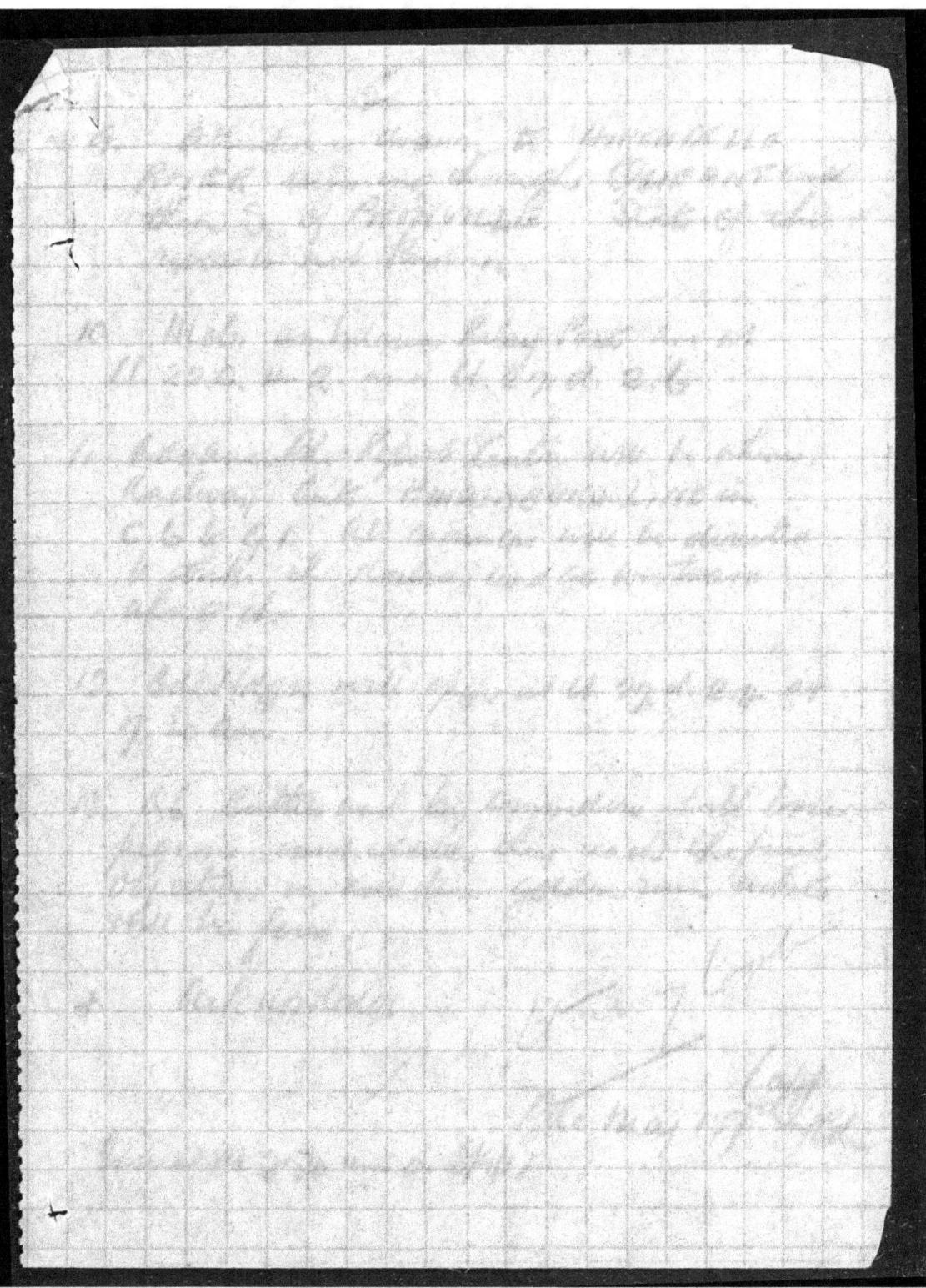

9. [illegible]

10. [illegible]

11. [illegible]

12. [illegible]

13. [illegible]

14. [illegible]

[illegible]

[illegible]

Secret. Copy No

157th Infantry Brigade

APPENDIX V

Order No 139

Ref Maps 1/20,000. 51.b. SW. 51.b.SE., 57.c.NE. 57.c.NW.

1. 157th Inf Bde Warning Order No OR/139 of 4/9/18 is confirmed.

2. The 157th Inf Bde will be relieved by the 169th Inf Bde.

3. Battalions and 157 T.M.B. will march out immediately they are relieved by the respective incoming units.

4. Units of the 157th Inf Bde will be billetted in the new area approximately as follows:-

5th H.L.I.	in	S.11.
6th H.L.I.	"	S.16.
7th H.L.I.	"	S.23.
157th L.T.M.B.	"	S.17.

5. During the march to the back area the following route will be used:-
QUEANT - NOREUIL - ECOUST - ST. LEGER - T.25.c.

A distance of 500 yards will be maintained between Battalions and 100 yards between platoons.

2

Battalion will march in the order in which they are relieved.

6. Guides One officer and 16 ORs per Battn to act as Guides to the incoming units will report to 157th Inf Bde HQ at 3. pm. today.

7. Arrival in the new area will be at once reported to 157th Inf Bde HQ by units.

8. Bde Hdqrs will close at D.7.d.1.9 and open at S.9.d.6.1 on completion of Relief.

9. Acknowledge.

A. J. Stirling Cookson Capt
Bde Maj 157th Inf Bde

Issued at. 10.30 am on 5/9/18

Copy No 1	to 5 HLI		8	155th Inf Bde
2	6 HLI		9	156th "
3	7 HLI		10	Staff Capt
4	157 LTMB		11 }	War Diary
5	2nd L FA		12 }	
6	413th Field Coy RE		13.	FILE
7	169th Inf Bde			

Secret 157th Infantry Brigade Order No 40 Copy No

ATTENDIX VII

Ref Map Sheets 51.b SW and 57c NW

1 The 52nd Divn will withdraw tomorrow the 7th inst, but will remain in Corps support.

2 The 157th Inf Bde will move by route march to T. 30 in the following order:–
6th H.L.I., 157th L.T.M.B., 5th H.L.I., 7th H.L.I.
Head of the leading Batt. to pass the point D.16.a. 2.9. where MELBOURNE STREET joins the road, at 6 am.

3 Units will march independently, observing the usual halts and maintaining 100 yards between platoons.

4. Route via QUEANT – NOREUIL – LONGATTE – thence LONGATTE – CROISILLES ROAD – T. 30.

5. Bde. H.dqrs will close at present site at 9. am. and open at T. 30. d. 4.7 at same hour.

6. Units will immediately report arrival in new area.

7. Acknowledge

A. C. Stirling Cookson Capt
Bde Maj. 157 Bde.

Issued at 10.30pm on 16/9/18

Copy No 1 to 5th A.F.A. [illegible]
2 6th A.F.A. [illegible]
3 7th A.F.A. [illegible]
4 [illegible] T.M.B.
5 2nd [illegible]
6 443 [illegible] R.E.
7 C Coy 32nd Bn M.G.C.
8 153rd Inf Bde
9 156th Inf Bde
10 } War Diary
11 }
12 File

Note Machine Guns will withdraw with Battery to which they are attached. Further instructions to "C" Coy are being issued by OC 32nd Bn M.G.C.

<u>SECRET</u> Copy No. 10.

157th Infantry Brigade Administrative Instructions issued with 157th Infantry Brigade Order No. 140

6th Sept. 1918.

Ref: Maps Sheet 57^B S.W. & Sheet 57^C N.W.

1. <u>CAMPING AREAS</u> are allotted to Units as under:–

5th H.L.I.	All ground in T30 a less that WEST of SUNKEN RD.
6th H.L.I.	All ground in T30 c
7th H.L.I.	All ground in T30 ~~b~~ d.
157th L.T.M.B.	in T30 b.
157th Bde H.Q.	T24 central o. 7.

2. Each unit will detail the usual advance parties mounted either on cycles or horses to report to Staff Capt at present Bde H.Q. at 6 a.m., 7th inst.

3. TRANSPORT ARRANGEMENTS are as follows:–

(a) Greatcoats will be carried on the man.

(b) The Transport Officers will send up to their Battalions, to be there by 4.30 a.m. on 7th inst, to collect Field Kitchens & G.S. Limber Waggons which are at present with the Battalion, also Officers Mess Cart if required and Limbers for the

2.

Lewis Guns.

The whole of the above will march behind the unit.

(c) The Brigade Transport Officer will arrange to send up 1 G S Wagon, 1 G S Limber Wagon and 10 Pack animals for the L T M Bty, to report to O.C. L T M Bty by 4-30 a.m on 7th inst.

(d) The remainder of the transport will be loaded up ready to move off at 7 a.m on 7th inst from the Transport Lines under the orders of the Staff Captain.

(e) On arrival in new area Transport will be Brigaded in U 25 a 3.5.

4. BAGGAGE left at the Brigade Dump will be brought to the new area under Brigade arrangements.

5. BIVOUACS will be issued as soon as they are received.

6. WATER will be delivered by Mobile tanks to the new area.
1 Water Cart per Battalion should be sent to U 25 a 6.5 where road crosses railway at 10 a.m, to-morrow 7th inst.

3.

7. Arrangements for bathing will be notified when they are received.

8. ACKNOWLEDGE.

H.M. Hewison
Captain
Staff Captain, 157th Inf. Bde.

Issued at 10.30 P.M. on 6th Sept. 1918.

Copy No. 1 to 5th H.L.I.
2 6th H.L.I.
3 7th H.L.I.
4 T.O., 5th H.L.I.
5 T.O., 6th H.L.I.
6 T.O., 7th H.L.I.
7 157th L.T.M.B.
8 Brigade major
9 }
10 } War Diary
11 File.

19th Inf Bde Administrative Instruction No 1.

Ref Administrative Instruction issue and Bde Order No 140.

1. Locations

2nd Low Field Ambulance	U. 25 a.
Divisional Train	T. 21. Central
SAA Section D.A.C	T. 13. BOYELLES
Mobile Vety Section	T. 21. Central
Divisional Reception Camp	MONCHIET.
D.A.D.O.S.	Sugar Factory BOYELLES

2. Water. Carts can be filled at:-
CROISILLES T. 24. c. 2. 8.
ST. LEGER
Horse watering Points:-
CROISILLES T. 24. c. 3. 9.
ST. LEGER

3. Baths (a) Baths with a capacity of 100 men per hour have been erected at:-
S. 10. d. 0. 5 and T. 1. d. 2. 1.
(b) Baths are allotted to units as follows:-

	S. 10. d. 0. 5.	T. 1. d. 2. 1.
Sept 9.	5 HLI 8 am - 1 pm.	6 HLI 8 am - 1 pm
"	7th HLI 1 pm - 5 pm.	Bde Hq. TMB 1 pm

Clean underclothing will be available at these places.

Salvage. Units will salve all material in the area as follows:-

5 H.L.I. T.24.c. N. to Railway Embankment and T.30.a.

6th H.L.I. T.30. c and d.

7th H.L.I. T.30.a. and U.25.a. and c to a N. and S. line through where road crosses Railway and as far N. as Railway.

L.T.M.B. T.24.d.

All salvage will be sent to Brigade Dump situated at U.25.a.3.5.

Sanitation. Units will erect latrines, incinerators, refuse pits, and field ovens in their areas as soon as possible.

Field Cashier. Field Cashier will be at D.H.Q. 8th inst. 9.30 am till 11 am.

[illegible]

7/9/18

Capt
Staff Capt 157th Inf Bde

APPENDIX VIII

Copy No. 12

SECRET.

157th Infantry Brigade Order No. 141.

Ref. Map. Sheet 57 c. N.E. 1/20,000.

15th September, 1918.

1. The 52nd Division, less Artillery, will relieve the 57th Divn. in the front line on the nights 15th/16th and 16th/17th September, 1918.

The 157th Infantry Brigade will relieve the 172nd Infantry Brigade in the Left Section on the night of the 16th/17th September, in accordance with Table "A" on the reverse, taking over dispositions as held by relieved units.

3. Units will not pass E. of MELBOURNE STREET, in D.10.a. & c. before 8. p.m.

The 6th and 7th H.L.I. entering the Front Line by the HINDENBURG SUPPORT Line and track running through D.4.c. & d., D.5.c. &.d., and D.6.c. &.d. The 5th H.L.I. entering by the track running through D.10.a. & b. and D.11.a. & b. The 157th L.T.M.B. by whichever of the above routes is more convenient.

4. Owing to the danger of gas shelling during the relief, the greatest care will be taken throughout the relief to conceal any extra movement by daylight, especially in the high ground between NORTUIL and ECOUST, and immediately W. of QUEANT. Closing up on the march will be specially guarded against.

5. All details of relief, including guides, will be arranged between C.O.s concerned.

6. In the event of alarm or enemy attack during the relief :-

(a) Troops will man the nearest defences, reporting their dispositions at once to ~~the nearest~~ Brigade Headquarters.

(b) C.O.s will remain with their opposite numbers and await orders.

7. There is a Listening Set at E.7.c.0.1.

O.C. 5th H.L.I. will be responsible for promptly warning this party of :-
(i) An impending attack.
(ii) Gas Alarm.

8. Completion of relief will be wire "Priority" to Brigade H.Q., using the code word "ACHI". No time will be lost in getting into position as the outgoing Brigade has to be out before daylight.

157th Inf. Bde. H.Q., will close at T.30.c.9.0. at 8. p.m. and at V.28.d.0.0. at same time.

10. ACKNOWLEDGE.

C.S. Stirling Cookson

Captain,
Brigade Major, 157th Infantry Brigade.

Issued at 6 P.m.

Copy No. 1 to 5th H.L.I.
2 6th H.L.I.
3 7th H.L.I.
4 157th L.T.M.B.
5 2nd L.F.A.
6 413th Field Coy. R.E.
7 220th Coy. A.S.C.
8 52nd Bn. M.G.C.
9 Staff Captain.
10 I.O.
11) War Diary.
12)
13 File.
14)
15) Spare.
16)
17 172nd Bde HQ

Copy No 18 to 155th Bde HQ
19 156th Bde HQ

Table "A".

Serial No.	Date.	Unit.	From.	To.	In Relief of.
1.	16th/17th.	157th Bde. H.Q.	T.30.c.9.0.	V.28.d.0.0.	172nd Infantry Brigade.
2.	16th/17th.	5th H.L.I.	Present Camp.	Front Line RIGHT.	1st Royal Munster Fusrs.
3.	16th/17th.	6th H.L.I.	Present Camp.	Front Line LEFT.	9th King's Liverpool Regt.
4.	16th/17th.	7th H.L.I.	Present Camp.	Support.	2/4th South Lancashire Regt.
5	16th/17th.	157th L.T.M.B.	Present Camp.	Line.	172nd L.T.M.B.

Remarks. Units will march via the ECOUST - NOREUIL - QUEANT Road in the following order :-

(1) 5th H.L.I. leaving Camp at 2.15 p.m.
(2) 6th H.L.I. " " " 3.15 p.m.
(3) 7th H.L.I. " " " 3.45 p.m.
(4) 157th L.T.M.B." " " 4.– p.m.

A distance of 500 yards will be maintained between Battalions and 100 yards between Platoons and every 4 vehicles on the march.

All units will halt about 1 mile W. of QUEANT, in HIRONDELLE VALLEY, where evening meal will be served. Order of march after halt, same as before.

SECRET. APPENDIX IX Copy No. 11

157th Infantry Brigade Order No. 142.

18th September, 1918.

1. Warning Order issued under this office B.M.2/55 of to-day's date is confirmed.

2. After Relief, the 157th Infantry Brigade will withdraw to bivouacs in the Area between [illegible] and [illegible].
Representatives are being taken by the Staff Captain on morning of 19th September, to be shown bivouac sites allotted.

3. Orders regarding the Listening Set at E.7.c.0.1., all trench stores and orders regarding defences etc., will be handed over.

4. Completion of Relief will be wired "Priority" to Brigade Headquarters by using the code word "GOOD BYE".

5. 157th Infantry Brigade Headquarters will close at V.28.d.0.9. on completion of Relief, and will open at same time at a place which will be notified later.

6. In the event of alarm or enemy attack during the relief :-
(a) Troops will man the nearest defences, reporting their dispositions at once to Brigade Headquarters.
(b) C.O.s will remain with their opposite numbers and await orders.

7. A C K N O W L E D G E .

C. S. Stirling Cookson.
Captain,
Brigade Major, 157th Infantry Brigade.

Issued at 9.20 p.m. on 18/9/18.

Copy No. 1 to 5th H.L.I.
2 6th H.L.I.
3 7th H.L.I.
4 157th L.T.M.B.
5 5th Canadian Infantry Brigade.
6 155th Infantry Brigade.
7 156th Infantry Brigade.
8 7th Scottish Rifles.
9 Staff Captain.
10 I.O.
11 } War Diary.
12 }
13 File.
14 52nd Division.
15 4th Cand. Inf Bde

157th Infantry Brigade.
Administrative Instruction No 2
with reference to Brigade Order No 142.

<u>Handing Over</u>

All bivouac shelters, latrine tins & ammunition taken over by Units from Units of 172 Bde will be retained and taken down to the new area.

All other trench stores will be handed over to Units of the relieving Brigade. Copies of receipts will be sent to Bde HQrs by 2 pm on 20th inst, also lists of battle stores taken from the area.

<u>Bivouac Area</u>

On relief Units will proceed to the following areas.

These have been pointed out to representatives of Units and guides will meet units at C11 d. [illegible] to lead them in.

Bde HQ	C11 a 5 2
5th HLI	C11 d 9 5
6th HLI	C18 a 3 9
7th HLI	C17 a 7 7
157th LTMB	C17 a 4 4

2.

Shelter.

50 Shelters for Battalions and 10 for L T M Bty will be handed over to Battalion representatives at the new area at 1800 to-day.

Transport

All transport has moved this afternoon from U 28 Central to the new bivouac area.

Bde T.O will send up one limber for the L T M Bty at 9 Pm to-night.

K M Harrison Captain

19/9/18. Staff Capt 157th Inf Bde

APPENDIX IX

H.Q., 157TH. INFANTRY BRIGADE. No. BM/753 Date 18/9/18

SECRET.

T. O.C. 5th Bn. H.L.I.	Headquarters, 155th Inf. Bde.
6th Bn. H.L.I.	156th Inf. Bde.
7th Bn. H.L.I.	5th Canadian Inf. Bde.
157th L.T.M.B.	O.C. 1/7th Scottish Rifles.

Warning Order.

1. The 5th Canadian Infantry Brigade will relieve the 157th Infantry Brigade INCHY Sector on the night of the 19th/20th September, 1918.

2. (a) The 25th Canadian Infantry Battalion will relieve all troops of 5th H.L.I. ~~on the Right~~ also the 2 Companies of 7th H.L.I. in the Right Section of the 157th Infantry Brigade Front.

(b) The 26th Canadian Infantry Battalion will relieve the 6th H.L.I. and the 2 Companies of 7th Scottish Rifles in the [illegible] SWITCH.

(c) The 24th Canadian Infantry Battalion will relieve the remaining Company of 7th H.L.I. located in D.6.d., also the 2 Companies of 7th Scottish Rifles in ADELAIDE STREET - also making use of the HINDENBURG SUPPORT LINE in D.5.d. if necessary.

(d) The 5th Canadian L.T.M.B. will relieve the 157th L.T.M.B.

3. The 25th Canadian Infantry Battalion will enter the front line by the track running through D.10.a. and b. and D.11.a. and b.
The 24th and 26th Canadian Infantry Battalions entering the front line by the HINDENBURG SUPPORT LINE and track running through D.4.c. and d., D.5.c. and d., D.6.c. and d.
The 5th Canadian L.T.M.B. using whichever track is more suitable.

Order of Relief :- 5th., 6th, 7th H.L.I., 7th Sco Rifles, 157th L.T.M.B.

First troops of 5th Canadian Infantry Brigade will not pass [illegible] STREET in D.10. a. and c. before 6. p.m.

4. Advance Parties. Small advance parties from units of 5th Canadian Infantry Brigade will proceed to Battalions' and L.T.M.B. Headquarters. tomorrow morning 19th Guides from units will meet these advance parties at the points stated below and will conduct them to the respective Headquarters.
Guide from 5th H.L.I. to meet Advance Party at Cross Roads S. of PRONVILLE at D.9.d.1.2.
" " 6th, 7th H.L.I. and 157th L.T.M.B. to meet Advance Party at PRONVILLE in the street at D.9.b.central.
Guides to be at Meeting Points at 8.30 a.m.

Guides for units in the evening at the rate of 1 per platoon, under an Officer.
Guides for 24th and 26th Canadian Infantry Battalions and 5th Canadian L.T.M.B. to meet incoming units at D.9.b.central (PRONVILLE).
Guides for 25th Canadian Infantry Battalion to meet that Battalion at D.9.a.7.8. (N.W. end of PRONVILLE).
O.C. 7th H.L.I. will arrange guides from Companies of 7th S.R.
Guides to be ready waiting at meeting place at 7.30 p.m.

The roads and way into the line to be previously reconnoitred by the Officer in charge, and guides.

5. ACKNOWLEDGE. (Units of 157th Inf. Bde. only)

(Sgd) C S Stirling-Cookson Captain,
18th September, 1918. Brigade Major, 157th Infantry Brigade.

URGENT.

SECRET.

APPENDIX X

B.M.7/206.
19/9/18.

O.C. 5th Bn. H.L.I.

1. 155th Infantry Brigade is going to re-establish itself in MOEUVRES under a barrage at ZERO this afternoon.

2. ZERO will be notified later.

3. When the 155th Infantry Brigade have established themselves in MOEUVRES and the Post in CEMETERY SUPPORT, 5th H.L.I. will re-establish themselves in the posts D.14.a.35.30. and D.14.a.30.70

4. The barrage will probably come down on the line of the Light Railway running through D.14.a.

5. Further information will be given as soon as known.

6. 5th Bn. H.L.I. to acknowledge by wire.

Captain,
Brigade Major, 157th Infantry Brigade.

19th September, 1918.

Copies to :- 6th H.L.I.
7th H.L.I.
157th L.T.M.B.

O.C. 5th H.L.I.
6th H.L.I.
7th H.L.I.
157th L.T.M.B.

Ref this Office BM 7/206 of today's date.

1. It is essential that MOEUVRES be captured forthwith and held at all cost.

The 155th Inf Bde will therefore take MOEUVRES this evening and consolidate a line on Ridge in E.20.b. and CEMETERY SUPPORT as far East as F.14.d.

2. Troops of the 157th Inf. Bde will assist the 155th Inf Bde with rifle and machine gun fire, keeping down the heads of any enemy in E.14.a. and E.8.c. Up to the time the barrage lifts the 5th H.L.I. to pay particular attention to this.

All troops of 5th & 6th H.L.I. who cannot fire on E.14.a and E.8.c. will fire on enemy posts to their front.

2

OC 7th H.L.I will send 2 Coys. to keep touch with the 4th R.S.F. who are operating on the Left of the 155th Inf Bde.
These 2 Coys of 7th H.L.I. will follow troops of the 4th R.S.F. along CEMETERY SUPPORT as far Eastwards as E. 14. d. 50.65.
Coy of 7th H.L.I. being in touch with 4th R.S.F. in Hindenburg Line (now our present front line, ie. enemy's 2nd Line) so as to advance with them.
These 2 Coys. 7th H.L.I. will then consolidate CEMETERY SUPPORT as quickly as possible, establishing 3 platoon posts, the most Eastern post being at E. 14. d. 50.65. then at E 14. d. 30. 85, and E. 14. central. and improving the whole of CEMETERY SUPPORT WEST of the advanced post at E. 14. d. 50.65.
After capture of CEMETERY SUPPORT these 2 Coys. will be under orders of GOC 155th Inf Bde. and will remain in the line instead of being relieved tonight.

3. The OC 5th H.L.I. will detail the Coy. in HOBART trench to re establish the former posts on the railway at E.14.a 35-30 and E.14 a. 30.70. These getting in touch with 7th H.L.I. in CEMETERY SUPPORT /

4. The attack will be supported by the 57th Divn. Arty and available XVII Corps Hy Arty. The former will provide a Creeping Barrage which will come down at ZERO on the following line :-

From E.15.a 1.8. to E. 14. a. 30.70 thence Southwards along the Light Railway to CEMETERY SUPPORT at E 14. a. 4. 0. thence Southwards through MOEUVRES to E.14.c.6.0. thence Southwards to E.20.a.6.5. thence SE. to E.20.a 85.75.

This barrage will roll forward at 100 yds. per 4 minutes at ZERO plus 5 minutes.

A. F.A. standing barrage will be placed on HOBART STREET from E 8.c.6.1. Eastwards, also along hedge from E.14.c.5.2 Eastwards.

5. Troops of the 155th Inf Bde and of the 7th and 5th H.L.I. will push forward immediately the barrage lifts at ZERO plus 5 minutes.

6. Arrangements re guides for incoming units of the ~~5~~ 5th Canadian Inf Bde remain as previously ordered.

7. OC. Y.57 M.T.M.B. and OC. 157th L.T.M.B will arrange to bombard enemy M.G. Posts.

4

along Light Railway in E. 8. a. and c. also in E. 14. a. The bombardment of latter portion to cease immediately the barrage lifts.

8. The Guards and 2nd Canadian Divn. are assisting with artillery fire on both flanks.

9. 3 Coy. 52nd Bn. M.G. will support the attack and provide a S.O.S. barrage in front of the new line.

10. Every man to carry 3 Sandbags and as many bombs as possible.
220 rounds per man.
Rations for 2 Coy. of 7th H.L.I. will be sent up during course of tonight.
Every man of assaulting Coys of 5th and 7th H.L.I. will carry a pick or a shovel.

19/9/18 Captain,
Brigade Major, 157th Infantry Brigade.

SECRET

APPENDIX XI

Copy No. 10

157th Infantry Brigade Order No 143.

21st September 1918

Ref. Map 1/20,000. 57c N.E.

1. The 52nd Division will extend its front Southwards to-morrow, 22nd inst, as far as the line K.11.b.0.7 – K.3.c.0.8 – D.30.b.0.3 – D.22.a.0.7.

2. The 6th HLI will relieve the troops of the 1st Guards Brigade in the new area after dark to-morrow.

The 6th HLI will come under orders of B.G.C., 156th Inf Bde, at present commanding the MOEUVRES Sector, at 6 P.M. to-morrow.

3. O.C., 6th HLI and his Company Commanders will report at Headquarters 156th Inf Bde at D.15.b.7.7 at 9.45 a.m. to-morrow morning.

4. The present Front Line, Outpost Line and Main Line of Resistance and Barrage Line are shewn on map issued to 6th HLI.

The Guards Main Line of Resistance is the Old British Line in J 5 and D 29 from where the spurs to the N.E. are heavily swept by M.G. fire. The Guards will not move their Machine Guns at present.

Owing to the above method of holding the ground, the Outpost and Main Line of Resistance marked in our new area are not dug, except where trenches are shewn on map. 1 Company 17th North'd Fus. (P) will be placed at the disposal of the B.G.C., 156th Inf Bde, to assist in this matter.

5. O.C., 52nd M.G. Bn, in consultation with O.C., Guards Division, M.G. Bn, and B.G.C., 156th Inf. Bde, will place as many Machine Guns as necessary in the new area up to half a Company. These Machine Guns will come from Divisional Reserve.

6. O.C. 6th Bn. H.L.I. will report completion of relief to 156th Inf. Bde. H.Qrs. by Priority wire using the code word "CAMBRAI".

7. 1st Guards Brigade, 156th Inf Bde. and 6th H.L.I. please acknowledge.

(Sgd) C.S. Stirling-Cookson Captain,
Brigade Major, 157th Infantry Brigade

Issued at 11-45 P.M.

Copy No 1 to 6th H.L.I.
2 156th Inf Bde
3 1st Guards Bde
4 52nd Division
5 5th H.L.I.
6 7th H.L.I.
7 157th L.T.M.B.
8 155th Inf. Bde
9 Staff Captain
10 }
11 } War Diary
12 File.

Secret

APPENDIX XII

Copy No

157th Infantry Brigade

Order No 104

1. 5th H.L.I. will relieve 6th H.L.I. in the Right Battalion area, in the line during the night 24th/25th Sept 1918. Commencement at [illegible]

2. Details of relief including guides will be arranged between C.Os concerned.

3. On relief 6th H.L.I. will move to quarters vacated by 5th H.L.I.

4. 5th H.L.I. will wire completion of relief to 157th Inf Bde. 6th H.L.I. will report their arrival in camp to 157th Inf Bde.

5. 5th & 6th H.L.I. to acknowledge.

[illegible] Capt.
Bde Major 157th Inf Bde.

21

Issued at [illegible] on 24/9/18.

Copy No. 1 to [illegible]

2	[illegible]
3	[illegible]
4	[illegible] Inns
5	1/5th [illegible]
6	[illegible]
7	[illegible] Bde.
8	[illegible]
9 }	War Diary
10 }	
11	File

ADDENDIX XIII

SECRET.

Copy No....15....

157th Infantry Brigade Order No.145.

Ref. Map MOEUVRES Special Sheet
parts of 57.c.N.W., N.E., S.W., and S.E., 1/20,000.

1. On a day and at a Zero hour to be notified later the British 1st and 3rd Armies will attack.

(a) The Canadian Corps (1st Army) on our left, attacking BOURLON WOOD from the North and West will direct.
In conformity with their action the 63rd Division, XVII Corps will attack with its left on the Corps Northern Boundary and its right on the MOEUVRES-GRAINCOURT ROAD(E.21.c., E.27.b., E.28.c. and d, K.5.a) exclusive.
The 52nd Division will conform to the action of the 63rd Division and attack with its left on the MOEUVRES-GRAINCOURT ROAD (inclusive).
On the South the Guards Division is likewise attacking, but not as a part of the concerted movement of the Canadian and XVII Corps.

(b) The objectives are given on Maps issued to C.O's.

1st objective			RED
2nd	do.	Canadian	GREEN
		Remainder	BROWN
3rd	do.		BLUE.

(c) (i) The XVII Corps barrage for attack of 156 Infantry Brigade will come down at Zero on line E.26.b.2.8. - E.20.d3.9. and at Zero plus 15 minuted will roll eastwards at the rate of 100 yards in 3 minutes to a line running north from E.27.a.5.5. Here it will pivot and swing round to a general line from E.27.a.5.5. to E.21.c.5.5. - E.17.c. which it will reach at Zero plus 110 minutes. The barrage will then again roll forward south eastwards at the rate of 100 yards in 4 minutes.
(ii) The 9th Brigade R.F.A. will place a block barrage on the line E.26.b.6.4. - E.26.a.8.6. at Zero for 157th Inf. Bde.
(iii) At Zero plus 40 minutes the block barrage will swing southwards at 100 yards per 5 minutes to the line South end of lock - K.3.a.7.5. - K.2.b.6.6. where it will pause for 5 minutes and then cease at Zero plus 95 minutes.
(iiii) Consequent on the above the 156th Inf. Bde. will attack and make good the line of the Canal by Zero plus 28 minutes. The assualting troops of the 157th Infantry Brigade (6th and 7th H.L.I.) will attack simultaneously with 156th Inf. Bde. at Zero plus 15 minutes and will capture and form a defensive flank down ALF Trench under which the remainder of the assaulting troops of 6th and 7th H.L.I. will form up, afterwards attacking southwards under the block barrage which will move forward at Zero plus 40 minutes.

(d) The 63rd Division will attack under the barrage with its right on the MOEUVRES - GRAINCOURT ROAD (exclusive), clear the HINDENBURG LINE and capture GRAINCOURT and ANNEUX.

(e) In conformity with the action of the 63rd Division the 52nd Division will attack as follows:-
(i) The 156th Inf. Bde. will take LEOPARD AVENUE from the MOEUVRES-GRAINCOURT ROAD (inclusive) to the bend at E.27.a.2.5. to which the barrage, while pivoting, will form a protection.
(ii) The 156th Bde. will then advance and clear the area shaded pink on map. The line KANGAROO TRENCH-SOW AVENUE must be made good and from here they will push forward on to high ground in K.4.a. and K.4.c.

(f) The 155th Inf. Bde. will hold their present line.

2. (a). The 157th Inf. Bde will mop up the HINDENBURG FRONT LINE and both banks of the CANAL in E.26., K.2.b., K.3.a. under a block barrage (vide para 1 sub para c and sub para 3.)

(b) The remainder of the area between 157th Inf. Bde, and Guards Division will be cleared without a barrage.

(c) It is most important that the 157th Inf. Bde. area be cleared of the enemy at the earliest possible moment.

3. 157th Bde.
The HINDENBURG FRONT LINE and the CANAL will be mopped up from North to South as follows:-
The 6th H.L.I. on the right, mopping up both lines of trenches and the Communication trenches between them.
The 7th H.L.I. on the left, dealing with the CANAL (including both banks) and the Communication Trenches leading from the most Easterly of the two Trench Lines to the CANAL.
The 5th H.L.I. will be in Brigade Reserve in their present position, but after the attack by the 157th Brigade has started the two rear Companies will close up into the two trenches running Northwest from each end of SAND LANE, one Company in each.

4. Prior to the assault the 6th and 7th H.L.I. will assemble in SAND LANE and front line of HINDENBURG FRONT LINE ~~running South east~~ running South east from the Northern end of SAND LANE.
They will ~~assault~~ ASSEMBLE here in accordance with the arrangement made at the Conference this morning.
To make room for this, the 5th H.L.I. will temporarily close down to the Southern end of SAND LANE and the trench running South from it, opening out again when the assaulting troops have moved forward.

5. The forming up trench will be ALF Trench (E.26.a.95.70. to E.26.b.60.55.) and North of it.
Only the leading Companies of 6th and 7th H.L.I. can form up here; the remaining Companies must push down from SAND LANE as far as possible and be ready to come into position behind the leading Companies as these latter move forward, as arranged at to-day's conference.
For this purpose gaps will be cut in the wire from E.26.a.8.9. to E.26.a.9.5., by the tanks.
The forming up place is at present in the hands of the enemy, the leading troops therefore, must expect, and be prepared to fight their way down; they will then form a defensive flank under cover of which the leading assault Companies will form up. The method of forming the defensive flank will be as arranged at the conference to-day.

6. The assault will be carried out as follows:-

(a) The barrage, consisting of shrapnel, thickened up by Machine Gun and Trench Mortar Fire, will move forward from the line given in para.1, (c), (iii). at the rate of 100 yards in 5 minutes. The depth of the barrage from North to South will be 100 yards and the breadth will stretch across both lines of trenches and the CANAL. It will be an oblique barrage.

(b) Immediately behind the barrage will follow 4 tanks in line abreast, one tank being just West of the trenches, two tanks between the two lines of trenches, and one tank between the trenches and the CANAL. The tanks will move from North to South but will zigzag about. Two of those tanks, on reaching the CAMBRAI Road, will cross to the East of the CANAL, the other two continuing to our Southern Boundary.
The Infantry will keep close behind the line of tanks.

(c) The 7th H.L.I. will mop up the canal from West to East, taking it in sections; the leading Company taking the 1st section, the 2nd Company leapfrogging through the 1st Company

(6) (e) Contd.

1st Company and taking the second section, and so on, care being taken in carrying out the leap frog principle not to lose the barrage.

The 6th H.L.I. will not leap frog, but will work straight down the trenches dropping moppers up as they go.

In both cases very detailed arrangements will be required; every man must know what his particular task is.

O.C. 7th H.L.I. must make special arrangements for dealing with the crossing over the canal by the CAMBRAI Road and also with the Lock at E.3.7.?. & the spoil heap in E.27.?.

Two tanks will, in the first case, deal with the former and one with the latter.

7. (a) As soon as the areas have been captured, the 156th Inf. Bde. will secure the line SOW AVENUE - KANGAROO TRENCH.

(b) The 157th Inf. Bde. front will be divided into two areas. The Right Area from our Southern Boundary to COW ALLEY (exclusive). The Left Area from COW ALLEY (inclusive) to the forming up ... ANT TRENCH.

(c) Immediately it is seen that the 156th Inf. Bde. are occupying SOW AVENUE and KANGAROO TRENCH, the new dispositions will be taken up:-

The 6th H.L.I. occupying the Right Area.
The 7th H.L.I. occupying the Left Area.

Each Battalion will be organised in depth, the CANAL being the Main Line of Resistance.

(d) Both Battalions will at once obtain close touch with the units on their flanks, i.e, the Guards on the Right and troops occupying MOEUVRES on the Left.

The 6th H.L.I. will send out troops to gain touch with the 2nd Guards Brigade at the following points, reporting when contact gained :-

(i) BEAR Trench K.3.a.5.2.
(ii) WORM Trench and Canal K.3.a.8.3.

The 7th H.L.I. will send out troops for a similar purpose to:-

(iii) PIG AVENUE.

The Guards will be at these points at Zero plus 60 minutes and will commence working North as soon as our barrage lifts at Zero plus 95 minutes.

The 6th H.L.I. will also arrange to send a patrol to get in touch, *and report having done so:-

*WITH 156 INF. BDE

(a) In LION Trench.

Similarly the 7th H.L.I. will send patrols:- TO GET IN TOUCH WITH 156TH INF. BDE

(b) On the CAMBRAI Road.
(c) In ZEBRA Trench.
(d) In KANGAROO Trench.

(e) Consolidation will be started and carried out as quickly as possible after capture of the area. Tools for this must be taken.

(f) While the 157th Inf. Bde. is capturing its area, the Heavy Artillery and the 52nd Bn. M.G.C. will be engaging LEOPARD AVENUE - LION, SOW and KANGAROO Trenches and the HINDENBURG SUPPORT LINE in Squares E.22. and 28.

8. (a) 6 Light Trench Mortars placed in position in the TRENCH approximately at the following points :- ~~E.26.a.6.0.~~ E.20c 4.3. - ~~E.26.c.6.0.~~ E.25b 9.6. E.26c 1.4., E.26.b.0.1., will fire on the enemy trenches, thickening the ... barrage, their fire moving Southwards with that of the

8. (a) Contd.
with that of the barrage.

(b) Two Light Trench Mortars will follow the Assaulting Companies moving down WILLY Trench,* thence down the trench running parallel to the Canal and next East of WOLF and FOX Trenches.
* The Trench from E 20c 8.1. to E 20c 3.3. Latter point being junction of HINDENBURG FRONT LINE with SAND LANE.

9. On Y/Z night the 157th Inf. Bde. will move into position prior to forming up for assembly, by track "G" marked on the map, and marked "157th" on the ground, in luminous paint. This track will not now run along the Light Railway in E.19.c.6.1. as previously arranged, but will run via Sunken Road running North and South through E.25.b. It will run Eastwards from about E.25.a.5.3. to Sunken Road about E.25.b.6.9. thence to WILLY Trench.
The above track will be thoroughly reconnoitred beforehand.

The 156th Inf. Bde. will move by track "H" on map and marked "156" in luminous paint on the ground.

10. An officer from Brigade Headquarters will be sent to each Battalion Headquarters to synchronise watches.

11. Medical Arrangements. - Issued with Administrative Instructions.

12. Signal Instructions, including position of Advanced Brigade Report Centre, routes for runners, etc. will be issued separately.

13. 157th Inf. Bde. Hqrs. will be at D.28.b.8.2.

14. ACKNOWLEDGE.

P. S. Stirling Cookson.
Captain,
Brigade Major, 157th Infantry Brigade.

Note.
Ref. Para. 3. [illegible] should get square behind this line, (ALF Trench) if time and space permit and if the 155th Inf. Bde. have by then made room.

Copy No. 1 to 5th H. L. I.
2 6th H. L. I.
3 7th H. L. I.
4 157th L. T. M. Bty.
5 B. G. C.
6 Hqrs. 155th Inf. Bde.
7 Hqrs. 156th Inf. Bde.
8 Hqrs. 2nd Guards Bde.
9 Hqrs. 52nd Division.
10 Hqrs. 63rd. Division.
11 Staff Captain.
12 Sigs. Officer.
13 S.A.A. Officer.
14 (
15 (War Diary.
16 File.

Copy No....15.

S E C R E T.

157th Infantry Brigade Administrative Instructions
Issued with Reference to
157th Infantry Brigade Order No. 145 of 25/9/18.

---

1. Supplies.

Railhead - BOISIEUX AU MONT
Refilling Point - ECOUST (C.1.d.9.9.)

(a) Preserved Meat will be issued (less a proportion of Fresh Meat for Transport Details) for consumption on 'Z' day.

(b) Supply Situation on Morning of 'Z' Day.

On the Man { One days Rations. P. Meat.
{ One Iron Ration.

Commanding Officers will ensure that the above rations have been distributed to and are carried by individuals prior to the advance.

2. AMMUNITION.

S.A.A. & Grenade Dumps.

Brigade Dumps are established at the following points:-

(i) Forward Dump E.20.c.6.3
(ii) " " E.25.c.1.9
(iii) Main Dump D.30.c.9.7.

These Dumps contain a supply of S.A.A., Grenades, Lewis Gun Magazines, S.O.S. Rockets, 1" D.I. Lights & Ground Flares. Box Respirators and Chlorid of Lime, and will be under charge of Lt. J.. STEWART, who will be situated at Main Dump (D.30.c.9.7.)

3. WATER.

"A" Men.

(a) An advanced Dump of Drinking water will be established at the Main Ammunition Dump (D.30.c.9.7.). For this purpose 20 Petrol Tins will be withdrawn from each Unit. In addition to these the Dump will contain 150 Petrol Tins and 250 full Water Bottles, i.e. a total of 210 Petrol Tins and 250 Water Bottles.

(b) Empty Petrol Tins should be sent back to the Dump. No man should come back without one.

"B" Animals.

(a) Available Water Points :-

PRONVILLE. (D.9.a.2.2.)
QUEANT. (D.1.d.central)

It is hoped to open up a water point at LOUVERVAL as early as possible.

4. TRAFFIC./-

4. TRAFFIC.

(i)

(A) As operations proceed the Main Line of Supply for the Division will become CROISILLES - LAGNICOURT - LOUVERVAL Road.

(B) MOEUVRES will be controlled by 63rd Division.

(C) Troops and empty H.T. must use Cross country Tracks as far as possible.

(D) Animals proceeding to and from water must on no account use Lorry Routes. All Transport Officers must be prepared to reconnoitre new routes to water and if necessary will cut wire or fill in old trenches to accomplish this end.

(E) Vehicles must not halt on Main Lorry routes. They must pull clear of the Road or down a side road.

(F) The QUEANT - PRONVILLE - MOEUVRES Road will be used as little as possible by Transport of this Division

(ii)

The following Road is allotted to this Brigade for Supply purposes from 'Z' day inclusive:-

LAGNICOURT - LOUVERVAL - CAMBRAI Road.

5. PROVOST.

(A) Stragglers.

(i) Brigade Stragglers Posts will be established at the following points:-

(a) Trench junction in E.20.c.3.3.
(b) Trench Junction in E.25.b.70.35.

Any Stragglers stopped by these posts will be sent back direct to their Units.

(ii) Behind these Brigade Posts a line of Stragglers Posts and a Straggler collecting station will be established under Divisional Control.

(B) Prisoners of War.

Divisional Cage, D.13.c.1.

Battalions will establish P. of W. collecting stations and will send back prisoners to Brigade Headquarters (D.23.b.8.2.)

(i) From ALF along trench in E.20.c., to North end of SAND LANE. Routes used should be down SAND LANE and along trench running through E.25.a & b, to Light Railway at E.19.c.5.1., thence along Light Railway to Bde. Hqrs. - and

(ii) Down APE Trench E.25.c. to trench running through E.26.c. past South end of SAND LANE on to Light Railway, and Bde. Hqrs. as for (i).

6. MEDICAL.

Locations. 1/1st Lowland Field Ambulance D.1.d.5.9. (Divisional Advanced Dressing Station)

Relay Posts.	Regtl. Aid Posts.
D.17.d.3.8.	E.13.d.0.8.
D.18.c.5.8.	D.18.d.2.6.
D.18.d.2.6.	E.19.a.8.3.
E.19.a.0.9.	E.19.a.1.0.
E.19.a.8.3.	

6. MEDICAL (Contd.)

Trolley Post.	Horsed Ambulance Post.
D.17.a.5.9.	D.17.b.1.3.

Motor Car Post.

D.15.d.5.5.

7. VETERINARY.

Advanced Collecting Station will be situated at D.7.c.5.8.

8. BURIAL.

The Burial Parties, detailed in this Office Z/3928 of 21/9/18, will report to Brigade Transport Officer at Transport Lines at 4 p.m. on 'Z' minus 1 day. They will be rationed to 'Z' day inclusive after which day they will be attached for Rations to 17th Northumberland Fus.

9. SALVAGE.

(A) As soon as the Tactical situation permits, Battns., will at once start Salvage operations in their immediate vicinity. The Salvage area allotted to this Brigade is - the Area to be captured.

Lists of material salved should be made out, particularly for Guns, Machine Guns, etc.

(B) Wherever possible Battn Salvage Dumps should be situated near a Road or Track.

(C) Every effort must be made to Salve British Rifles in serviceable condition. If left exposed to weather they deteriorate rapidly. These Rifles must therefore, when collected, be placed under extemporised cover at once.

(D) Returning vehicles of 1st Line Transport will be systematically used to evacuate salvage to Divnl. Salvage Dump. British Rifles and equipment must be evacuated first.

(E) All Roads or Tracks must be cleared of loose boxes or rounds of ammunition.

10. TENTAGE.

(A) For the purposes of these operations the following number of Tents and shelters may be retained by Units for Transport Lines etc.

	Tents.	Shelters.
Brigade Hqrs.	1	7
Each Battalion.	2	13
L.T.M. Bty.	1	4

(B) Every precaution must be taken to prevent of this Tentage during operations as it cannot be replaced at present. Units will be held responsible for any losses.

(C) All/-

10. TENTAGE (Contd.)

(C) All tentage in excess of the scale laid down in para (A) will be returned to D.A.D.O.S. by noon 'Z' minus day. Unit will report when this has been done and the amount returned.

11. RECEPTION CAMP.

From 'Z' day inclusive, reinforcements and personnel returning from Leave will remain at Divnl. Reception Camp, pending Orders to rejoin their Units.

12. PERSONNEL FOR ADMINISTRATION PURPOSES.

The parties who have already been earmarked (reference Z/3928 of 21/9/18) for the above duties will report as follows:-

Duty.	Unit.	Number	Report to.
Escort for P. of W.	5th H.L.I. 7th H.L.I.	1 N.C.O. & 5 men 1 N.C.O. & 5 men	Bde. Hqrs. at Transport Lines at 0900
Salvage.	6th H.L.I.	1 N.C.O. & 2 men	do.
Burial.	5th H.L.I. 7th H.L.I.	10 men. 1 N.C.O. & 10 men	do.
Pack Dump.	Each Unit.	1 man.	do.
Bde. S.A.A. Carrying party.	5th H.L.I. 6th H.L.I. 7th H.L.I.	4 men 4 men 4 men	do.

13. ACKNOWLEDGE.

H.W. Hewison
Captain,
Staff Captain, 157th Infantry Brigade.

Issued at 11 P.M. 25/9/18.

Copy No. 1 to 5th H. L. I.
2 6th H. L. I.
3 7th H. L. I.
4 157th L. T. M. Bty.
5 B.G.C.
6 Hqrs. 155th Inf. Bde.
7 Hqrs. 156th Inf. Bde.
8 B. T. O.
9 S. A. A. Officer.
10 }
11 } Battn. Quartermasters.
12 }
13 }
14 } War Diary
15 File.

NC 7

W A R   D I A R Y .

157th I N F A N T R Y   B R I G A D E   H E A D Q U A R T E R S .

O C T O B E R 1 9 1 8 .

V O L U M E   I I I.

Instructions regarding War Diaries and Intelligence Summaries are contained in F. S. Regs., Part II. and the Staff Manual respectively. Title pages will be prepared in manuscript.

WAR DIARY
or
INTELLIGENCE SUMMARY.
(*Erase heading not required.*)

Army Form C. 2118.

October 1918 — 157th Inf. Bde — Vol III — (01)

Place	Date	Hour	Summary of Events and Information	Remarks and references to Appendices
Near MOEUVRES	1/10	2 p.m.	Bde. moved to Divnl. Support just E. of CANAL D'ESCAUT (F30. 57c N.E) relieving 188 Bde of 63rd. Div.	
F30 a. (57c N.E)		5 p.m.	Wire received from Div giving Divnl. policy and attack to be carried out by Bdes – 157th Bde to attack NIERGNIES and AWOINGT.	
		6 p.m.	B.G.C's conference with C.O's to discuss plans of attack.	
		5.40 p.m.	155 Bde. attacked FBG de PARIS but failed to gain objective. Attack of 157 Bde therefore cancelled.	[illegible]
	2/10	1800	Nothing of interest to report. Bde. remained throughout last 24 hours in same position.	[illegible]
	3/10	1800	Nothing of interest to report. Bde remained throughout last 24 hours in same position.	
		1900	Working party of 250 men (supplied by 7 HLI) provided for 155 Bde.	
		2300	155 Bde again attacked FBG de PARIS but failed to gain objective. 157 Bde. ordered by Divn. to be ready to send out battle patrols at dawn if 155 Bde found no signs of enemy. 5 HLI ordered to comply.	[illegible]
	4/10	0600	Enemy still in position and patrols of 5 HLI did not go out.	
		1100	Orders received from Div that Bde would relieve 155 Bde in line tonight. Orders issued to units accordingly (App I)	App I
		1400	Conference of C.O's held to discuss new dispositions.	[illegible]
		1900	Relief commenced.	

[illegible signature] Capt.

D. D. & L., London, E.C. (A8001) Wt. W1771/M2031 750,000 5/17 Sch. 52 Forms C2118/14

Instructions regarding War Diaries and Intelligence Summaries are contained in F. S. Regs., Part II. and the Staff Manual respectively. Title pages will be prepared in manuscript.

Vol III

WAR DIARY
or
INTELLIGENCE SUMMARY.
(Erase heading not required.)

157th Inf. Bde
October 1918

Army Form C. 2118.

O2

Place	Date	Hour	Summary of Events and Information	Remarks and references to Appendices
F30a 6.3 (Sheet 57c N.E)	5/10	0200	Relief completed. Delay due to M.G. and shell fire	
		0600	Patrols report all quiet on front during night. Several enemy M.G's located	
		1800	Orders received from Div. that Bde would be relieved tonight by Bde of 57th Div. Bde order issued (App II)	App II
		2200	Relief commenced.	MB
	6/10	0300	Relief complete and Bde moved to positions just W. of CANAL du NORD all units arriving in new area by 0600.	
			Division advised that whole Division was proceeding by train the following day to rest area in vicinity AVESNES-LE-COMTE	MB
		1400	Billeting parties proceed.	
	7/10		Bde Order issued for move by rail (App III). Train due to arrive 2300	App III MB
GRAND RULLECOURT.	8/10	0600	Train with Bde arrived PETIT HOUVIN 9 hours late. Brigade billeted as follows Bde Sign & 6th HLI GRAND RULLECOURT. 5 HLI LIGNEREUIL. 7 HLI & 157 L.T.M.B LIENCOURT.	MB
		1600	All troops including transport which came by road arrived in billets	
	9/10	1000	Conference held at Div. & attended by B.G.C. B.M. all C.O.'s & 2nds in command Subject Training.	MB
			Bde employed day for cleaning up etc. & settling down.	

D. D. & L., London, E.C. (A5004) Wt. W1771/M2031 750,000 5/17 Sch. 52 Forms/C2118/14

Instructions regarding War Diaries and Intelligence Summaries are contained in F. S. Regs., Part II. and the Staff Manual respectively. Title pages will be prepared in manuscript.

WAR DIARY or INTELLIGENCE SUMMARY.

(Erase heading not required.)

157 Inf. Brigade

Oct. 1918. O.3.

Army Form C. 2118.

Place	Date	Hour	Summary of Events and Information	Remarks and references to Appendices
Grand Rullecourt	10th to 19th		The Brigade remained in this area training – The weather was practically all the time so that good progress was made –	MG
Mont St Eloy.	19th		The Brigade Group march in accordance with Bde. order No. 151 to the Camps at Mont St. Eloi. The last unit getting into camp at 5.30. pm. The march was 14 miles –	Appendix IV MG
Henin Liétard	20th		The Bde. Group marched to Henin Liétard where it was billeted for the night. The last unit reaching the new area at 5.45. pm. A 15 mile march over very bad roads indeed. 15 men in whole group only fell out. Showers off and on the whole day. Bde. order 152.	Appendix V MG
Wagnonville	21st		The Brigade group less the 413 Field Co RE & 2 sects. of ½ Lowl. Fld. Amb. march in accordance with Bde. order No. 153. to following villages. Bde. H.Qr. & 157 L.T.M.B. to WAGNONVILLE. 5th H.L.I. to PLANQUE. 6th & 7th H.L.I. to FLERS. A 6 miles march. Brig. Gen. Hamilton Moore C.M.G. D.S.O. left to attend an Inter allied Tank demonstration at FONTAINEBLEAU. Lt.Col. Romanes Comdg. 1/7 Scottish Rifles 157 Bde assumed temporary Comd. of the Bde –	Appendix VI – MG

D. D. & L., London, E.C. (A8001) Wt. W1771/M2031 750,000 5/17 Sch. 52 Forms C2118/14

Army Form C. 2118.

Instructions regarding War Diaries and Intelligence Summaries are contained in F. S. Regs., Part II. and the Staff Manual respectively. Title pages will be prepared in manuscript.

WAR DIARY
or
INTELLIGENCE SUMMARY.
(Erase heading not required.)

157 Inf Brigade
October 1918 O. 4.

Place	Date	Hour	Summary of Events and Information	Remarks and references to Appendices
WAGNONVILLE –	22nd Oct.		Units spent the day cleaning up and doing specialist training. A very wet day indeed –	
WAGONVILLE	23rd		Training –	
FLINES.	24.		Bde. moved to FLINES & MONTREUIL in accordance with Bde. order No. 154.	App. VII
"	25th		Repairing roads. The whole Bde. was employed on this work –	
"	26th		Training –	
LANDAS – AREA	27th		The Bde. group less 413 Fd Co. R.E. marched in accordance with Bde. order No. 156. General Hamilton-Moore rejoined the Bde.	Appendix VIII
LECELLES. AREA.	28th		The Bde. group less 413 Fd Co. R.E. marched in accordance with Bde order No. 157.	App. IX
"	29th		The Brigade spent the day cleaning up equipment, clothing, and billets –	

D. D. & L., London, E.C.
(A8001) Wt. W1771/M2031 750,000 5/17 Sch. 52 Forms C2118/14

Instructions regarding War Diaries and Intelligence Summaries are contained in F. S. Regs., Part II. and the Staff Manual respectively. Title pages will be prepared in manuscript.

WAR DIARY
or
INTELLIGENCE SUMMARY.
(*Erase heading not required.*)

157. Inf. Brigade
O.S.

Army Form C. 2118.

Place	Date	Hour	Summary of Events and Information	Remarks and references to Appendices
LECELLES AREA.	29/30		During the night LECELLES was shelled heavily at intervals by the enemy. The 6 H.L.I. had one casualty, & the 7. H.L.I. 9 – The latter Bn. also losing 6 horses	MC
"	30th		Training during the morning. On orders from Div. the 6th & 7 H.L.I. were moved out of LECELLES as result of shelling during previous night. The 6 H.L.I. went to RUMEGIES and 7th H.L.I. to RUE DES FÈVES	MC
RUMEGIES	31st		Bde H.Qrs., on orders from Division were moved to RUMEGIES during the afternoon & the L.T.M.B. from LECELLES to RUE DES FÈVES – Training was carried out as usual.	MC

B. Stirling Cochrane Capt
for Brig. Gen. Comdg
157th Inf Bde

D. D. & L., London, E.C.
(A8001) Wt. W1771/M2031 750,000 5/17 Sch. 52 Forms C2118/14

CASUALTIES FOR MONTH OF

OCTOBER, 1918.

Killed.		Wounded.		Missing.	
Officers.	O. R.	Officers.	O. R.	Officers	O. R.
-	8	5	42	-	4

STRENGTHS AT END OF MONTH OF

OCTOBER, 1918.

UNIT.	Effective Strength.		Fighting Strength.	
	Officers	O. R.	Officers.	O. R.
1/5th BN. H. L. I.	41	662	24	457
1/6th Bn. H. L. I.	40	627	25	411
1/7th Bn. H. L. I.	48	660	37	443
157th. L. T. M. Bty.	4	46	4	46
157th. Inf. Bde. Hqrs.	9	103	9	103
TOTAL.	142	2098	99	1460

Secret Appendix I Copy No —

154th Infantry Brigade Order No. 146

4/10/18.

I. The 154th Inf Bde will relieve the 155th Inf Bde in the front line tonight, the 4/5th October, 1918 in accordance with table "A" attached. Relief to commence as soon as it is dark enough.

II. All details of relief, including guides will be arranged between C.O's concerned.

III. Completion of relief will be wired "Priority" to Bde Hqrs using the code word "A.C.E."

IV. 154th Inf Bde will close at F30. a. 6.3 at 2030 and open at F20. a 7. 4 at same time.

V. Acknowledge.

(Sgd) C. S. Stirling Cookson Capt.
Bde Major 154th Inf Bde.

Issued at— — — —

Copy No	1	5 A.S.H.	6	156 Inf Bde.
	2	6 H.L.I.	7	52 Divn.
	3	7 H.L.I.	8	172 Inf Bde.
	4	154 LTMB.	9	6 Inf Bde.
	5	155 Inf Bde.	10, 11	War Diary.

TABLE "A"

Serial	Date Oct	Unit.	from	to.	In relief of.
1	4/5th.	157 BHQ.	F30a.6.3	F30a 7.4	155 Inf Bde HQ F30 a - 7. 4
2	"	5 HL.I.	Right Support.	Front Line LEFT	1/5 R.S.F (Bn HQ. A20 C 1.0).
3	"	6 HLI	Left Support.	Front Line RIGHT	1/4 R.S.F (Bn HQ A26 d 6.0)
4	"	7 HLI.	Centre Support	Left Support.	6 H.L.I.
5	"	157 LTMB.	Support.	Line	155th L.T.M.B (HQ F30a 5.3)

The 1/7th Royal Scots will take over area at present occupied by 5th & 7th HLI. also Battn Hqrs F30.c.4.4.

SECRET. *Appendix 2* Copy No......

157th Infantry Brigade Order No. 149.

5th October, 1918.

1. 157th Inf. Bde. will be relieved in front line tonight the 5th/6th October by 172nd Inf. Bde.

2. On relief units of 157th Inf. Bde. will withdraw to E.26, West of CANAL DU NORD and occupy same area held by them after operations on 27th September to 1st October, except that the 6th H.L.I. will only occupy the area so far south as the Battalion Headquarters in that area.

3. Representatives of incoming units on arrival at Brigade Headquarters will be sent at once to the Headquarters of units of this Brigade to enable arrangements regarding the relief to be completed.

4. Completion of relief will be reported by wire, using the code word "CANAL".

5. Units will at once report arrival in new area by the code word "NORD".

6. Brigade Headquarters will close at present site and open at same headquarters as before (E.25.b.7.4.) on completion of Relief.

7. A C K N O W L E D G E.

(Sgd) C.S.Stirling Cookson, Capt.,
Brigade Major, 157th Infantry Brigade.

Issued at 2145.

Copy No. 1. to 5th H.L.I.
2. 6th H.L.I.
3 7th H.L.I.
4. 157th L.T.M.B.
5. 52nd Division.

Copy No. 6. to 172nd Inf. Bde.
7) War Diary.
8)
9 FILE.

SECRET. Appendix VII Copy. No.

157th Infantry Brigade Order No. 150.

6th Oct. 1918.

Ref. Maps. LENS II - VALENCIENNES 12, both 1/100,000.

1. The 52nd Division, less R.A. and M.G. Battalion will move from XVII Corps to VIII Corps.

2. The 157th Inf. Bde. Group will proceed tomorrow, 7th October, to the HOUVIN area, entraining at VAULX VRAUCOURT and detraining at PETIT HOUVIN in accordance with Administration Instruction issued by the Staff Capt.

3. The following will be the order of march to the entraining Station:-

	Time to pass starting point.
157th Bde. Hqrs.	1430.
7th H.L.I.	1435
6th H.L.I.	1500
157th L.T.M.B.	1515
5th H.L.I.	1520.

Adistance of 500 yards between Battalions and 100 yards between Coys. will be maintained on the march.

A 10 minutes halt will be observed at 10 minutes to every clock hour.

4. (a) Starting Point. The Cross Roads where the MOEUVRES - DEMICOURT Road crosses the CAMBRAI - BAPAUME Road (K.1.a. 95.45.)

(b) Route. From present Camp - BOURSIES - Cross Roads N. of Z. on BEAUMETZ-les-CAMBRAI - MORCHIES - VAULX VRAUCOURT.

5. Dismounted personnel of 413th Field Coy., R.E. and personnel of 2nd L.F.A. will march independently to the entraining station - Route as desired.

6. ACKNOWLEDGE.

(Sgd) C.S.Stirling Cookson, Capt.,
Bde. Major, 157th Infantry Bde.

Issued at 2355.

Copy No. 1 to. 5th H.L.I.
2. 6th H.L.I.
3. 7th H.L.I.
4. 157th L.T.M.B.
5. 413th Field Coy, R.E.
6. 2nd L.F.A.
7. Staff Capt.
8.)
9.) War Diary.

appendix IV

SECRET. Copy No. ....

187th Infantry Brigade Order No.181.

Ref. Map. LENS 11. 1/100,000. 12th October, 1918.

1. The 62nd Division will move EAST from present area, commencing to-morrow, 13th inst.

2. The 187th Inf. Bde. Group will proceed by route march on the 13th inst. to [illegible] Area.
The Starting Point will be the meeting of the roads immediately West of AVESNES-LES-COMTE, i.e. where the [illegible] - AVESNES-LES-COMTE and GRAND RULLECOURT - AVESNES-LES-COMTE Roads meet.

3. The following will be the order of march :-

Bde. Hqrs.	Time to pass Starting Point	0945
5th [illegible]	------ Do ------	1000
7th [illegible]	------ Do ------	1020
9th [illegible]	------ Do ------	1040
460th Field Coy. R.E.	------ Do ------	1100
2nd L.F.A.	------ Do ------	1120

The 187th L.T.M.B. will follow immediately in rear of the 7th [illegible].
The 230th Coy. A.S.C. will follow in rear of the Field Ambulance, leaving [illegible] at 1100, joining the AVESNES-LES-COMTE - HABARCQ Road by the most direct route

4. A distance of 500 yards will be maintained between units and 100 yards between Companies. Transport will accompany units.

5. Route:- As follows:- STARTING POINT, HABARCQ, Junction of Roads Southeast edge of BOIS-DE-HABARCQ, [illegible], [illegible].

6. O.C. 2nd L.F.A. will detail one horse ambulance wagon to be attached to, and to follow in rear of each Battalion, joining the Battalions at the [illegible] entrance to AVESNES-LES-COMTE, the remainder of ambulance following in rear of the column.

7. A halt of one hour will be observed approximately from 1300 to 1400. This halt will be ordered by Brigade Headquarters in the most suitable place.

8. The mid-day meal must be ready for issue from cookers immediately the halt takes place. On no account will the halt be extended.

9. A rear party under an officer will be left by each unit to clean up the billeting area. The officer will obtain a certificate from the Area Commandant that billets have been left clean. This will be sent to Brigade Headquarters on arrival at [illegible].

10. ACKNOWLEDGE.

[signature]
Captain,
Brigade Major, 187th Infantry Brigade.

Issued at 2215 on 12/10/18.

Copy No. 1 to 5th [illegible]. Copy No. 6A 230th Coy. A.S.C.
2 6th [illegible]. 7 62nd Division.
3 7th [illegible]. 8 Area Commandant Cd. [illegible].
4 187th L.T.M.B. 9 Staff Capt.
5 460th Field Coy. R.E. 10) War Diary.
6 2nd L.F.A. 11.
12 File.

Appendix V

Copy No. ....

SECRET.

157th Infantry Brigade Order No.152.

19th October, 1918.

Ref. Map. LENS 11, 1/100,000.

1. The Division will continue its move towards [illegible] to-morrow 20th October, 1918.
The 157th Infantry Brigade Group will proceed by route march to the HENIN LIETARD Area where it will bivouac for the night.

2. The Starting Point will be Brigade Headquarters (the WHITE HOUSE).
The following will be the order of March :-

Brigade Headquarters.	Will pass Starting Point	0820
7th H.L.I. followed by 157th L.T.M.B.	------- Do -------	0835
	------- Do -------	0900
5th H.L.I.	------- Do -------	0915 0915
6th H.L.I.	------- Do -------	0930 0930
412th Field Coy. R.E.	------- Do -------	0945 0945
1/2nd L.F.A.	------- Do -------	1000
220th Coy. A.S.C.		

The 157th L.T.M.B. will follow immediately in rear of 7th H.L.I.

3. A distance of 200 yards will be maintained between Units, and 100 yards between Companies.

4. March discipline must be improved, particularly as regards keeping well to the right of the road. Transport must not be allowed to straggle.

5. Route. From the Starting Point - NEUVILLE ST.VAAST - THELUS - WILLERVAL - ARLEUX-EN-GOHELLE - DROCOURT - HENIN-LIETARD.

6. O.C. 2nd L.F.A. will detail one Horse Ambulance Wagon to be attached to and follow in rear of each Battalion, joining Battalions at the Starting Point.

7. A halt of one hour for the midday meal will take place about 1230 on receipt of orders from Brigade Headquarters.
Brigade Headquarters will be at the head of the column.

8. Brigade Headquarters will close at The WHITE HOUSE at 0820.

9. Advanced Parties as for today will report to the Staff Captain at Brigade Headquarters (the WHITE HOUSE) at 0800 mounted on bicycles.

10. A rear party under an Officer will be left by each Unit to clean Billets. Each Officer will obtain a certificate from the Area Commandant or his representative that the Billets have been left clean. Certificates to be forwarded to Brigade Headquarters.

11. Each Unit of the Brigade Group will detail an Orderly to report to Brigade Headquarters at ~~2000..........~~ 1900 tomorrow.

12. A C K N O W L E D G E.

Captain,
Brigade Major, 157th Infantry Brigade.

Issued at ....on 19/10/18.

Copies to all recipients of Brigade Order No. 151, and S.A.A. Section, D.A.C., and Mob. Vet. Section.

After Order.

Motor lorries will report at 0700 as follows :- 2 to 7th H.L.I and 157th L.T.M.B., 2 to 5th H.L.I., 1 to 6th H.L.I. and 1 to Bde. Hqrs for carrying baggage.

appendix VI

SECRET. Copy No............

157th Infantry Brigade Order No. 153.

Ref. Map. 44A 1/40,000. 20th October, 1918.

1. The 52nd Division will continue its move eastwards tomorrow.

2. The 157th Infantry Brigade Group, less the 413th Field Coy, R.E., and Headquarters and 2 Sections of 1/2nd L.F.A., will proceed by route march to FLERS, FLANQUE, and WAGNONVILLE.

3. The Starting Point will be point O.29.b.7.4. (i.e., Road junctions in HENIN LIETARD where the road turns due east and near which point on the left hand side is a large Y.M.C.A. Marquee.
The following will be the order of March :-

Brigade Headquarters,
5th H.L.I.
6th H.L.I., immediately followed by 157th L.T.M.B.
7th H.L.I.
220th Coy., A.S.C.
1 Section, 2nd L.F.A.

Brigade Headquarters will pass the Starting Point at 0900, and units will follow in the order of march at the regulation distance of 500 yards between each Unit and 100 yards between Companies.
The Section of the Field Ambulance to join the tail of the column by the most direct route.

4. Route. From Starting Point - Main HENIN LIETARD-DOUAI Road - to FLERS, FLANQUE, WAGNONVILLE.

5. Advance Parties as for today will report to the Staff Captain at the Y.M.C.A. Tent at the Starting Point at 0730.

6. A Rear Party under an Officer will be left by each unit to clean billets.

7. Brigade Headquarters will close at its present site at 0830 to-morrow.

8. On reaching destination after move each unit will invariably send an orderly to Brigade Headquarters.

9. A C K N O W L E D G E.

[signature]
Captain,
Brigade Major, 157th Infantry Brigade.

Issued at 2130 on 20/10/18.

Copies to all recipients of Brigade Order No. 152, less, S.A.A., Sect. D.A.C., 413th Field Coy. R.E. Mob. Vet. Sect. D.A.C.

SECRET. *Appendix VII* Copy No. *8*

157th Infantry Brigade Order No.184.

Ref. Map. 44A. 1/40,000. 23rd October, 1918.

1. The 52nd Division will concentrate in the FLINES Area, commencing to-morrow, 24th October, 1918.

2. The 157th Infantry Brigade Group, less 413th Field Coy. R.E., will proceed by route march to billets at [illegible].
The Starting Point will be the road junctions at W.21.c.0.2. West of the North end of DOUAI.

3. The following will be the order of march :-

Brigade Hqrs.	Head of unit to pass the starting point	0915.
157th L.T.M.B.	(Immediately followed by 157th L.T.M.B.)	
5th H.L.I.	Head of unit to pass the starting point	0930.
7th H.L.I.	------------------ Do ------------------	0945.
6th H.L.I.	------------------ Do ------------------	1010.
1/2nd L.F.A.	------------------ Do ------------------	1025.
250th Coy. A.S.C.	------------------ Do ------------------	1040.

4. A distance of 500 yards will be maintained between units and 100 yards between Companies.
Brigade Headquarters, 157th L.T.M.B., and 1/2nd L.F.A. will march to the starting point by the WAGNONVILLE – DOUAI Road running approximately North and South through W.14.b., W.15.a. & c. W.21.a. & c. to starting point.

5. ROUTE.
FLERS – DOUAI – FAUBG. [illegible], (W.17.d.) – RACHES – PT. [illegible] (R.33.b.) – [illegible].
The route through DOUAI will be carefully reconnoitred beforehand.

6. A rear party under an officer will be left by each unit to clean billets.

7. The usual advance parties, mounted on bicycles, will report to the Staff Captain *at Bde Hqrs* by 0800.

8. Brigade Headquarters will close at present site at 0830.

9. A C K N O W L E D G E.

[signature]
Captain,
Brigade Major, 157th Infantry Brigade.

Issued at *2030* 23rd October, 1918.

Copy No.	1	to 5th H.L.I.	7	52nd Division.
	2	6th H.L.I.	8	Staff Captain.
	3	7th H.L.I.	9	Bde. Sigs. Officer.
	4	157th L.T.M.B.	10)	War Diary.
	5	1/2nd L.F.A.	11)	
	6	250th Coy. A.S.C.	12	File.

S E C R E T. *appendix VIII* Copy No....9....

157th Infantry Brigade Order No. 156.

27th October, 1918.

Ref Map. Sheets 44 and 44A, 1/40,000.

1. The 52nd Division will relieve the 12th Division in the Front Line on the night of 28th/29th.

2. The 157th Brigade Group, less the 413th Field Coy. R.E., but plus 'C' Coy., 52nd Bn. M.G.C., will march to the LANDAS Area on the 27th October. The starting point will be the Road Junction at M.13.d.7.2. (i.e. where the LE HEM Road joins the LA PLACETTE - FLINES - ORCHIES Rd.)

3. The following will be the order of March :-

157th Bde. Hqrs.	Head of Unit to pass Starting Point at	1130
6th Bn. H. L. I.	" " " " " " " "	1135
7th Bn. H. L. I.	" " " " " " " "	1200
5th Bn. H. L. I., followed by L.T.M.B.	" " " " " " " "	1215.
'C' Coy 52nd Bn. M.G.C.	" " " " " " " "	1230
1/2nd L. F. A.	" " " " " " "	1240

Route.-
From Starting Point -.COUTICHES - ORCHIES - RUE D'ORCHIES - LANDAS.

4. A distance of 500 yards between Units and 100 yards betw een Coys will be maintained.

5. SUPPLIES.

(a) The 220th Coy A.S.C. will load supplies for 28th inst at 1000 on 27th., and will subsequently march to new Brigade Area by same route as the Brigade Group.
Meeting Place (where Unit representatives will meet Train at end of March)
220th Coy. A.S.C. LANDAS Church.
(b) Above Train Coy., will not pass through COUTICHIES before 1300.
After delivering supplies to Units the Coy., will Concentrate at LES ARCINS (on ORCHIES - MARCHIENNES Road)
(c) Refilling Point for 27th inst.

Unit.	Refilling Point.
157th Brigade Group.	On ORCHIES - MARCHIENNES Road in neighbourhood of LES ARCINS

(d) Supply arrangements for 29th inst will be notified later.

6. The usual advance parties on bicycles will report to the Staff Captai n at Brigade Headquarters at 0830.

7. BLANKETS.

Blankets, extra Stores and Kits which cannot be carried on Normal Transport Echelons, will be sent to Divisional Blanket Dump, FLINES, before the march.
One man per Unit will be left as Guard to these stores. These men will be rationed from 28th inst. inclusive by Town Major, FLINES.
A nominal roll of these men (in duplicate) will be sent to Brigade Headquarters on receipt of these Orders.

8. RECEPTION CAMP.

The Reception Camp will start moving to the new site selected in DOUAI on 27th inst., in preparation for the move of Railhead to that place, which will probably take place on 29th inst.

O.C. Reception Camp, will, however, arrange to leave an Officer and sufficient men at VITRY to receive and despatch personnel of the Division, until the Div. Railhead leaves that place.

9. A rear party under an Officer will be left by each Unit to clean Billets. Each Officer will obtain a certificate that the billets have been left clean - certificates to be forwarded to Brigade Headquarters.

10. Brigade Headquarters will close at FLINES at 1100.

11. A C K N O W L E D G E.

A.S. Whitingham Cook [signature]

Captain,
Brigade Major, 157th Infantry Brigade.

Issued at.........0230.........

Copies No. 1 to 5th H. L. I.
2 6th H. L. I.
3 7th H. L. I.
4 157th L.T.M.B.
5 'C' Coy., M.G.C.
6 1/2nd L. F. A.
7 220th Coy. A.S.C.
8 Hqrs. Division.
9)
10 War Diary.)
11 File.

Appendix IX

SECRET. Copy No.............

157th Infantry Brigade Order No. 157.

Ref. Map. Sheet 44. 1/40,000. 27th October, 1918.

1. The 52nd Division will continue its march East to-morrow, 28th, the 156th Inf. Bde. taking over the front line on the night of 28th/29th inst.

2. The 157th Inf. Bde. Group will march from LANDAS to LECELLES to-morrow 28th inst. Starting Point will be the Cross Roads at H.23.b.7.4. West of VIEUX CONDE.

3. The following will be the order of march :-

Brigade H.Q.	Head of Unit to pass Starting Point at.....	1215
7th H.L.I.	——— Do ———	1220
6th H.L.I. followed by 157th L.T.M.B.	——— Do ———	1235
5th H.L.I.	——— Do ———	1300
"C" Coy. 52nd Bn. M.G.C.	——— Do ———	1315
2nd L.F.A.	——— Do ———	1325

4. Route. From Starting Point - North end of VIEUX CONDE (H24.a.5.9.) - through H.18.d. - Cross Roads H.15.c.4.4. - RUMEGIES (Church) - LECELLES.

5. The usual distances will be maintained between Battalions and Companies on the march.

6. Advance Parties as for to-day will report to the Staff Captain at Brigade Headquarters LANDAS (H.23.b.3.5.) at 0900

7. A rear party under an officer will be left behind by each unit to clean billets, the officer to obtain certificate that the billets have been left clean. Certificates will be forwarded to Brigade H.Q.

8. Brigade Headquarters will close at present location at 1115.

9. A C K N O W L E D G E.

10. Separate orders will be issued to 220 Coy. A.S.C. by Div.

11. Troops will be given midday meal before marching off.

J. S. Stirling Cookson

Captain,
Brigade Major, 157th Infantry Bde.

Issued at 2000 on 27/10/18.

Copy No. 1 to 5th H.L.I.
2 6th H.L.I.
3 7th H.L.I.
4 157th L.T.M.B.
5 2nd L.F.A.
6 "C" Coy. 52nd Bn. M.G.C.
7 52nd Division.
8 52nd Bn. M.G.C.
9 Staff Captain.
10) War Diary.
11)
12 F I L E.

220 Coy. A.S.C.

SUMMARY OF OPERATIONS.

157th INFANTRY BRIGADE.

From midnight 7th/8th September, 1918,

to

Midnight 7th/8th October, 1918.

------ooOoo------

Date.	Time.	
Sept.		
7th		In accordance with Brigade Order No.140 dated 6th inst. the Brigade marched from the area near QUEANT to T.30. thus becoming Corps Reserve. The Brigade bivouacked in T.30. the last Battalion, the 5th H.L.I. reaching the area at 1130 - delay being due to the fact that this Battalion was heavily gas shelled East of PRONVILLE.
8th. to 14th.		The Brigade remained in the T.30. area training, and salving the area. A considerable amount of rain fell during the week, somewhat interfering with the training. A Warning Order was received from the Division stating that the Brigade would take over the INCHY SECTOR in the front line from the 172nd Infantry Brigade, on the night of the 16th/17th inst.
15th.		After I visited the 2nd Canadian Infantry Brigade in the line, Brigade Order No. 141 was issued, giving orders for the relief on the following night.
16th.		The Brigade started marching from T.30. at 4. p.m. Units halted on the way about one mile West of QUEANT, where the evening meal was served prior to continuing the march up to the fron t line. The 5th H.L.I. took over the Right of the line. The 6th H.L.I. took over the Left of the line with 7th H.L.I., plus 2 Companies of 156th Inf. Bde. under orders of 157th Inf. Bde. in support.
17th.	4. a.m.	The Relief was completed at 4. a.m. Brigade Headquarters being situated in the QUARRY at V.28.d.0.0.
	10. a.m.	At 10.30. a.m. the enemy put down a barrage on the 155th Inf. Brigade front, on our immediate Right in the MOEUVRES Sector. The S.O.S. Signal was fired and the S.O.S. barrage came down. No hostile Infantry Action took place and the barrage was stopped shortly after 1100
		At 6.30 p.m. the enemy put down a barrage on the 155th Inf. Bde. front, it gradually increased in intensity and extended North as far as INCHY. Under cover of this barrage the enemy attacked and captured MOEUVRES including the two most Southern Posts (of 5th H.L.I.) on this Bde. front. (One of these posts however, was still found intact when we retook MOEUVRES two days later).
		As a result of MOEUVRES having been captured by the ee enemy, the troops of the 155th Infantry Brigade on the immediate Right of the 5th H.L.I. were driven back out of CEMETERY SUPPORT Trench to the HINDENBURG LINE on the West edge of the village. This necessitated the 5th H.L.I. forming a defensive flank facing S.W. along HOBART STREET, the extreme Right being in the HINDENBURG SUPPORT LINE in touch with the 155th Infantry Brigade troops. Between HOBART STREET and CEMETERY SUPPORT at avout E.13.d.4.9.
18th.		The situation at MOEUVRES remained unchanged.
	1. p.m.	At 1. p.m. a Warning Order was received stating that the 5th ~~2a~~ Canadian Infantry Brigade would take over the front line from the 157th Infantry Brigade on the following night. All quiet on the front throughout the day, but there was a considerable amoun of shelling throughout the night of 18th/19th and the early morning of the 19th. Several bombing attacks were made by the enemy on our Right Post in HOBART STREET at E.14.a.2.9. they were, however, repulsed.

Date. Time.

Sept.
19th. 1.p.m. At 1.p.m. Orders were received from the Division that the 155th Infantry Brigade, assisted by two Coys, of the 157th Infantry Brigade would attack and recapture MOEUVRES this evening. The two Right Posts which had been lost by the 5th H.L.I. were to be re-established at the same time. On receipt of the above orders the Brigade Major went over to the 155th Infantry Brigade Hqrs., to get in touch with the G.O.C., of that Brigade and get details of the arrangements for the attack. Few details were, however, at the time available, as the G.O.C. 155th Inf. Bde. had not then had time to see the Battalion Commander concerned in the attack. It was, however, arranged later that the two Companies of the 7th H.L.I. which were detailed for the attack, would form up in the S.W. end of HOBART STREET and the HINDENBURG SUPPORT LINE S.E. of junction of HOBART STREET and HINDENBURG SUPPORT LINE as far South as about E.13.d.4.8. on Left of troops of 155th Infantry Brigade.

The attack on the two posts on this Brigade front at E.14.a.35.30. and E.14.a.30.70. was to be carried out by a company of 5th H.L.I. attacking from HOBART STREET simultaneously with the two Coys. of the 7th H.L.I. and troops of the 155th Inf. Bde. The 2 Coys. of 7th H.L.I. being detailed to retake CEMETERY SUPPORT from its junction with the HINDENBURG LINE to E.14.d.50.65. (Brigade Orders issued under B.M.7/209).

The attack was carried out under a barrage which started at 7.p.m. Owing to short notice the two Coys. 7th H.L.I. only just reached the jumping off line in time.

By 8.p.m. the situation had been successfuly restored with the exception of the post at E.14.a.35.30. which the enemy managed to retain. This post was, however, shortly afterwards retaken by the 5th Canadian Infantry Brigade which came up during the night and relieved the 157th Inf. Brigade.

According to Orders the 5th Canadian Infantry Brigade relieved the 157th Infantry Brigade in the line, less the 2 Coys. of the 7th H.L.I. which had taken part in the attack and which had come under Orders of the G.O.C. 155th Inf. Brigade from Zero Hour.

20th. 12.30a.m. The relief was completed by 12.30a.m. on the 20th, the 157th Infantry Brigade withdrawing into bivouacs in C.17.a.&.b.

21st. The day was spent in cleaning up etc. the two Coys. 7th H.L.I. which had been attached to the 155th Infantry Brigade for the attack on MOEUVRES, rejoined their Battalion during the night 20/21st.

22nd. Brigade at C.17.a. & b.

7. a.m. At 7.a.m. Orders were received that the Division was extending its front South as far as the line K.4.b.0.7. - K.3.c.0.8. - D.30.b.0.3. - D.22.a.0.7. The 6th H.L.I. were therefore placed under orders of 156th Infantry Bde. in the MOEUVRES Sector, and in accordance with 157th Bde. Order No.143, took over the line from troops of the 1st Guards Brigade during the night.

23rd. Brigade at C.17.a. & b. training.

24th. The 5th H.L.I. moved up to the line to-night relieving the 6th H.L.I. the latter Battalion withdrawing to C.17.b. after relief. The remainder of the Brigade continued training.

Date. Time.

Sept. 25th. Orders for the attack which was to take place on the 27th instant were received and in consequence, the 157th Infantry Brigade moved after dark to D.14. c. &. d.

26th. Brigade Headquarters moved up to D.28.b.8.8. on the morning of the 26th instant.

26th. The 5th H.L.I. in the line S. of MOEUVRES under orders of G.O.C. 155th Inf. Brigade are occupying WILLY Trench, SAND LANE and the line running from the latter down to the CAMBRAI Road. The remainder of the Brigade arrived into bivouac just S.E. of QUEANT. Brigade Headquarters established in the HINDENBURG LINE D.28.b.2.8.

This movement was in preparation for the attack the following day by the 1st and 3rd Armies on the BOURLON WOOD and crossing the CANAL DU NORD.

The particular task of the 157th Infantry Brigade being to capture that portion of the HINDENBURG LINE and the CANAL DU NORD between the Northern end of squares E.26.a. & b. and K.2. and 3. central.

During the afternoon a conference of Commanding Officers was held and the plan of attack carefully gone into, actual Orders being issued at 8.p.m. (Brigade Order No.145).

Briefly the plan for the following day was as follows:-

Under cover of darkness the Brigade (less 5th H.L.I. already in the line) was to move up into positions of Assembly WILLY Trench and the Northern end of SAND LANE, the 5th H.L.I. to close in on their right to make room for this assembly as the assualting troops arrived and to spread out again the moment the assualting troops had gone over the top.

For this purpose a track across country had been laid out and marked by luminous boards.

The 7th H.L.I. was detailed to mop up the canal and the 6th H.L.I. the two lengths of trench and the communication trenches between them of the HINDENBURG LINE.

The 5th H.L.I. was in Brigade Reserve.

The CANAL was to be mopped up from West to East, taking it in Sections, the leading Coy. taking the first Section, the second Coy. advancing in echelon on its right to leap frog through it and take the second section and so on, care being taken in carrying out the leap frog principle not to lose the barrage under which they were advancing.

The 6th H.L.I. in mopping up the HINDENBURG LINE were not to leap frog but to work straight down the trenches dropping moppers up as they went.

Special arrangements were to be made by the 7th H.L.I. for dealing with the crossing over the CANAL by the CAMBRAI Road with the lock at K.3.b.7.7. and the Spoil Heap in E.27.c.4.2. Two tanks being told off in the first case to assist with the former and one with the Spoil Heap.

The forming up trench was to be in ALF Trench (E.26.a. 95.70 to E.26.b.60.55.) and N. of it.

Owing to the artillery barrage for the 156th Infantry Brigade coming down W. of the Canal close up to ALF TRENCH, immediately to the North of us, it was calculated that there would only be room for three Coys. in ALF Trench, i.e. 1 Coy. of 7th H.L.I. at the Eastern end and close to the CANAL then 2 Coys. of the 6th H.L.I. opposite the end of their respective bit of the HINDENBURG LINE. For this reason the assembly in WILLY Trench was arranged as follows:-

One Coy. 7th H.L.I. with a few moppers up of 6th H.L.I. then 2 Coys. 6th H.L.I. The head of the 7th H.L.I. leading Coy. to be as far down WILLY Trench as the block established in E.20.c.8.1. then 2 Coys. of 6th H.L.I. and 1 Coy. of 7th H.L.I., then the continuation of WILLY Trench W. of

Date. Time.

Sept.

26th. N. of its junction with SAND LANE to contain the remaining 2 Coys. of 7th H.L.I. and the Northern end of SAND LANE the remainder of the 6th H.L.I.

In endeavouring to cut down wire in front of the enemy position just outside the block at E.20.c.8.1. on the previous night, it had been reported that the enemy had 3 Machine Gun posts within 50 to 100 yards of the block, located as follows :- E.26.a.9.8., E.20.c.9.0. and E.20.c.95.25. It was clear therefore that these would have to be captured immediately at Zero Hour or the troops would be delayed in the forming up place, also ALF Trench, the forming up place, and the two short lines of trench running S.W. from the W. end of it were held by the enemy and had also to be captured before the troops could form up.

The following arrangements were therefore made :-

Firstly: To deal with the three Machine Gun positions 3 scuppering parties from the 5th H.L.I. in Brigade Reserve were detailed to go out at Zero Hour and each to capture one of the Machine Gun Posts.

Secondly : As regards ALF Trench, two Trench Mortars situated in SAND LANE, were at Zero Hour to put down rapid fire on the most Westerly of the two trenches running S.W. from the W. end of ALF LANE. At Zero plus 5 they were to stop. During this 5 minutes the head of the assaulting troops in WILLY Trench were to push down as close to ALF LANE as the Trench Mortar fire would allow them. At Zero plus 5 the Trench Mortar situated in WILLY Trench was to put down rapid fire on the second trench running Southwards from ALF LANE and to cease fire at Zero plus 10. At Zero plus 5 the head of the assaulting troops was to push into ALF TRENCH and a portion of the moppers up of 5th H.L.I. attached 7th H.L.I., to be pushed into the most westerly trench running S.W. from ALF Trench. Meantime the whole of the assaulting troops were closing down WILLY Trench.

At Zero plus 10 the 4th Trench Mortar situated in WILLY Trench was to open rapid fire on the remaining portion of ALF Trench close to the CANAL and to cease fire at Zero plus 14. The assaulting troops were then to close down and form up ready to advance South at the allotted time.

According to the Divisional Order, at Zero Hour (which was subsequently fixed at 5.20. a.m.) the general barrages covering the whole of the advance of the 1st and 3rd Armies were to come down. In our immediate neighbourhood there were two barrages, one running N. and S. from E.26.b.4.8. to E.20.d.4.9. which was to cover the advance of the 156th Inf. Bde. from West to East across the CANAL, and secondly an enfilade barrage stretching from the CANAL at E.26.b.7.4. to E.25.a.8.5., this latter barrage was to move southwards. The barrage for the 156th Inf. Bde. was to move forwards at Zero plus 15 reaching the Eastern bank of the CANAL at Zero plus 23 and then continue moving Eastward. The ~~as~~ latter barrage which was to cover the advance from North to South, of the 157th Infantry Brigade, was to come down at Zero and remain standing until Zero plus 40, and then creep forward at the rate of 100 yards every 5 minutes.

Four Tanks were allotted to the Brigade to assist in the operation. These were to form up before Zero on the low ground behind SAND LANE. At this same place there were also to be four tanks working under the 63rd Division.

Date.	Time.	
26th		63rd Division and which were to go up N. to join the Division, exactly at Zero hour. I requested therefore, that the 4 tanks of the 63rd Division might, en route, cross SAND LANE and go through the wire covering the HINDENBURG LINE just West of ALF TRENCH. There was a considerable amount of wire which it was necessary to cut and which I had not been previously able to do owing to the proximity of the enemy Infantry and the three Machine Gun nests previously mentioned. My request was granted and very considerable help was gained by their cutting this wire.
		The necessity for cutting this wire was due to the fact that my forming up ground was practically limited to ALF TRENCH and had no depth in it, as the 156th Inf. Bde. was at Zero plus 15 attacking from West to East with its Right very nearly on ALF Trench. The result being that the two rear Companies of each of my assaulting Battalions had to come down over the open from SAND LANE and WILLY Trench in a South Easterly direction and get into position as the leading assault troops were moving forward under the barrage.
		The role of the 4 tanks allotted to this Brigade was as follows :- To be formed up behind the barrage line at Zero plus 38, the barrage being timed to move forward at Zero plus 40. They were then to follow as close under the shrapnel barrage as they could, one tank moving down the wire immediately West of and close to the most Westerly trench of the HINDENBURG LINE., two tanks between the two trench lines, and one tank between the trench lines and the CANAL. They were to zigzag down behind the barrage with the Infantry following straight but close behind them; On reaching the CAMBRAI Road two tanks were to cross to the East bank of the CANAL and after dealing with any Machine Gun Nests at the crossing and also in the Spoil Heap in E.27.c.5.0. were to move N.E. and come under the orders of the 156th Inf. Bde. The remaining two tanks were to continue Southwards, one going ahead to get touch with the Guards Division on our Right, who were mopping up the HINDENBURG LINE Northwards, and the other after working down to the lock, to pay attention to that place which was supposed to have Machine Gun nests.
		The guns of my Light Trench Mortar Battery were distributed in pairs from WILLY TRENCH down SAND LANE and continuation of SAND LANE towards the CAMBRAI Road, their role being to fire into and thicken up the shrapnel barrage as it moved South.
		After the objectives had been captured and it was seen that the 156th Inf. Bde. had made good their objectives opposite to us on the Eastern side of the CANAL, Battalions were to reorganise in depth as follows :- 6th H.L.I. from our Southern Boundary by the lock in K.3.a. to COW ALLEY - just North of the CAMBRAI Road. 7th H.L.I. from COW ALLEY (exclusive) to ALF Trench, meantime 5th H.L.I., who at Zero hour had come back under my orders, were to close in and move down SAND LANE and its continuation to the CAMBRAI Road - to be in Brigade Reserve.
	7. p.m.	About 7. p.m. the 7th H.L.I. began to move up from its bivouac area S.E. of QUEANT, to take up its position in WILLY Trench. The 6th H.L.I. starting at mid-night and following them.
27th.		All the assaulting troops were ready in their positions of assembly one hour before Zero hour.

Date. Time.

Sept.

27th. 5.20 a.m. At Zero Hour, 5.20. a.m., all barrages came down as arranged, and the head of the 157th Infantry Brigade assaulting troops began to move down WILLY Trench towards ALF Trench. Three enemy Machine Gun posts were close to our starting point were rushed by parties from the 6th H.L.I. After very little opposition the leading Coy. of the 7th H.L.I. forced its way into the Western end of ALF Trench, closely followed by two Companies of 6th H.L.I.

Immediately the 156th Inf. Bde. barrage began to move Eastwards, at Zero plus 13, the leading Coy. of 7th H.L.I. and the two leading Coys. of 6th H.L.I. occupied ALF Trench and formed up facing South, ready to advance at Zero plus 40 under our own barrage.

Meantime the remainder of the assaulting troops were closing down, ready to get into position behind the leading assaulting Coys. when they advanced.

Just before Zero plus 40, when the barrage was due to roll forward, three out of the four tanks, took up their allotted positions, the fourth tank having been left behind SAND Trench owing to engine trouble.

At Zero plus 40, the barrage, tanks and assaulting troops moved Southwards in accordance with the time table.

The 6th H.L.I. on the Right carried out their programme absolutely according to previous arrangements, mopping up both lines of trenches of the HINDENBURG LINE and the communication trenches between them.

Considerable opposition was met with as the enfilade shrapnel barrage had had very little effect on the enemy.

The 6th H.L.I. followed the barrage right down to the Southern Boundary and finally gained touch with the Guards Division in the neighbourhood og Lock No.6.

The 7th H.L.I. had not started off quite according to arrangements, for instead of starting off 2 Coys. deep at the forming up place, so that these Coys. might move forward in echelon, ready to leap frog, they had started off with only one Coy. in ALF Trench, the other Coy. having lost its bearings and had not turned up to time.

The section of the CANAL given to the leading Coy. was from ALF Trench to COW ALLEY. This Coy. followed the barrage at Zero plus 40 and as it advanced, dropped platoons at intervals along the Western bank of the CANAL. These platoons at once turned Eastwards and attacked and captured the Western Bank of the CANAL as far as COW ALLEY, but owing to strong opposition from the Eastern Bank, they were, at first, unable to go across the CANAL. A Lewis gun section and party, which endeavoured to cross near the Eastern end of ALF Trench so as to enfilade the Eastern bank, were driven back with heavy loss.

When the leading platoon of the Company which reached the Canal where COW ALLEY cuts it, the second Coy. of the 7th H.L.I. should have been on its immediate Right, echeloned slightly behind it. Owing, however, to its lost direction at the start, it was unable to get to the forming up place and follow alongside the leading Coy. The Company Commander, however, guiding his direction by means of the barrage after it had moved forward, moved along parallel to it and immediately West of the HINDENBURG LINE, and when the barrage passed over COW ALLEY, he led his Coy. across the front og the 6th H.L.I. over the HINDENBURG LINES and cut into his proper place just in time.

This Company had no difficulty in taking the Western bank of the CANAL, but were greatly hampered by nests of enemy Machine Guns in the Spoil Heap on the Eastern Bank

Date. Time.

Sept.

27th. Eastern Bank of the CANAL at the bottom of Square E.27.c.

Parties were, however, got across the canal and in conjunction with the tanks mopped this place up.

The third Coy. of this Battalion was now coming up and was dribbled across the CANAL at, and near the CAMBRAI Road Crossing, and by its aid the Eastern Bank of the CANAL From the CAMBRAI Road to ALF Trench was eventually cleared; but this was not completed until about one hour after the bar age had ceased.

All the objectives allotted to this Brigade had now been captured, but I did not consider it wise to start reorganising in Battalion areas at present, as the attack for the Eastern side of the CANAL in Squares E.27.a., b, c, and d. and K.3. &. 4. had been held up and the enemy were still holding the ground in some strength. In case the enemy counter attacked I therefore decided to wait until events had further developed.

About 4.0pm the 156th Inf. Bde. Had captured the whole of the ground in squares E.27.a.,b.,c., and d. as far South as KANGAROO Trench, I therefore gave orders to reorganise as previously arranged. into Battalion areas in depth.

Shortly after this was completed information was received that the attack on the Eastern side of the CANAL was held up by the enemy who were holding SOW Trench and its neighbourhood and the HINDENBURG LINE Support Line behind it in great strength, in consequence I was ordered to launch an attack against SOW AVENUE and pay particular attention to HOG POST.

I at once issued a Warning Order to O.C. 5th H.L.I. to close up his Battalion down towards the CAMBRAI Road to be prepared to move across the CANAL to carry out an attack at a moment's notice. Directly definite information was received from the 52nd Division I issued orders to the 5th H.L.I. to assemble on the Western Bank of the CANAL at Lock No.6.

The Battalion proceeded to assemble there and I went down to interview the Commanding Officer and make a ~~provisional~~ personal reconnaissance with him; but before the attack was launched, orders were received that the enemy had retired and that our own troops were in possession of SOW AVENUE. The attack was therefore abandoned and the 5th H.L.I. sent back into Brigade Reserve.

28th Sept. to 4th Oct. The Brigade was in Support to the 155th Inf. Bde. in the front line just S. of CAMBRAI; Brigade Hqrs., being in the farm building F.30.a.6.3. with the Battalions disposed in F.30.a. &.c. (The MARCOING LINE).

October. 4th/5th. On the night of 4/5th Oct the 157th Inf. Bde. relieved the 155th Inf. Bde. in the front line in accordance with Brigade Order No. 146. Relief was completed at 0200.

5th. The enemy shelled the CANAL Crossings and approaches to them intermittently by day and night.

At 1600 a Warning Order was received that the 157th Inf. Bde. would be relieved in the line by the 172nd Inf. Bde. to-night.

5th/6th. Brigade Order. No.149. was issued and the relief carried out and completed by 0230. The 157th Inf. Bde. withdrawing on relief to E.26. W. of the CANAL DU NORD.

Date.	Time.	
Oct.		
6th.		The Brigade rested and cleaned up during the day. During the evening orders were received, notifying that the 52nd Division, Less Artillery and the Machine Gun Battalion, would move on the 7th October, from XVII to VIII Corps. Brigade Order No. 150 was issued accordingly.
7th.		The 157th Infantry Brigade moved in accordance with Brigade Order. No.150. and entrained at VAUX VRAUCOURT, reaching its detraining Station at PETIT HOUVIN, next morning.

LESSONS LEARNT; SUGGESTED IMPROVEMENTS IN TRAINING,

TACTICS AND EQUIPMENT.

1. Owing to the mode of warfare having changed from trench to open fighting, objectives now being far distant, it is strongly advocated that a larger number of pigeons should be issued to Battalions. The pigeons should be in baskets containing two birds. They would be given to Company Commanders to let loose on reaching their objective.

2. It is strongly advocated the Light Trench Mortars should be made mobile. It is, at present, impossible to carry the loads; the value of the Mortars being thus lost.

3. From experience gained, Battalions cannot carry all their Lewis Gun Magazines, it is therefore necessary to withdraw a proportion of them to form an Advance Brigade Dump.

PRISONERS AND WAR MATERIAL CAPTURED.

Prisoners   1 Officer   254 Other Ranks.

War Material.

Machine Guns.	44
Trench Mortars.	2
Anti-Tank Rifles.	2

CASUALTIES.

KILLED.		WOUNDED.		MISSING.	
Officers.	O.R.	Officers.	O.R.	Officers.	O.R.
4	35	20	340	NIL.	28

STATEMENT OF CASUALTIES FOR PERIOD.

Date.	Killed.		Wounded.		Missing.		Total.	
Sept.	Off.	O.R.	Off.	O.R.	Off.	O.R.	Off.	O.R.
7th.	-	-	-	47	-	-	-	47
8th.	-	-	-	-	-	-	-	-
9th.	-	-	-	-	-	-	-	-
10th.	-	-	-	-	-	-	-	-
11th.	-	-	-	-	-	-	-	-
12th.	-	-	-	-	-	-	-	-
13th.	-	-	-	-	-	-	-	-
14th.	-	-	-	-	-	-	-	-
15th.	-	-	-	-	-	-	-	-
16th.	-	-	-	-	-	-	-	-
17th.	1	-	-	2	-	-	1	2
18th.	-	5	3	17	-	-	3	22
19th.	-	2	2	14	-	-	2	16
20th.	3	5	1	45	-	12	4	62
21st.	-	-	-	-	-	-	-	-
22nd.	-	-	-	-	-	-	-	-
23rd.	-	-	1	16	-	-	1	16
24th.	-	-	-	2	-	-	-	2
25th.	-	-	-	-	-	-	-	-
26th.	-	1	-	3	-	-	-	4
27th.	-	15	9	156	-	12	9	183
28th.	-	-	-	-	-	-	-	-
29th.	-	-	-	-	-	-	-	-
30th.	-	-	-	4	-	-	-	4
October.								
1st.	-	1	-	-	-	-	-	1
2nd.	-	1	-	7	-	-	-	8
3rd.	-	1	4	18		4	4	23
4th.	-	2	-	4	-	-	-	6
5th.	-	2	-	5	-	-	-	7
6th.	-	-	-	-	-	-	-	-
7th.	-	-	-	-	-	-	-	-
TOTAL.	4	35	20	340	-	28	24	403

Instructions regarding War Diaries and Intelligence Summaries are contained in F. S. Regs., Part II. and the Staff Manual respectively. Title pages will be prepared in manuscript.

WAR DIARY
or
~~INTELLIGENCE SUMMARY.~~
(Erase heading not required.)

Army Form C. 2118.

HQ 157th Inf. Brigade – November 1918. 1.

Place	Date	Hour	Summary of Events and Information	Remarks and references to Appendices
RUMEGIES	Nov. 1st 1918		Training Continued – Weather continued fine.	MC
"	2nd			
"	3rd			
FONTAINE BOUILLON (P.17.b.6.7.) Sheet 44 S.E.	4th		The 157. Bde. moved in accordance with Bde. order No. 158 relieving 28th Inf. Bde in front line. 7th H.L.I. took over front line from FRESNES to NORTH of ODOMEZ (Map 44 S.E.) 6th H.L.I. to support billeted in the MINERAL SPRING ESTABLISHMENT. 5th H.L.I. in Bde. Reserve in billets at St. AMAND. The relief was completed by 8.15 p.m. Brig. Gen. HAMILTON-MOORE. CMG. DSO left for England on one months leave. Lt. Col. ROMANES DSO. Comdg 1/5 Scottish Rifles. took over command of the Bde.	app. I MC
"	5th		A quiet day. Nothing to report.	
"	6th		Bde received orders from Div. to be prepared to follow up enemy in case of enemy's withdrawal. 157th Inf. Bde Order 159 issued accordingly. Orders issued to 5th H.L.I., in view of fact that the Bde was taking over part of the 8th Canadian Bde front, to be prepared to move up to line on night of 7/8 Nov.	app II WEG
"	7th		Div. order No 245 received that 157th Inf. Bde would clear their new area W. of ESCAULT RIVER. 157th Bde orders 160 issued accordingly & the operation was timed to take place at 1200 on 8th.	WEG
"	8th		In accordance with Bde order No 160 the 5th H.L.I. came up into the front line taking over on a two Coy. front, partly from 7 H.L.I. & partly from 8th Canadian Inf. Bde. on our right.	App IV

A7092. Wt. W12839/M1293 750,000. 1/17. D. D & L., Ltd. Forms/C2118/14.

Instructions regarding War Diaries and Intelligence Summaries are contained in F. S. Regs., Part II. and the Staff Manual respectively. Title pages will be prepared in manuscript.

WAR DIARY
or
INTELLIGENCE SUMMARY.
(Erase heading not required.)

~~WAR DIARY or~~ 157 Inf Brigade — November 1918 — 2.

Army Form C. 2118.

Place	Date	Hour	Summary of Events and Information	Remarks and references to Appendices
	8th	7. am	The early morning patrols of 5th & 7th H.L.I. reported that there were no signs of the enemy in front of the Bde –	
		0800	At 0800 the Code word "Kuiri" was received from Divn – vide Bde order No. 159 (App II) On receipt of the above Code word operations as ordered in Bde order No 159 started. The Coy. of 7 H.L.I. ferrying across the Scheldt and JARD canal on Jerusalem rafts. The 6 H.L.I. were East of the CANAL by 1130, they advanced through the Coy. of 7 H.L.I. which was covering the bridge heads and ~~advance~~ without opposition reached the FIRST OBJECTIVE at 1630, taking over the line from the Cavalry & Cyclists at dusk – The 7 H.L.I. crossed to East of the CANAL at 5.30 pm and concentrated at RIEU CONDE for the night. The 5 H.L.I. concentrated for the night at ODOMEZ & CONDE where they remained for night 8/9th	App II. [illegible]
	9th		Advance continued east. 6th H.L.I. leading no opposition met with and by 1600 reached the line H1 cent – H33 cent – H27 cent – NW of GRAND GLISE in touch with 156th Bde on left & 8th Cans on right. Bde Hqs. POMMEROEUIL	
		2200	Orders received for 10th inst (vide Bde order No 161 appendix V) Advance to be in NE direction with MONS – JURBISE Road between K6a03 and D13a03 as objective at midnight 9/10th orders received that 8th Div would not be up in time to advance eastward consequently Bde was ordered to advance on K19d34 – D23a03 as final objective.	App V. [illegible]

A7092). Wt. W12839/M1293 750,000. 1/17. D. D & L., Ltd. Forms/C2118/14.

Instructions regarding War Diaries and Intelligence Summaries are contained in F. S. Regs., Part II. and the Staff Manual respectively. Title pages will be prepared in manuscript.

WAR DIARY
or
INTELLIGENCE SUMMARY. 157 Inf Bde
(Erase heading not required.)

Army Form C. 2118.

November

3

Place	Date	Hour	Summary of Events and Information	Remarks and references to Appendices
	10th		The advance was started at 0800 two battns being in the front line - 5 HLI on the left, 7th HLI on the right with the 6th HLI in support and in rear of the 5th HLI. (vide Bde Order 162)	App. VI
			5 HLI advanced in NE direction without opposition until reaching line C 18 cent - I 12 cent where mounted troops were held up by MG fire at 1130. Similarly advance of 7th HLI was held up by MGs from J 21 a and from the N and E outskirts of GHLIN.	
		1215	Advanced Guard of 5 HLI was ordered to work forward, followed by one company 6th HLI which was to debouch from the BOIS DE BAUDOUR and attack NE to clear VACRESSE & HERCHIES of the enemy. Owing to MG fire 5 HLI advance Guard was held up on a line J 2 a cent - J 7 a cent. Coy of 6 HLI detailed to clear VACRESSE & HERCHIES therefore debouched from the wood in J 16 attacked & captured VACRESSE shortly after 1630. Meanwhile 156 Bde on left had cleared HERCHIES. After capture of VACRESSE advance was ordered to halt for the night on line gained ie C 30 cent - J 1 cent - J 8 a 0 0 - I 18 b 8 4 - J 19 cent - J 26 cent - J 32 b 8 0 - due south. Bde Hqrs remained for the night at SIRAULT RAILWAY STN where it had been established at 1100.	
			During the night 10/11th orders were received to advance at 0700 next morning. Bde Orders No 1162 (appendix VI) were accordingly issued	
			Bt Col (Temp Brig Gen) B G Price CMG DSO took over command of Bde vice Lt Col Romanes DSO	WCB

A7092). Wt. W12839/M1293 750,000. 1/17. D. D & L., Ltd. Forms/C2118/14.

Instructions regarding War Diaries and Intelligence Summaries are contained in F. S. Regs., Part II. and the Staff Manual respectively. Title pages will be prepared in manuscript.

WAR DIARY
or
INTELLIGENCE SUMMARY. 157 Inf Bde.

(*Erase heading not required.*)

Army Form C. 2118.

November 1918

4.

Place	Date	Hour	Summary of Events and Information	Remarks and references to Appendices
	11th	0800	5 H L I advanced to attack at 0800 (delay being due to lateness in receipt of orders) and captured the final objective i.e. line of MONS–JURBISE Road between J6a00 and O23a23 without opposition. The 7 HLI did not advance but were relieved by 2nd Middlesex Regt (23rd Bde) who advanced thro' them. The 7 HLI withdrew to VACRESSE into Bde reserve.	
			Bde Hqrs which had moved at 0645 to I4d37 moved to VACRESSE at 0900.	
			At 0800 orders were received that an armistice would commence at 1100 today and that a defensive line would be taken up with sentry groups about 1000 yds in front of the objective. These orders were carried out and Bde halted and took up following positions	
			BDE HQRS – VACRESSE ; 5 HLI – front line ; 6 HLI in support at ERBISOEUL ; 7 HLI in Bde Reserve at VACRESSE	WCS
	12th		No change in above dispositions	WCS
	13th		6th HLI took over front line from 5 H L I ; the latter battn withdrawing into Bde Support	WCS
	14th		Orders received for Bde to increase its front. On the 15th 7th H L I	WCS
	15th		took over 8th Div line from 2nd Middlesex Regt 23rd Inf Bde Relief completed by 1315. (Bde Order No. 163)	App. VII
		1030	150 men 5 H L I and 50 men 6 HLI with massed pipe bands represented the Bde at the Army Commds official entry into MONS.	WCS

A7092/. Wt. W12839/M1293 750,000. 1/17. D. D & L., Ltd. Forms/C2118/14.

Army Form C. 2118.

Instructions regarding War Diaries and Intelligence Summaries are contained in F. S. Regs., Part II. and the Staff Manual respectively. Title pages will be prepared in manuscript.

WAR DIARY
or
INTELLIGENCE SUMMARY. 157 Inf Bde

(Erase heading not required.)

November 1918. 5.

Place	Date	Hour	Summary of Events and Information	Remarks and references to Appendices
	16th		no change Training &c	
	17th	1100	Special Divisional Thanksgiving service held at D20b83. 200 men from Bde attended. Brig Gen B.G. Price in command of parade.	W.C.S.
			Bde was ordered to withdraw outpost. This was carried out (vide Div wire GA140)	App 8 W.C.S.
	18th		no change Training &c	
	19th		Bde HdQrs moved to Chateau at J.16b4.7 and opened at 0930. Brig Gen Price took over Comm^d of 52 Div ~~while~~ during absence of Major Gen Marshall on leave	W.C.S.
	20th 21st 22nd		Training &c	W.C.S.
	23rd	1015	Brigade Ceremonial Parade at Drill Ground K9 &10. The following units took part 5th 6th, 7th H.L.I. "D" Coy 52 M.G. Battn. 2nd L.F.A and 19th Battery 56th Bde R.F.A.	W.C.S.
	24th		no change	W.C.S.
	25th		LTM Bty moved into billets at BRUYERE K16.7.0.	W.C.S.
	26th 27th 28th 29th 30th		Training &c	W.C.S.

H.M. Hewison Capt
157 Infy Bde

A7092). Wt. W12839/M1293 750,000. 1/17. D. D & L., Ltd. Forms/C2118/14.

Report on Operations

From 1st November, 1918 to 14th November, 1918.

-------oooOooo-------

157th INFANTRY BRIGADE.

Date. Time.

Nov. 1st to Nov. 3rd. From 1st to 3rd November, inclusive, the Brigade was situated in the RUMEGIES Area where training and road repairs were carried out.

Nov. 4th. On November, 4th, in accordance with Divisional Orders and Brigade Order No.158 (appendix I), the Brigade relieved the 23rd Infantry Brigade in the front Line. The 7th H.L.I. holding the line, the 6th H.L.I. being in support and the 5th H.L.I. in Reserve at ST. AMAND.

The front extended along the West bank of the River ESCAUT, the Northern Boundary being at K.3.a.0.0. and the Southern Boundary being at R.14.d.0.0. The 156th Infantry Brigade and the 8th Canadian Infantry Brigade being on the Left and Right respectively.

The Policy (Brigade Order No.159 Appendix II) was that of active patrolling the whole front so as to detect at once and follow up, any retirement of the enemy from the JARD CANAL.

Nov. 7th. On November 7th, and in accordance with Divisional Order No.145, the Brigade extended its right and took over part of the 8th Canadian Infantry Brigade front, as far South as the Railway line running through R.26.a.&.b., R.21.c. R.16.c.&b. As a result of the Brigade Front being lengthened, it was necessary to order the 5th H.L.I. up into the front line. This ~~Company~~ Battalion taking over on a two Company front, relieving the Right Company of the 7th H.L.I., and placing the 2nd Company in the position taken over from the 8th Canadian Infantry Brigade.

This relief was completed at 2100 on the 7th inst. In accordance with para 5, of Divisional Order No.145 (appendix III) Brigade Order No.160 was issued.(Appendix IV) By the former order, the Brigade was detailed to clear the ground between the ESCAUT River and FRESNES Road as far South as the Corps Boundary. By later orders, one Coy. 5th BN. H.L.I. was to make good the ground South of a line East and West through R.20.central, and one Coy. 7th Bn. H.L.I. was ordered to establish posts at the Copse at R.20.b.7.8. and at FORT MAZY and thence patrol North.

The attacks was to be carried out at 1300 on 8th November in conjunction with Artillery and Machine Gun support.

8th Nov. On the morning of the 8th, however, patrols reported that there were no signs of the enemy in front, consequently, Divisional Order No.143 A., and Brigade Order No.159, came into operation on receipt of the code word "H U N T", thereby cancelling the operation which was to take place at 1300.

On receipt of " H U N T " , the two support Coys. of 7th H.L.I. began carrying forward the rafts to the positions selected for the construction of the two pairs of foot bridges (i.e. at Q.5.c.25.85., Q.5.b.7.7. and K.34.d.5.1. K.34.d.7.7.) respectively. The rafts, on reaching the ESCAUT River, were launched and the Left Front Line Coy. of 7th H.L.I. which had been detailed as the covering party to cross East of the JARD CANAL, boarded the rafts and ferried across. When this Coy. reached the East bank of the ESCAUT, half the rafts were then carried across the ground between the River and the Canal, launched in the Canal, ferried across and in time made into a footbridge by a Section of 413th Field Coy. R.E. detailed for the purpose. By 1130 the covering party had taken up a line K.34.b.cent.- K.26.a.25.70.- through RIEUX DE CONDE - K.36.c. - Q.6.b. - Canal; forming ~~the~~ bridgehead. At the same hour the 6th H.L.I. which was detailed to push through the covering party of 7th H.L.I., started crossing to East of the JARD Canal by both bridges. The first Coy. of 6th H.L.I. to cross the/

Date: Time. to cross the Canal, linked up with 156th Infantry Brigade on the Left at K.29.central, taking up the line K.29.central - Q.6.a. - where it halted. As soon as this line was reached

Nov. 8th. the remainder of the 6th H.L.I. started to advance on a 2 Coy. front, keeping touch with the Squadron 4th Hussars, and VIII Corps Cyclist Battalion, who were in front forming a screen (these mounted troops having crossed to East of the Canal on the 156th Infantry Brigade front), and followed closely by one Section "D" Coy. 52nd Bn. M.G.C. and one section of 157th L.T.M.B.

The advance of the 6th H.L.I. was carried out without a hitch, there being no opposition, and at 1630 this Battalion had reached the final objective (i.e. the line L.28.d.5.5. to L.22.b.7.0.) where it took over from the mounted troops and established a line of outposts for the night.

Owing to the pace at which the 6th H.L.I. advanced, it lost touch with the 156th Infantry Brigade on the Left, and owing to flooded country on the Right was unable to get in touch with the Canadians. The mounted troops, however, reconnoitred roads on both flanks before dusk and reported all clear.

On the Right one Coy. of the 5th H.L.I. had been detailed to capture and advance through CONDE, form a bridgehead there and so enable the R.E.s to build bridges South of the town. This Coy. was to cross the river either by means of footbridges or by floating down the ESCAUT on rafts from FRESNES. The former method of crossing, was, however, adopted, as a partially broken down bridge was discovered and quickly repaired, enabling the Coy. to enter the town. Owing to all the bridges on the East side of CONDE being destroyed, the Coy. was not able to get beyond the Eastern outskirts of the town where it remained until the following morning, when it rejoined the Battalion at Dawn.

1730. By 1730 the remaining three Coys. of 7th H.L.I. and three Coys. of 5th H.L.I. West of the ESCAUT had concentrated in RIEUX DE CONDE and ODOMEZ respectively, where they remained for the night, 8th/9th. "A" Coy. of the 7th H.L.I. relieving the Coy. of the 6th H.L.I. which had taken up the line K.29.central - Q.6.a. in the morning, the Coy. of 6th H.L.I. thus relieved, rejoined its Battalion at LORETTE.

9th Nov. On the 9th November, the advance was continued at daylight, the 6th H.L.I. again leading and advancing due East on a two Company front, followed up by 7th and 5th H.L.I. in turn, the two latter Battalions marching by the LE CORON VERT - CHENE RAOUL - LORETTE-BERKESART - Lock I - HARCHIES Road. Again no opposition was met with and by 1600 the Brigade had taken up a line H.1.central - h.33.cent. - H.27.central. - N.W. to GRAND GLISE in touch with the 156th Infantry Brigade on the Left and the 8th Canadian Infantry Brigade on the Right; Brigade Hqrs., having moved to POMMEROEUIL.

At 2200 on the 9th. the Brigade received orders that the advance would continue on the following morning, the 10th inst., (vide Brigade Order No.161 Appendix V) but that as two Battalions of the 8th Division were being bussed up to take over the front at present held by this Brigade, the advance would be made in a N.E. direction with the line of the MONS - JURBISE Road between the points K.6.a.0.3. - D.23.a.0.3. as our final objective. At midnight 9th/10th however, orders were received that the two Battalions 8th Division could not be expected to arrive in time to relieve this Brigade. In consequence therefore, of the non arrival of the 8th Division Battalions, the Brigade was ordered to continue the advance on the morning of the 10th on to a final objective K.19.d.3.4. - D.23.a.0.3.

This alteration necessitated two Battalions being placed in the front line . The advance was started at 0800, the 5th H.L.I. being on the left and the 7th H.L.I. on the Right, 6th H.L.I. being in Support and in rear of 5th H.L.I. The Brigade Boundary running as follows :-

Date. Time.

10th Nov. The Brigade Boundary running as follows :- On the South, O.11.central - RIVAGE to Southern outskirts of GHLIN - K.19.d.6.6. On the North, H.10.c.0.0. - H.12.c.0.0. - C.29.b.0.0. - D.22.central. Inter Battalion Boundary being, H.22.c.0.0. - I.22.c.0.0. - I.17.c.0.0. to I.18.c.0.0. - I.2.a.5.6. - J.6.a.0.3.

The 5th H.L.I. advanced therefore in a N.E. direction in touch with 7th H.L.I. on the Right and 156th Infantry Brigade on the Left.

The advance of 5th H.L.I. continued without opposition until reaching the line ~~C.22~~- C.18.central. -I.12.central. where the mounted troops were held up by hostile Machine Gun fire at 1130. Similarly the advance of the 7th H.L.I. was held up by Machine Gun fire from J.21.a. and from the Northern and Eastern outskirts of GHLIN where this Battalion gained touch with the 8th Canadian Infantry Brigade on their Right.

The advanced guards pushed forward level with the mounted troops, but owing to heavy Machine Gun fire were

1215. unable to continue advancing. At 1215 the Advance Guard of 5th H.L.I. was ordered to work its way forward among the trees on the Northern edge of the BOIS DE BAUDOUR, one company of 6th H.L.I. at same time being ordered forward on the right of 5th H.L.I. to work through the BOIS DE BAUDOUR and keep touch with 7th H.L.I. on its right, another Company of 6th H.L.I. was ordered to follow the ~~adv~~ advance guard of 5th H.L.I. in the Northern edge of the wood until it reached J.3.d. where it was ordered to debouch from the wood, attack in a North East direction and clear the villages of HERCHIES and VACRESSE, of the enemy. Owing, however, to Machine Gun Fire, the 5th H.L.I. advance guard was held up on a line J.2.a.central - J.7.a.central. The company of 6th H.L.I. detailed to clear HERCHIES and VACRESSE, therefore debouched from the wood in J.1.b., attacked and captured VACRESSE shortly after 1630. Meanwhile the 156th Infantry Brigade on the Left had cleared HERCHIES . After the capture of VACRESSE, just before dusk, the advance was ordered to halt for the night on the line gained i.e., C.30.central - J.1.central - J.8.a.0.0. - I.18.b.8.4. - J.19.central - J.26.central - J.32.b.8.0. - due South. Brigade Headquarters remaining for the night at STRAULT Railway Station where it had been established at 1100.

During the night of 10th/11th, the Brigade received orders that the advance would continue at 0700 next morning. Brigade Orders No.162 (appendix VI.) were issued accordingly.

11th.

0800. At 0800 the 5th H.L.I. therefore advanced to the attack (the delay of one hour in commencing the attack having been caused through lateness in receipt of orders) and captured final objective i.e., the line of MONS - JURBISE Road between J.6.a. 0.0. - D.25.a.2.3. without opposition, the enemy having withdrawn during the night. The 7th H.L.I. did not advance but were relieved by the 2nd Middlesex Regt. (23rd inf. Bde. 8th Div.) who advance through them , the former Battalion withdrawing to Brigade Reserve at VACRESSE on relief. Brigade Headquarters, which had moved forward to I.4.d.3.7. at 0645, moved to VACRESSE at 0900.

At 0800 orders were received that an armistice would commence at 1100 to-day, and that after capture of the objectives, a defensive line would be taken up, the sentry groups being pushed out about 1000x in front of the Objective.

These orders were therefore carried out, and the Brigade halted and took up positions as follows :-

Brigade Headquarters .... VACRESSE

5th Bn. H.L.I. .... In Front Line.

6th Bn. H.L.I. In Support at ERBISOEUL.

7th Bn. H.L.I. in Brigade Reserve at VACRESSE.

Date. Time.

11th Nov.

12th. Nov. On the 12th no change took place in the above dispositions, on the 13th, however, the 6th H.L.I. took over the front line from the 5th H.L.I., the latter Battalion withdrawing into Brigade Support.

13th. Nov.

14th. Nov. On the 14th orders were received that the Brigade would increase its front, taking over from the 2nd Middlesex Regt. (23rd Inf. Bde. 8th Div.) on the 15th. Relief to be completed by 1800.

Throughout the above operations the Brigade was supported by the 9th Brigade Royal Field Artillery and by "D" Coy., 52nd Battalion, Machine Gun Corps.

Appendix No. 1.

Copy No..........

SECRET.

157th Infantry Brigade Order No. 158.

3rd November, 1918.

Ref. Map. Sheet 44.1/40,000.

1. The 52nd Division will take over the whole VIII Corps front by relieving 8th Division in the right sector of the Corps.
The policy will continue to be that of closely watching the enemy by patrols, so as to detect at once and follow up any retirement of the enemy from his line on the JARD CANAL.

2. The 157th Infantry Brigade will relieve the 23rd Infantry Brigade in the front line in accordance with Table "A" on the reverse.

3. All details of relief, including guides, will be arranged mutually between C.Os. concerned.

4. All maps, defence schemes, trench stores, etc., will be taken over.

5. Completion of relief will be wired "PRIORITY" to Brigade Headquarters, using the code word "TURK".

6. The 157th Infantry Brigade H.Q. will close at RUMEGIES and open at P.17.b.6.7. at an hour to be notified later.

7. Orders as regards time units will march off from their present billets will be notified later.

8. A C K N O W L E D GE.

S. Stirling Cookson

Captain,
Brigade Major, 157th Infantry Brigade.

Issued at ....on 3/11/18.

Copy No.	1 to	5th H.L.I.
	2	6th H.L.I.
	3	7th H.L.I.
	4	157th L.T.M.B.
	5	2nd L.F.A.
	6	220th Coy. A.S.C.
	7.	23rd Infantry Brigade.
	8	155th Infantry Brigade.
	9	156th Infantry Brigade.
	10	52nd Bn. M.G.C.
	11	52nd Division.
	12	Staff Captain.
	13	Brigade Sigs. Officer.
	14) 15)	War Diary.
	16	File.

Table "A".

Serial No.	Date. Novr.	Unit.	From.	To.	Relieving.	Remakks.
1	4/5th.	157th Bde. Hqrs.	RUMEGIES. (I.20.b.5.9.)	Line. (P.17.b.6.7.)	23rd Inf. Bde. Hqrs. (P.17.b.6.7.)	
2	4/5th.	5th H.L.I.	BOUR BOTIN. (H.Q. I.35.a.)	Brigade Reserve. (H.Q. P.8.a.2.1.)	2nd Devon Regt.	
3	4/5th.	6th H.L.I.	RUMEGIES. (H.Q. I.14.d.1.5.)	Brigade Support. (H.Q. P.17.b.8.8.)	2nd Middlesex Regt.	
4	4/5th.	7th H.L.I.	RUE LASSON. (H.Q. J.19.a.3.5.)	Front Line. (H.Q. Q.2.d.9.9.)	2nd West Yorks Regt.	
5	4/5th.	157th L.T.M.B.	RUE LASSON. (H.Q. J.19.c.2.2.)	Front Line. (H.Q. P.17.a.0.9.)	23rd L.T.M.B.	

Appendix No. 2

SECRET. Copy No........

157th Infantry Brigade Order No.159.

Ref. Sheet 44. 1/40,000 6th November, 1918.

1. It is ~~the~~ not intended to force a crossing of the JARD CANAL, active patrolling will however, be carried out from dusk till dawn to ensure that the enemy does not retire without our knowledge.

2. When the enemy withdraws, the 52nd Division will follow him up to gain and maintain touch with his main force. It is not the intention that Battalions should become heavily engaged.

3. (a) As soon as the enemy's withdrawal from the JARD CANAL is ascertained, the following will be the procedure :-

(i) Single file bridges will be thrown across the river and canal as under :-

(Q.5.c.25.85.	to be known as	G	bridge.
(Q.6.b.7.7.	--- do ---	K	"
(K.34.d.5.1.	--- do ---	L	"
(K.34.d.7.7.	--- do ---	M	"

(ii) Covering parties for each of the above pairs of Bridges (G. &. K., L. &. M.) will be found from the Left Coy. of the Front Line Battalion: two platoons to each pair.

These platoons will ferry across the river in the rafts and make good the ground between the river and canal. Similarly on arrival of the rafts for the canal bridges these two platoons will ferry across the canal and make good a bridgehead along the line K.34.b.central - K.36.a.25.70. - along the Road running S.E. through RIEUX DE CONDE to about K.36.c.central - about Q.6.b.0.6. - Canal.

The Centre Coy. of the Front Line Battalion will be responsible for watching the ground between the river and the canal in Q.6.c. and d. from positions along the Southern bank of the river. This Coy. will also have one anti-aircraft Lewis Gun mounted.

(iii) Carrying parties for material for the above bridges will be found as follows :-

For G. &. K. Bridges by the Reserve Coy. of Front Line Battn.
For L. &. M. Bridges by one Coy. of Reserve Battalion.

The latter Coy. being billetted in Q.9.b.

The above Coys. will provide not less than 40 carriers each. On completion of work the carrying parties will return to their billets and stand by.

Anti-aircraft Lewis Guns will be placed in the vicinity of the bridges by Companies furnishing the carrying parties.

(iv) Bridging operations will be supervised by an officer and one Section to be detailed by O.C. 413th Field Coy. R.E.

(b) Support Battalion. When the bridges are completed the Support Battalion will push over one Coy. through the Coy. of the Front Line Battalion (vide para 3, (a) sub-para (ii)) to link up with the Right of the Left Brigade at K.29.central and to take up the line K.29.central - Q.6.a. The Company will halt on this line.

The remainder of the Support Battalion, accompanied by the Section of D. Coy. 52nd Bn. M.G.C., at present in Brigade Reserve, and one Section 157th L.T.M.B., will then cross to East of the Canal, push forward through the line Q.6.a. - K.29.central - K.16. central and advance on a 2 Company Front, making good the following successive objectives, taking over each from the VIII Corps Cyclists Battalion, (less 1 Coy.) which will have already crossed East of the Canal by bridges on the Left Brigade Front :-

(i) VIEUX CONDE - PERUWELZ Railway.
(R.1., L.31., L.25., L.19., L.13.)

3. (b), ~~(iii)~~ Contd.

(ii) CONDE - MONT DE PERUWELZ - PERUWELZ Road.
(L32., L.26., L.20., L.14., L.8.)

(iii) CONDE - CHATEAU de L'ERMITAGE - BOUQUET Road.
(L.33., L.27., L.21., L.15., L.8.b. & d.)

(iv) The line LORETTE - BONSECOURS - PERUWELZ.

Battalion Hqrs., moving forward on the RIEUX DE CONDE - GD. QUENOY - CHENE RAOUL Road.

Touch will be maintained throughout with the Left Brigade who are advancing on to the same objectives on our immediate Left.

Reports will be rendered on gaining toudh with troops on flanks :-

(a) On line Q.6.a. - K.29.central - K.16. central.
(b) VIEUX CONDE - PERUWELZ Railway.
(c) On line LORETTE - BONSECOURS - PERUWELZ.

(c) Reserve Battalion. One Coy. as in para 3, (a), (iii).
One Coy. will be detailed to proceed through CONDE either by ligh bridges or by rafts down the ESCAUT Canal, in order to cover the construction of bridges in CONDE by C.E. VIII Corps.
This Battalion, less two Coys., will remain in Brigade Reserve and concentrate about Q.3.d.central.

(d) D. Coy. 52nd Bn. M.G.C.) 157th L.T.M.B.) Less Sections mentioned in para 3, (b) will concentrate in Brigade Reserve at about Q.3.d.2.0.

4. As soon as the Bridgehead is taken over by the Support Battn. the Left Front Line Coy. of Battalion in Line, vide para 3, (a), (ii), will block the Western and Northern exits from VIEUX CONDE, reconnoitre VIEUX CONDE and report as to its occupation or otherwise by hostile troops.

5. Orders for the concentration of the Front Line Battalion will be issued by Brigade Headquarters.

6. Action of Artillery. In addition to the Artillery at present supporting the Brigade, the 9th Brigade R.F.A. will come forward from NIVELLE to HAUTE RIVE preparatory to pushing one Battery to East of the Canal when the Heavy Traffic Bridges "A" and "B" , and "X" and "Y" have been completed by the C.R.E. at K.27.d.3.1. and PONT DE LA VERNETTE, respectively. After crossing to East of the Canal this Battery willswing Southwards to assist the advance of the Support Battn to whose Hqrs., it will send a liaison Officer.

7. Boundaries.

Northern Brigade Boundary.

P.3.central - K.35.central - K.36.b.2.7. - K.33.d.0.5. - K.28.d.2.0. - L.25.a.0.7. - L.22.central - L.23.central and then due Eastwards.

Southern Brigade Boundary and Corps Boundary.

The Southern Boundary is as follows :- Q.9.c.2.4. - Q.16.c.9.5. - R.13.c.5.4. - R.20.a.1.1. - R.9.c.9.1. - along HAISNE RIVER, but, with the exception of one company of the Reserve Battalion detailed to push through CONDE, no troops of the Brigade will move into or South of the CONDE - BOLT FACTORY - LE COCQ Railway unless tactically necessary.

8. The Code word " H U N T " will bring the above orders into operation without further orders.

9. A central visual Signalling Station will be established by Division about K.25.a.10.8. Further Orders as regards communications will be issued later.

10. First Line Transport will cross to East of the Canal as soon as practicable and on orders from Brigade Hqrs.

11. Brigade Headquarters will open near HAUTE VILLE as soon as the River Bridges are open.
The exact location will be notified later.
On moving East of Canal Brigade Headquarters will be in the vicinity of the RIEUX DE CONDE - GD. QUENOY - CHENE RAOUL Road.

12. A C K N O W L E D G E .

J.S. Stirling Cookson

Captain,
Brigade Major, 157th Infantry Brigade.

Issued at .... on /11/18.

Copy No. 1 to 5th H.L.I.
2 6th H.L.I.
3 7th H.L.I.
4 157th L.T.M.B.
5 2nd L.F.A.
6 413th Field Coy. R.E.
7 220th Coy. A.S.C.
8 D. Coy. 52nd Bn. M.G.C.
9 155th Inf. Bde.
10 156th Inf. Bde.
11 8th Canadian Inf. Bde.
12 9th Bde. R.F.A.
13 33rd Bde. R.F.A.
14 C.R.A.
15 52nd Division.
16 VIII Corps Cyclists Battalion.
17 4th Hussars.
18 52nd Bn. M.G.C.
19 Staff Captain.
20 Brigade Major.
21 G.O.C.
22 Bde. Sigs. Officer.
23) War Diary.
24)
25 F I L E .

Appendix No 3.

SECRET.

Copy No. 1.

52nd Division Order No.145.

7th November, 1918.

1. The Boundary between the Canadian and VIII Corps will be adjusted so that the dividing line will run according to the attached map.

2. The 157th Infantry Brigade will extend its Right and take over up to the new Boundary on night 7th/8th November.
Relief ~~will~~ to be completed by 0600 on 8th November.

3. O.C. 52nd M.G. Battalion will arrange relief of any Machine Guns in the new area with O.C. M.G. Battalion, 3rd Canadian Division.

4. Details of relief will be arranged between G.O.s C. 157th Inf. Bde. and 8th Canadian Inf. Bde.
H.Q., 8th Canadian Inf. Bde. - S.8.b.3.8. (from 0800 to-day.)
7th Canadian Infantry Brigade relieve 8th Canadian Infantry Brigade on night 7th/8th inst.

5. After the relief the 157th Infantry Brigade will clear their new area West of the ESCAUT River of the enemy.

6. A C K N O W L E D G E .

(sgd) H.V. Curtis, Major,
General Staff.,
52nd Division.

Issued at 0600.

Copy No. 1 to 157th Inf. Bde.
2 C.R.A.
3 52nd M.G. Battalion.
4 VIII Corps.
5 3rd Canadian Division.

Appendix No. 4.

SECRET. Copy No........

157th Infantry Brigade Order No. 160.

Ref. Map. 44 S.E. 1/20,000. 7th November, 1918.

1. The 157th Infantry Brigade will clear the ground between the River ESCAUT and the CONDE - FRESNES Road as far SOUTH as the Corps Boundary tomorrow , 8th November.

2. 1 Coy. 5th H.L.I. will make good the ground SOUTH of a line East and West through R.20.central.
1 Coy. 7th H.L.I. will establish posts at the Copse at about R.20.b.7.8. and FORT MAZY, and thence patrol northwards. All of the above points are held by the enemy.
At ZERO hour the Coy. of 5th H.L.I. will attack due EAST from about R.20.a.5.2. followed by the Coy. of 7th H.L.I. which will attack along the road R.20.a.5.2. - R.20.d.9.8.(a post will be established at the latter point) - through the Copse entering FORT MAZY from the NORTHEAST.

3. Machine Guns will support the attack from R.20.c.7.5. and R.26.b.0.7.

4. Trench Mortars. One 6" Trench Mortar will demolish the three most northerly houses of FRESNES (R.14.a.85.10.) on the east side of the FRESNES - CONDE Road before ZERO.

5. Artillery.
(a) Two preliminary bombardments of half an hour each are being put down by the heavy artillery on to FORT MAZY and Copse at R.20.b.75.90. also on the house R.20.b.70.85. The artillery is also directing steady fire on to these points up to ZERO plus 5.
(b) Neutralising fire will be directed by heavies on to houses at R.15.a.85.00. also on to group of houses R.14.b.4.4. and FORT FRANQUET R.14.b.25.50. The above firing being carried out from ZERO to ZERO plus 30.
(c) 4.5" Hows. are demolishing the three houses at R.20.d.3.9. and also bombarding the two houses at R.20.d.10.95. and R.20.d.30.95.
(d) 4.5" Hows. are neutralising FORT MOULIN A VENT from ZERO to ZERO plus 20. from which hour an 18 pdr. barrage will be directed against this point.
(e) A standing barrage of 18 pdrs. is being put down on the Copse and house R.20.b.75.90. and R.20.b.70.85. respectively also on FORT MAZY.
(f) A standing barrage of 18 pdrs. and heavies is being put down on the following line from Zero to Zero plus 20 :- From the Railway Crossing R.8.d.1.0. to the River bank at R.15.a.3.8. thence south along the East bank of the River ESCAUT to R.20.b.9.9. This standing barrage will, however, continue till Zero plus 30 along the line mentioned north of FORT DU PIGEONNIER.

6. The artillery is cutting gaps in the existing wire about R.20.b. cent. and about R.20.central.

7. Artillery fire ceases at Zero plus 30.

8. Os.C. 5th and 7th H.L.I. will arrange O.Ps. in our present lines and make frequent reports as to progress.

9. Zero hour will be notified later by the code word "R A T I O N S".

10. A C K N O W L E D G E.

J.S. Stuky Cookson

Captain,
Brigade Major, 157th Infantry Brigade.

Issued at 21000 on 7/11/18.

To all recipients of 157th Infantry Brigade Order No.160.

RATIONS .... 1 3 0 0 .

W. Cumming Lt. for
Captain,

7/11/18.

Brigade Majorr, 157th Infantry Brigade.

SECRET.   Appendix No. 5   Copy No..........

157th Infantry Brigade Order No. 161

Ref. Map. Sheet 45.   10th November, 1918.

1. In formation. Small bodies of the enemy have been located in woods East of WILLEROT also East of TERTRE, which village a Company of a Canadian Battalion holds. These Canadians are crossing new Corps Boundary to-day.

2. (a) The Division will continue the advance to-day.
(b) The 7th H.L.I. leaving present billets at 0700 will advance on a two Company front and cover 157th Infantry Brigade front up to the line O.10.b.0.5. - Railway line through O.4. - I.34.d., c. &. a. - I.27.d. thence up road I.27.a. to I.21.a.2.0. from which point the 156th Infantry Brigade continue the line North alone NEUF MAISON Road.
(c) 5th H.L.I. will march at 0700 by roads HARCHIES - VILLE POMMEROEUIL - HAUTRAGE, at last place they will halt until further orders.
(d) 6th H.L.I. will be prepared to move to HAUTRAGE after 0800 on receipt of orders.
(e) The Section 157th L.T.M.B. at present with 6th H.L.I. will accompany the 7th H.L.I.Remainder of the battary will accompany 5th H.L.I.
(f) "D" Coy. 52nd Bn. M.G.C. will assist 7th H.L.I. in their advance. Sections not detailed for this purpose will march in rear of 157th L.T.M.B.
(g) 7th H.L.I. Hqrs., will advance along the VILLE POMMEROEUIL - CHENE - TERTRE Road.
(h) Brigdde Headquarters will remain at POMMEROEUIL (Rue DE BOIS) until 0930, when it will open at HAUTRAGE.

3. Boundaries.
(i) Corps Boundary. On the North runs ~~along~~ G.9.central - East along Canal to H.2.c.6.5. - thence South of STAMBRUGES - NEUF MAISON Road to C.20.c.0.6. North of HERCHIES to D.10.b.6.6. (approx.)
Southern Boundary. O.11.central - RIVAGE (exclusive) to Southern outskirts of GHLIN to K.19.d.6.6.
Inter Brigade Boundary at present unaltered.

4. The 8th Division take over part of the Corps front to-day, time uncertain, but probably not before we reach our objectives given in para. 2 (b). When this relief is complete the Inter Divisional Boundary will will run :- H.22.c.0.0. due East to I.22.c.0.0. thence I.17.c.0.0. to I.18.c.0.0. up Railway as far as road crossing J.2.a.5.6. - along road (inclusive to 8th Division) to J.6.a.0.3.
Inter Brigade Boundary after relief by 8th Division will be :- H.10.c.0.0. - H.12.c.0.0. thence North Eas t to C.29.b.0.0. - Railway at D.22.central.
The moves consequent on this re-arrangement will be notified later.

5. Transport. Transport will accompany units except that of 7th H.L.I. which will only accompany the Battalion as far as H.30.c.central, where it will halt (7th H.L.I. Hdqrs., probable final destination WILLEROT.)

6. A C K N O W L E D G E .

Issued at 0145 on 10/11/18.

Copy No. 1 to 5th H.L.I.
2 6th H.L.I.
3 7th H.L.I.
4 157th L.T.M.B.
5 "D" Coy. 52nd Bn. M.G.C.
6 9th Bde. R.F.A.
7 O.C. Mounted Troops.
8 Staff Captain.
9 } War Diary.
10 }
11 F I L E.

SECRET. *Appendix No. 6* Copy No..........

157th Infantry Brigade Order No.162.

Ref., Map Sheet 45, 1/40,000. 10th November, 1918.

1. The 157th Infantry Brigade will continue its advance to-morrow 11 th November, and capture the MONS - TURBISE Road, to-day's objective, in conjunction with the 155th Infantry Brigade on the Left, who will pass through 156th Infantry Brigade at 0700 on a North and South line through HERCHIES. A further advance from this objective should only be made for Local protection and patrolling up to 1000 yards.

2. The 5th H.L.I. will advance at 0700, move direct on HERBISEUF advancing North and South of the village to the objective. One Company should be specially detailed to search and hold HERBISEOUEL.
6th H.L.I. will move before daybreak and assemble in support at I.4.central, to be in position before 0645, under cover.

3. Artillery. O.C. 9th Brigade R.F.A. will arrange for:- (i) one battery to work under orders of O.C. 7th Bn. H.L.I. South of the wood. (ii) one battery at HERCHIES to cover the advance of the 5th H.L.I. and the capture of HERBISEOUEL and afterwards to move in close support to about D.14. (iii) One battery 18 pdrs. will cover and support the advance of the 5th H.L.I.also, first from about I.5.central, afterwards from about J.2.central. (iv) One battery 4.5" Hows. will be in position about I.4.central and await orders.

4. "D" Coy. 52nd Battalion M.G.C. 1 Section will be attached to 7th H.L.I., 2 Sections will be attached to and advance with 5th H.L.I. The Reserve Sections will be in position at I.4.central.

5. Trench Mortars. 157th L.T.M.B. Sections not already detailed to Battalions will rendezvous at I.4.central at 0645.

6. During the course of the morning the 23rd Infantry Brigadw will relieve the 7th H.L.I. and Machine Guns. On relief the 7th H.L.I. and Machine Guns will withdraw to VACRESSE.

7. All regimental Transport will remain at SIRAULT and go forward later on orders from the Staff Captain.

8. Brigade Headquarters will be at I.4.d.3.7. at 0645, but will afterwards move to VACRESSE.

9. O.C. "D" Coy. 52nd Bn. M.G.C. will be at Brigade Headquarters at 0645.

10. A C K N O W L E D G E .

(sgd) C.S.Stirling Cookson, Captain,
Brigade Major, 157th Infantry Brigade.

Copy No. 1 to 5th H.L.I.
2 6th H.L.I.
3 7th H.L.I.
4 157th L.T.M.B.
5 "D" Coy. 52nd Bn. M.G.C.
6 9th Bde. R.F.A.
7 2nd L.F.A.
8 156th Inf. Bde.
9 155th Inf. Bde.
10 8th Canadian Infantry Brigade.
11 Staff Captain.
12)
13) War Diary.
14 F I L E .

appendix 1.

157th Infantry Brigade Order No. 163.

Ref. Sheet 45, 1/40,000. 14th November, 1918.

1. The 157th Infantry Brigade will relieve the 23rd Infantry Bde. in the front line to-morrow, 15th November, by 1800

2. The 7th H.L.I. will relieve the 2nd Middlesex Regt. (Bn. H.Q. at MAISIERE) taking over the dispositions as they stand at present.

3. All details of relief will be arranged between Os.C. concerned.

4. O.C. "D" Coy. 52nd Bn. M.G.C. will arrange to relieve the Machine Guns of the 8th Bn. M.G.C.

5. Completion of relief will be reported to Brigade Headquarters.

6. Acknowledge.

(Sgd) C.S.Stirling Cookson, Captain,
Bde. Major, 157th Infantry Brigade.

Issued at 2000 on 14/11/18.

Copy No. 1 to	5th H.L.I.	No. 7 to	220th Coy., A.S.C.
2	6th H.L.I.	8	23rd Inf. Bde.
3	7th H.L.I.	9	52nd Division.
4	157th L.T.M.B.	10)	War Diary.
5	"D" Coy. 52nd M.G.C.	11)	
6	2nd L.F.A.	12	File.

Appendix

Priority.

To. 157th Bde.

GA.140 17. AAA

2nd Army having taken over responsibility for front outposts will be withdrawn by 2200 today AAA

Report completion AAA.

Addsd 155 & 157, Reptd 3rd Cans, 58th Div, 8th and 22nd Corps etc.

52nd Div. 1730

Instructions regarding War Diaries and Intelligence Summaries are contained in F. S. Regs., Part II. and the Staff Manual respectively. Title pages will be prepared in manuscript.

WAR DIARY
157 INFANTRY BRIGADE
~~INTELLIGENCE SUMMARY.~~
(Erase heading not required.)

Army Form C. 2118.

DECEMBER 1918

9

Place	Date	Hour	Summary of Events and Information	Remarks and references to Appendices
MAISIERE - ERBISOEUL - GLIN AREA	1–2		TRAINING ETC.	W.C.G.
	3–5		Brig Gen C.D. Hamilton-Moore CMG DSO returned from UK leave and assumed duties vice Brig Gen C.B. Price CB. CMG. DSO. returned to duty 3rd Army Infantry School	W.C.G.
	6–31		TRAINING. ETC	W.C.G.

[illegible] Capt
for B.G.C. 157 Bde

A7092. Wt. W12839/M1293 750,000. 1/17. D. D & L., Ltd. Forms/C2118/14.

Instructions regarding War Diaries and Intelligence Summaries are contained in F. S. Regs., Part II. and the Staff Manual respectively. Title pages will be prepared in manuscript.

WAR DIARY

or

~~INTELLIGENCE SUMMARY.~~

157 INFANTRY BRIGADE

(~~Erase heading not required.~~)

Army Form C. 2118.

JANUARY 1919

V.B. 10

Place	Date	Hour	Summary of Events and Information	Remarks and references to Appendices
MAISIERE — ERBISOEUL AREA	1 2 3 4 5 6 7 8 9 10 11 12 13 14 15 16 17 18 19 20 21 22 23 24 25 26 27 28 29 30 31		TRAINING, RECREATION, EDUCATION &c.	W.C.G.

C. B. Hamilton Moore Brig Gen

Commdg 157 Inf Brigade.

A7092). Wt. W12839/M1293 750,000. 1/17. D. D & L., Ltd. Forms/C2118/14.

Instructions regarding War Diaries and Intelligence Summaries are contained in F. S. Regs., Part II. and the Staff Manual respectively. Title pages will be prepared in manuscript.

WAR DIARY
or
~~INTELLIGENCE~~ SUMMARY.
(*Erase heading not required.*)

157. Inf. BRIGADE — H.Qrs.
FEBRUARY 1919.

Army Form C. 2118.

VR 11

Place	Date	Hour	Summary of Events and Information	Remarks and references to Appendices
MAISIÈRE – ERBISOEUL AREA	1st to 28th		Training, Recreation, demobilization and Education	[initials]

J. S. Stirling Cookson Capt.
for Brig. General
Comdg. 157 Inf. Brigade

A7092). Wt. W12839/M1293 750,000. 1/17. D. D & L., Ltd. Forms/C2118/14.

Instructions regarding War Diaries and Intelligence Summaries are contained in F. S. Regs., Part II. and the Staff Manual respectively. Title pages will be prepared in manuscript.

WAR DIARY
or
INTELLIGENCE SUMMARY.
(Erase heading not required.)

Army Form C. 2118.

157. Inf. Brigade H.Qrs.
March 1919.

Vol 12

Place	Date	Hour	Summary of Events and Information	Remarks and references to Appendices
Maisières – Erbisoeul area	1st to 30th		Continuation of demobilization –	MC
Soignies	21st		The Brigade moved by route march to SOIGNIES where the Divn. is to concentrate prior to entraining for U.K.	MK
"	22nd to 31st		demobilization –	MC

[illegible] – Cookson Capt
for B.G.C. Comdg 157 Bde.

A7092). Wt. W12839/M1293 750,000. 1/17. D. D & L., Ltd. Forms/C2118/14.

Instructions regarding War Diaries and Intelligence Summaries are contained in F. S. Regs., Part II. and the Staff Manual respectively. Title pages will be prepared in manuscript.

WAR DIARY
or
INTELLIGENCE SUMMARY.
(Erase heading not required.)

Army Form C. 2118.

157. Inf. Brigade H.Qrs.
APRIL 1919.

Vol 13

Place	Date	Hour	Summary of Events and Information	Remarks and references to Appendices
SOIGNIES	1st to 27th		Nothing to report.	
	28th		Cadres of 1/5th 1/6th & 1/7th HLI all entrained at SOIGNIES en route for U.K. (CALAIS). The train left SOIGNIES at 1830	[illegible]
	29th		Nothing to report	[illegible]
	30th		Nothing to report.	[illegible]

B. Stirling-Cookson Capt.
for 157 Bde. Comdr.

52

Instructions regarding War Diaries and Intelligence Summaries are contained in F. S. Regs., Part II. and the Staff Manual respectively. Title pages will be prepared in manuscript.

Army Form C. 2118.

WAR DIARY
or
INTELLIGENCE SUMMARY.
(Erase heading not required.)

HQ 157 Infy Bde

LR 15

Place	Date	Hour	Summary of Events and Information	Remarks and references to Appendices
Soignies	To 14/6/19		Nothing to report	Ceased
	14/6/19		Equipment Guard entrained with equipment for Antwerp	
Antwerp	21/6/19		Loaded equipment on barge	
"	24/6/19		Equipment Guard entrained for Boulogne	
Boulogne	25/6/19		Equipment Guard embarked to UK for disposal.	

E Russell Lieut
a/. Bde Major 157th Inf. Bde

(A9175) Wt W2358/P360 600,000 12/1 D. D. & L. Sch. 52a. Forms/C2118/55

www.ingramcontent.com/pod-product-compliance
Lightning Source LLC
Chambersburg PA
CBHW080836010526
44114CB00017B/2318
* 9 7 8 1 4 7 4 5 2 9 2 1 1 *